Letting the People Decide

Letting the People Decide

Dynamics of a Canadian Election

RICHARD JOHNSTON   ANDRÉ BLAIS
HENRY E. BRADY   JEAN CRÊTE

Stanford University Press
Stanford, California
1992

Stanford University Press
Stanford, California
© 1992 McGill-Queen's University Press
Originating publisher: McGill-Queen's
    University Press, Montreal
First published in the U.S.A. by
    Stanford University Press, 1992
Printed in the United States
Cloth ISBN 0-8047-2077-0
Paper ISBN 0-8047-2078-9
LC 91-68213
This book is printed on acid-free paper.

Contents

Acknowledgments

Writing this book has been rather like forming a government: it involved building a coalition. The four of us who happen to sit in the cabinet have drawn upon moral support and money from many sources.

None of this could have happened but for the generosity of the Social Sciences and Humanities Research Council of Canada (SSHRCC). Our proposal challenged SSHRCC to consider a wholly new way of conducting a Canadian Election Study, to take a major analytical risk. The council rose to the challenge. We hope this book vindicates its faith in us. At the start we were helped by the Institute for Research on Public Policy, especially by John Langford. Later we also drew upon the Fonds pour la Formation des Chercheurs et aide à la Recherche (FCAR) in Quebec, the US National Science Foundation, and a UBC Izaak Walton Killam Research Prize. A timely arrangement with the Royal Commission on Electoral Reform and Party Financing (the Lortie Commission) allowed us to collect data on third-party newspaper advertising. Each of us also received support from his respective home base. The Department of Political Science at the University of British Columbia committed space and other resources right from the beginning and facilitated extended stays by Blais and Crête. The departments at Laval and Montréal made space available for planning sessions both before and after fieldwork, and Laval has provided storage space for our embarrassment of videotape. Brady has been supported along the way by individuals and institutions at three universities: the Data Center at

Harvard: the Center for the Study of Politics and Society at the National Opinion Research Center (NORC) and the Dean of the Social Sciences, both at Chicago; and the College of Letters and Sciences and the Survey Research Center at the University of California, Berkeley.

Then there is our equivalent of the party machine, the people who did the fieldwork and the research assistants who took it from there. Fieldwork for the 1988 Canadian Election Study was conducted by the Institute for Social Research at York University, Toronto. Gordon Darroch, sometime director of the institute, persuaded us of its commitment to the project. The commitment was borne out by our subsequent dealings with the associate director who had immediate responsibility for the project, Michael Stevenson, and with the technical staff, especially David Northrup, the project director, David Bates, who drew the sample, and John Tibert, who gave us a whole new appreciation of the virtue of obsessiveness. Our research assistants were vital to what came next. These were: at the University of British Columbia, Sandra Bach, Pablo Policzer, and Brenda O'Neill; at the Université de Montréal, Stéphane Dupuis, Michael Mendelsohn, and Benoît Sanscartier; at Université Laval, Denis Bastien, Cheryl Jones, James Comyn, Patrick Vincent, Alfredo Brandolino, Yves Bernier, Donald Paget, and Victor-Manuel Sanchez-Velarde; at the University of Chicago, Fay Booker, Patti Conley, Robert Eisinger, and Carrie Fisher; and at Berkeley, Martin Petri and Chris Downing. Synita Booker at NORC provided Henry Brady with administrative support during the project's critical early stages.

At a crucial point in the design of the study, personnel at the Institute for Social Research, University of Michigan, gave us invaluable advice (so invaluable they graciously never charged us for it) on how to design a rolling cross-section. We must thank the American National Election Studies for pioneering the rolling cross-section design, and we especially thank Santa Traugott and Steve Heeringa for telling us about their experience with it. Don Kinder at ISR-Michigan also provided help in the design of the questionnaire.

We did not lack for advice and informal support. We thank our colleagues at UBC, Montréal, Laval, Harvard, Chicago, and Berkeley. A handful of individuals proved especially steadfast supporters and penetrating critics: Ken Carty, David Elkins, Jean Laponce, Avigail Eisenberg, and Donald Blake in Vancouver; Richard Nadeau and Stéphane Dion in Montreal; John Courtney in Saskatoon; Larry Bartels in Princeton; Chris Achen in Chicago (now in Ann Arbor); Bruce Cain, Raymond Wolfinger, Nelson Polsby, Austin Ranney, and Laura Stoker in Berkeley. For three colleagues there is even more to be said. Percy Tannenbaum, director of the Berkeley Survey Research Center, has been especially helpful to both Brady and Johnston. Paul Sniderman provided both intellectual and practical guidance throughout this project and has been a friend to all four of us. It is fair to say that this study would never have taken the shape it did but for Paul: he was critical to getting the CASES system from the Computer Assisted Survey Methods (CSM) Program at the University of California, Berkeley established at ISR-York; and he introduced two of the authors to each other. And it was Paul who encouraged us to seek out Stanford as an American publisher for the manuscript. Merrill Shanks deserves special mention both as the progenitor of the CSM-CASES software without which this book would not have been imaginable, much less possible, and as a wise and calming presence. We trust that Merrill too will see this book as a kind of vindication.

We have benefited from advice and counsel by some of the campaign's key players. Ian McKinnon, formerly of Decima Research, convinced us that campaigns had to be taken seriously and was a source of advice about design and of delicate hints about what to look for. Among active politicians and their advisors, we are particularly grateful to: the Right Honourable John Turner MP, Tom Axworthy, and Gerry Robinson of the Liberal party; Patrick Boyer MP, of the Conservative party; and Johanna den Hertog of the New Democratic Party. Especially important for us were two remarkable forums: the Conference on Media and Elections, Queen's University, February 1989, attended by Blais and Johnston; and the Lortie Commission, of whose gatherings Blais, Crête, and Johnston each attended at least two. Both forums brought together media, polling, and party figures. Although each forum was on the record and all participants were careful about what they said, the participants were numerous enough and sufficiently at cross purposes for us to gain a strong sense of the texture of campaigning and of campaign coverage. Each forum provided ample opportunity for informal contact.

We must also thank our collaborators on other projects who have waited graciously until this one was completed.

Finally, there are the key individuals at the McGill-Queen's and Stanford University Presses. Philip Cercone at McGill-Queen's and Grant Barnes and Muriel Bell at Stanford gave us critical early support. Diane Mew and Joan McGilvray banished many infelicities, even as they had to put up with others, as the manuscript stumbled to the finish.

No person and no organization mentioned here bears any responsibility for outrages against analytical rigour, common sense, or either of Canada's official languages perpetrated by us.

From conception to execution this effort has taken, by the shortest count, some six years. Along the way we have been repeatedly taken away from our families, even when we were physically present. We thank them all – Suzanne, Geneviève, François-Yves, and Louis, Patricia, Daniel, and Julia, Olivier, Kathryn, Patrick, Rory, and Ellen – for their love and their support even when this book took us away from models, hikes, soccer, hockey, baseball, and weekends in the country, not to mention bedtime stories, cooking, and appliance repair.

As befits a book which is almost as much about history as it is about contemporary politics, we dedicate it to our parents. Some of our parents are still among us; some have been gathered to the rest of our ancestors. Their lives have been intertwined with the events that set the stage for this book's subject. The loss of his father in January 1992, just as this manuscript was coming to completion, gives Henry the last word: he would like to believe that Donald L. Brady's playful use of words and Myrtle C. Brady's careful use of numbers were not lost on their son.

Letting the People Decide

PROLOGUE

Gambling on the People

On 20 July 1988 John Turner, leader of Canada's opposition Liberal party, took the biggest gamble of his career. He instructed the Liberal majority in the Senate to hold up a comprehensive free trade agreement with the United States until the issue was referred to the people in a general election. In a press conference announcing his instructions, Mr Turner responded to criticisms that an appointed Senate had no right to block legislation passed by a democratically elected House of Commons: "the issue is so fundamental that the people of Canada deserve and must have the right to judge ... I think the issue becomes democracy. *Let the people decide.*"[1] John Turner evoked the image of the electorate which dominates popular discussion of mass politics: the people as a free-standing body, with its own indomitable collective opinion. This image, the people deciding, is also a recurring one in the classic studies of electoral behaviour. Voters are typically presented as the prime movers in the electoral drama.[2]

Letting the People Decide suggests a different emphasis. Elections are not just about how voters choose. They are also about how parties and leaders shape the alternatives from which the choice is made. The parties let the Canadian people divide over free trade, but they consciously suppressed divisions on other issues. The Conservative prime minister, Brian Mulroney, took the risk of negotiating a trade agreement because he believed that Canadians could be convinced of its necessity. John Turner forced the election on the same issue because he thought that over one hundred years of history would weigh heavily against the Conservatives. Both the Liberal and Conservative parties, as well as Canada's third major party, the social democratic and labour-oriented New Democratic Party (NDP), scrupulously avoided another issue: the recurring question of French Canada's place in the larger nationality. Once the campaign began, parties made decisions, calculated to gain strategic advantage, from week to week – indeed, from day to day – about advertising, debates, issues, and rhetoric.

Party strategies are chronicled in histories of campaigns, but little proof is offered that the electorate responds to them, or even notices them. Political scientists tend to treat claims about the impact of strategy and counter-strategy with scepticism. We are not so sceptical. This book shows that the strategies Canadian parties chose in 1988 made sense in terms of the structure of opinion on key issues. The parties chose to evoke certain responses and not others. The book also shows how the electorate responded and how this response led parties to revise their strategies. The 1988 Canadian campaign was a picture of dynamics and contingencies, far more so than the picture of campaigns that prevails in the voting literature. We do not believe that the 1988 campaign was all that exceptional, either for Canada or for other representative democracies.

Political parties face a fundamental problem each election: they must give citizens reasons for supporting them. To be sure, some voters will vote for a party simply out of loyalty, and this is part of the reason why party identification is always the single best predictor of the vote. But even party identifiers will soon tire of supporting a party that provides no reasons for their support. People, the psychological literature has taught us, are so fond of reasons they will manufacture them instead of conceding the randomness of some events.[3] Lack of reasons was critical, we suspect, to the end – or the interruption – of Liberal dominance that occurred in the 1984 election, the last one before 1988. Liberal dominance had spanned nearly a century, and yet John Turner could offer no cogent reason why he should be prime minister.[4]

By providing reasons, parties "prime" voters to consider the deep-seated values which motivate their choice of party. This, in turn, strengthens voters' party identification and ensures future support for the party. But priming, and the position-taking that goes with it, forces parties apart from each other and often away from the bulk of the voters as well. This conflicts with the need to make a wide appeal, to move towards the average voter. These opposing imperatives – to take stands which give voters reasons for supporting the party, on one hand, and to move towards the centre to avoid alienating voters, on the other – create one of the essential tensions in campaigns.

To show how politicians choose issues strategically from an historically determined menu to evoke fundamental considerations which mobilize voters, we weave four literatures together:

– The work on party realignments and the social and issue bases of party systems (Lipset and Rokkan, 1967; Burnham, 1970; Sundquist, 1973) shows how issue cleavages are created. These cleavages define the terrain over which parties manoeuvre to mobilize voters. This book shows how the Canadian case exemplifies notions out of this literature. This places us at odds with other interpreters of the Canadian system, notably LeDuc (1984).

– The literature on party alignments, which emphasizes abiding differences between parties and groups, is not always easy to reconcile with the spatial modelling literature, which usually emphasizes how parties choose issue positions at the average or "median" voter, to maximize the votes they receive (Enelow and Hinich, 1984; Ordeshook, 1986; Shepsle, 1991). We employ measures explicitly designed to represent the evaluative space employed by a real electorate in a real moment of choice, and then show how both centrist and non-centrist strategies can make sense.

– The spatial modelling literature assumes that voters immediately perceive where parties stand. Recent work in cognitive psychology reveals both the limitations on people's information-processing capabilities and the shortcuts that overcome these limitations (Kahneman, Slovic, and Tversky, 1982; Wallsten, 1980). Priming simplifies the cognitive task confronting voters. This much has been argued by Iyengar and Kinder (1987), Lodge, McGraw, and Stroh (1989), Aldrich, Sullivan, and Borgida (1989), Krosnick and Kinder (1990), and Popkin (1991). Now this cognitive literature must be linked to the spatial modelling literature. It is the role of priming in meeting voters' needs for cognitive simplification that makes parties' struggle over the campaign agenda so critical. To understand the strategic choices confronting politicians, then, a notion of priming must be incorporated in spatial models of elections. In the reformulated model, politicians prime issues to provide people with reasons for supporting them.[5] This causes parties to move away from the median voter. One of the long-term consequences of this is the development of party identification among voters. But the cognitive limitations of voters that make priming so critical also make campaigns potential sites for dynamics. The campaign raises both the stakes and the sound level for politics.

– Parties get their messages out in anticipation of the campaign and during the campaign itself by staged media events, advertising, and leaders' debates. In studying campaign dynamics, we follow in the footsteps of the Columbia school (Lazarsfeld et al., 1944; Berelson et al., 1954), recent work on American presidential primaries (Bartels, 1988; Brady and Johnston, 1987), and other works on American presidential elections (Patterson, 1980). Unlike the Columbia studies, we find campaign effects that are more than the unfolding of the historically inevitable. This is not to deny that campaigns, among other things, rebuild old coalitions. Indeed, we argue that because strategic politicians often find it useful to choose historically rooted cleavages as the basis for their appeals, campaigns are the place where these cleavages are reasserted and re-established. The deeper and more fundamental the considerations evoked, the more efficiently can voters be mobilized. This inevitably leads Canadian parties to return again and again to the same issues, to the mainsprings of Canadian politics. Campaigns strengthen party identifications through the issue updating central to "summary judgment" models of the phenomenon (Fiorina, 1977). But this is not all they do. To prime is to choose. Not every identification with the party will necessarily be reinforced by a particular issue emphasis. The more distinctive the party's position on a specific element in its overall inventory of positions, the more it risks losing identifiers at the margin. The campaign can also cut through coalitions.[6] In showing how new coalitions are formed we take seriously some of the newer, often frankly speculative, literature on the media and elections.

HOW DOES HISTORY SET CAMPAIGNS UP?

John Turner was not going to be without his reasons in 1988. But he could not emphasize just any issue that came to mind; he had to choose from the potluck of history. We argue in chapters 2 and 3 that by 1988 this meant three major issues: *commercial policy* – tariffs and trade relations with the United States; the *national question* – the place of Quebec and the French language within Canada; and *class questions* – the degree of welfarism and union power. In 1988 only the first two had serious strategic potential.

For much of its history Canada sat at the intersection of two empires, American and British. The conquest in 1760 which attached New France to the British Empire dictated that Canada, the synthesis of the old French empire and what remained of Britain's possessions in North America, would be a binational state. Immigration in the twentieth century added further complexity to the country's demography. Out of Canada's geopolitical location and fragmented sociology evolved the central features of its party system. Country and party system were destined to divide over church and state, over the moral and practical claims of the Empire, over the British-ness of Canadian state and society, and over the distinctive claims of the French-Canadian nation within the nation. Earlier divisions shaped later ones and imparted a high degree of continuity to the system.

Canada's attachment to the British Empire, with all that it entailed for party division, made practical as well as sentimental sense. If Canada was to deal with its neighbour to the south on a plane of equality, it could do so only by association with a countervailing power. The Empire served this purpose. And if over much of Ca-nadian political history the United States was in the background, occasionally it came to the foreground. In the 1891 and 1911 elections Canada-US trade relations were the central issue. Each time, the party advocating closer ties to the United States lost. But after 1935 the closeness of those ties became more and more the central external relations question for Canadian parties.

The cleavages created by disputes over commercial policy and the national question were far from anachronisms by the time the Con-servatives supplanted the Liberals in 1984. Between the 1984 and 1988 elections, the Conservative government approached these his-toric issues in new ways. The Meech Lake Accord of May-June 1987 attempted to meet Quebec's conditions for joining the other nine provinces in ratifying the Constitution Act, 1982. Quebec would be recognized as a "distinct society" within Canada and the position of provincial governments would be strengthened. The Canada-USA free trade agreement (henceforth FTA), initialled in October 1987, promised to reverse a century of commercial policy.

Both agreements were long, convoluted, and difficult – more the stuff of dingy governmental documents libraries than of thirty-second television commercials, memorable campaign rhetoric, or everyday conversation. Nevertheless, as we show in chapter 3, each issue presented the parties with both strategic possibilities and mortal danger. The Meech Lake Accord was especially perilous. The na-tional questions raised by the accord clearly divided Quebec and the rest of Canada in 1988. When Brian Mulroney announced the Meech Lake Accord, the Liberals and the New Democrats went immediately on record as approving its major features.[7] The parties struck a tacit bargain, roughly halfway between the preferred positions of English Canada and Quebec. The parties thus ensured that the potentially explosive Meech Lake Accord would not be the issue in the 1988 election. Chapter 3 shows how keeping the accord off the agenda made sense in national politics. The chapter also shows how the accord risked coming unravelled at the provincial level, as happened shortly after the 1988 campaign ended.

Chapter 3 also shows how emphasis on the FTA did make electoral sense. This was not because the FTA was a simpler issue than the Meech Lake Accord, nor was it an easier one to manage. The agreement placed the Liberals and especially the NDP in a difficult position. With its ties to organized labour, the NDP had to oppose an agreement that threatened its basic constituency. The Liberals had more freedom of movement but, for that very reason, less credibility as opponents of closer ties to the United States. But John Turner's need for an issue and his desire to elbow the NDP out of contention made opposition to the FTA useful to him. Only he actually had it within his power to stop the agreement: his party controlled the Senate. His 20 July pre-emptive strike, one news report suggested, "left the New Democratic Party gasping for breath, scrambling to recapture the attention of nationalist [anti-free-trade] voters as the original hard-line opponents of free trade."[8]

STUDYING CAMPAIGN DYNAMICS IN 1988

The 1988 Canadian Election Study was designed to study the interplay between strategic decisions like Mr Turner's and the electorate's response to them. To do this, we employed a design that has, to our knowledge, never been tried before in a parliamentary election, indeed in any general election: a rolling cross-section.[9] Between seventy and eighty telephone interviews were completed with a random sample of Canadians each day of the campaign; the date of interview was, to all intents and purposes, a random event. With this instrument, we could study day-to-day changes in vote intentions, issue positions, leader evaluations, and many other measures. Most of our respondents were interviewed again after the election, to establish "baselines" for each respondent, to allow us to separate true dynamic effects in the campaign from abiding cross-sectional differences.[10]

The novelty of our study was not limited to its design. We also made use of the full capabilities of computer-assisted telephone interviewing (CATI) by embedding experiments on question wording. These experiments and a related set of items in which we "challenged" respondents by asking them to consider opposing arguments would have been, at best, difficult with standard paper-

and-pencil telephone interviews. With CATI technology, the experiments were invisible even to the interviewers and were executed
flawlessly. The experiments allowed us to mimic the rhetoric of the
campaign.

In addition, we collected information on published polls, news,
and advertising. We identified every poll published during the campaign. We coded daily news on English and French CBC for every
night of the campaign and all prime time-party advertising on the
major Toronto and Montreal television channels. The coding scheme
sought to capture the rhetorical ebb and flow of the campaign. Finally, we measured the volume of "third-party" (which means, non-
party) advertising on the FTA in fourteen metropolitan dailies. Media
data were then stacked on top of the campaign wave of the CES, by
day of interview. Chapter 4 shows how media factors shifted over
the campaign and subsequent chapters assess the impact of media
factors on opinions, perceptions, expectations, and vote intentions.

THE MEDIA AND THE MESSAGE

The media stand between the electorate and the parties in all industrialized democracies. The parties can choose issues and take
stands, but without the media, the electorate is unlikely to get the
message. What kinds of sources are the media? Do people learn
about the campaign from the media, and do they learn what the
parties want them to learn, or do they pick up a message shaped
primarily by the media's own imperatives?

In the Columbia studies of the 1940 and 1948 elections, Lazarsfeld
and his colleagues showed that people did learn about campaign
issues from the media, but they were surprised by the minimal
effects of the media on attitudes and voting: "Despite the flood of
propaganda and counterpropaganda available to the prospective
voter, he is reached by very little of it. And, when we examine what
exactly does reach him, we find that he elects to expose himself to
the propaganda with which he already agrees, and to seal himself
off from the propaganda with which he might disagree."[11] Because
of this selective exposure and the related processes of selective perception and retention, the media can, at most, activate predispositions or reinforce pre-existing opinions. Since the publication of
Klapper's 1960 synthesis of media research, the notion that the media
have minimal effects has been the starting place for all media
research.

It is not, however, the end of the story. Today, the limited effects
model is simply not believed by most media researchers.[12] New

pathways for media influence, especially television, have yielded surprisingly strong effects. The two most important findings have been the importance of the media in setting the agenda and in priming. Iyengar and Kinder (1987) argue that "television news powerfully influences which problems viewers regard as the nation's most serious" (p. 4, emphasis omitted). They go on the argue that television may not only determine the problems citizens view as important, it may also prime citizens on what considerations to take into account when evaluating political issues and candidates.

We argue in chapter 3 that the parties first set the agenda for the election: free trade and not Meech Lake. In chapter 4 we show that they succeeded, with help from the media, in emphasizing free trade throughout the course of the campaign. We also show that the media's evaluation of the FTA and the three party leaders went up and down over the course of the campaign. Media coverage of John Turner had an impact on free trade opinion and on perceptions and evaluations of the Liberal leader himself. In chapter 8 we show that it had an impact on voting decisions.

What are we to make of this? It does not necessarily prove that the media have an autonomous impact. They may have done nothing more than mirror the events of the campaign, as media spokespersons are inclined to argue. Our analysis indicates that the media certainly did not just reflect voters' own autonomously formed opinions, perceptions, and preferences. It is true that the events of the campaign are unlikely to have an impact but for media coverage. And campaign events are not random; they are contrived, aimed at the audience the media bring to them. This still leaves open the question of impact from the media *as media*.

THE IMPACT OF DEBATES

Debates are the most direct form of political communication. Citizens of all sorts watch debates and those who watch them almost inescapably see all three party leaders in action.[13] Yet the common wisdom on debates is mixed, at least in the United States, where debates have been studied most extensively. There is general agreement that through selective perception, judgments about who won are strongly coloured if not absolutely controlled by partisanship.[14] Apart from prior partisanship, what dominates judgments of debate performance? Observers disagree over the relative power of independent judgment by viewers as opposed to influence from post-debate media coverage. The primary evidence for media dominance comes from polls on the 1976 Carter-Ford debate, in which Gerald Ford seemed to imply that the Soviet Union did not control Eastern Europe: where polls taken within twelve hours of the debate indicated Ford had won, those taken later in the week, after several days of media commentary on Ford's "disastrous" mistake, indicated Carter had won.[15]

Although there is some evidence that people learn about candidates' positions from debates,[16] the literature is almost unanimous in its conclusion that voting preferences are not changed. It is also conventional belief that "debates are more about accidents and mistakes than about enlightenment on the capabilities of candidates to govern" (Polsby and Wildavsky, 1991, p. 246). Evidence from other countries, including Canada, is also mixed. Outside the United States it seems fairly clear that at least some debates have actually moved voter preferences. Earlier Canadian debates seem not to have made much difference (LeDuc and Price, 1985).

In 1988 the English debate on 25 October provided a moment of extraordinary intensity. John Turner took his second major gamble and accused the prime minister of having sold the country out. Narratives of the campaign characterize this as its defining moment.[17] We agree. Chapter 4 shows that a consensus emerged early on the winner, John Turner. Those who watched the debate seemed to come to this conclusion immediately, but those who did not watch it took a week to ten days to come to rally to the consensus formed by viewers.

How did the non-viewers come to the conclusion that John Turner had won the debate? Their reaction appears to be one of following cues from television news and advertisements. Even though non-viewers tended to be inattentive and uninterested in politics, the lion's roar of Mr Turner's accusation was so prominently covered that no one could miss it. Voters also reacted to the message of the debates by becoming more positive about Mr Turner, by decreasing their support for free trade, and increasing the weight they placed on free trade in their voting preference, all of which fed through to vote intentions.

THE ROLE OF ADVERTISING

Although political advertising may be the most controversial aspect of modern elections, we know surprisingly little about its impact. Non-academic work on elections seems preoccupied with advertising and its tone often is apocalyptic. Scholarly work is more cool and tends to be dismissive of the whole non-academic controversy. In their judicious review of media factors, Sears and Kosterman (1987) note that advertising effects

are notoriously difficult to measure directly. They are brief moments in a complex sequence of campaign events, and their effects are difficult to single out. Most likely their effects, such as they are, are cumulative over repeated presentations, rather than the effect of any one particular ad, which adds to the complexity of measuring them. So claims about their effectiveness should be taken with some measure of skepticism – not that they are not often effective, but it is difficult to know how effective they are, and media consultants' self-serving hype about the wonders of their own products should be distinguished from careful and scientific measurement of effect in today's political environment. (p. 40)

This book undertakes the measurement and analysis Sears and Kosterman implicitly call for. In 1988 party advertising both set the tone of the campaign and reacted to its major events. Advertising, in turn, helped move opinion on the FTA and perceptions of John Turner. Advertising's impact is personalized, in two ways: the advertisements that really mattered talked about individual leaders; and the impact of these personalized advertisements was greatest of all on the evaluation of the person in question. The advertising pattern validates Popkin's (1991) observations about low-information rationality.

THE PLACE OF RHETORIC

Any student of rhetoric knows that different descriptions can yield vastly different reactions. The content of the news, advertisements, and the debates was explicitly rhetorical in this sense. The 1988 study sought to mimic the campaign's rhetoric in two ways. One was to present subtly differing versions of a question, the other was to challenge respondents once they had taken a position.

Experimental differences in question wording tended to be factual, selectively giving or witholding facts about a question, or choosing to emphasize some facts and not others. For this book the most critical experiment was on free trade: the identity of the negotiator made a serious difference to support for the agreement, an instance of the personalization of issues mentioned above. The experiment allows us to verify the success of one key opposition rhetorical ploy – always to refer to the FTA as "the Mulroney Trade Deal" – and even to map out the time path over which the ploy bit into the electorate, as the randomization in the experiment interacted with the "natural experiment" of the campaign. One other experiment helped to drive home our emphasis on the issue that ultimately did not matter, the Meech Lake Accord. Here an experiment was designed to bring out the coalition-building and coalition-splitting possibilities of alternative glosses on the accord. The power of one wording, which simply supplied the fact that the accord recognized Quebec as a distinct society, to undermine support for the accord helps bring out why the parties chose to suppress the issue.

Challenges helped flesh out arguments for and against the FTA. Five arguments – three against the FTA and two in favour – were cast as challenges to respondents on the other side of the issue. Response to challenges indicates which side, if any, had the rhetorical advantage. In 1988 it lay with FTA opponents. Again the time path of challenges' effect helped us plot the impact of campaign rhetoric.

PERCEPTIONS OF LEADERS

On the day after John Turner instructed Senate Liberals to block free trade, the Toronto *Globe and Mail* wondered in an editorial: "Could John Turner's poor personal stature as leader be the problem? He is running far behind his own party in the polls and behind the other national leaders. Is Mr Turner's dramatic invocation of a higher power meant to demonstrate personal control over his party in the face of its often conspicuous absence?"[18]

John Turner knew that people doubted his leadership. In his 20 July press conference, he presented a decisive face: "The Senate's not the issue here. I'm the issue. I asked the senators to do this. I'll take that responsibility."[19] Did John Turner's decisiveness here and later, in the English debate, have any impact on voters?

Leaders and their campaign managers may worry about their images, but political scientists are equivocal about the importance of leadership and other personality traits. The last decade has brought growing interest in traits in American and Westminster-style parliamentary elections (Kinder, Peters, Abelson, and Fiske, 1980; Miller, Wattenberg, and Malanchuk, 1986; Bean and Mughan, 1989). That leaders are important has been something of a staple of commentary on Canadian elections (Clarke et al., 1979; 1984), although little attention has been paid in Canada to the substance of leaders' appeal.

But there remains a lingering doubt that talk about the leadership qualities of a politician is nothing more than a repackaging of vote intentions formed for other reasons. This seems especially likely in the American system, where voters cast ballots directly for each party's *de facto* leader and the situation fairly begs for personalistic attributions for behaviour even where other forces are at work. Even in Canada, where the parties as teams and candidates as local representatives of the teams are interposed between voters and leaders, it is not unreasonable to expect that assessment of leaders' traits is moulded by selective perception. Sure enough, we find that party identification has a substantial impact on how party leaders are described by voters.

We also find, though, that leaders' traits have a life independent of prior party commitments. Not all traits vary in the same way over the course of the campaign, nor do they always move in tandem with voting intentions. Voters were able perceive trade-offs between leaders and traits: Brian Mulroney was high on competence but low on character, for instance. For all leaders competence proved to be especially critical to the dynamics of overall evaluation. And ratings – certain critical ones – *did* shift and usually did so in advance of vote shifts. None of this is consistent with a view of trait ratings as nothing more than restatements of vote intentions. Competence and character perceptions have a life of their own, in response to events in the campaign. These perceptions are causes, not merely consequences, of vote intentions.

THE ROLE OF EXPECTATIONS IN A PLURALITY ELECTORAL SYSTEM

In a three-party election, an additional consideration lies beyond issues, leaders, and the substance of the campaign. Supporters of the weakest party must think about the possibility that their behaviour will only help their least-preferred party to form the government. Will they "waste" their vote by supporting their first choice instead of going over to their second choice? Chapter 7 shows that voters were aware of parties' relative strengths and that their awareness reflected, among other things, published poll results. In 1988 all strategic considerations lay with opponents of the FTA, who had to choose between the NDP and the Liberals. Chapter 8 shows that expectations independently affected party choice, and that published polls had a significant impact on the Liberal and NDP votes, just as models of strategic voting would predict.

Strategic voting was not the whole story. In Quebec there is evidence for a bandwagon. Voters there not only made the strategic decision of choosing the Liberals over the NDP, they also moved away from the Conservatives after the debates, a movement over and above that induced by lowered support for the FTA. No conceivable version of a strategic voting calculus can account for such a shift. The existence, even if fleeting, of this bandwagon challenges us to consider whether other groups in an electorate have a large enough stake in being on the winning side to make a bandwagon possible.

Another challenge in our findings arises from the scale at which expectations work: both strategic voting and the bandwagon were driven by *national* expectations. There was, to be sure, also a role for local expectations, but these just did not exhibit the time-series dynamics that national ones did. Why would voters allow expectations for a race they, as individuals, could not possibly affect to alter their own behaviour? Although our expectations-driven models look at first glance to confirm the canonical model of political rationality, expected utility maximization, in fact they pose a major challenge to how we think about rationality in elections.

GAMBLING ON THE PEOPLE?

John Turner's decision to force an election on free trade was a gamble. He even risked being accused of trying to "hijack democracy."[20] The accusation did not stick and the constitutional question about the role of an unelected body like the Senate disappeared from view. Instead John Turner got to be a tribune, at least for a while. He took credit for forcing the government to let democracy work, to let the people decide.

But the people got to decide the question the parties wanted them to. This book is about why that question, and not some other, dominated the agenda. The one which did, the free trade agreement, contained surprises for both sides. For all the strategizing in advance of the campaign, the Canadian people could not be pinned down until very near the campaign's end. They entertained a wide range of considerations. They attended to debates, news, and advertising. They puzzled over the ancillary strategic questions thrown up by the campaign. Conceivably, 1988 raised more of these questions than any campaign before or since. In doing so it revealed the potential for campaigns. It also revealed the capacity of Canadian voters to deliberate, to behave remarkably like actors who rarely appear on the stage of voting research: *citizens*.

1 The Campaign Roller-Coaster

The Thirty-Second Parliament of Canada was dissolved on 1 October 1988, following the impasse over the FTA. All three of Canada's parties – the New Democratic Party as well the Conservatives and Liberals – seemed eager to let the people decide the issue in a federal election. The NDP leader, Ed Broadbent, wondered aloud about the propriety of a non-elected body such as Canada's Senate blocking, even temporarily, the will of a duly elected majority government. But, like John Turner, he opposed the agreement and hoped that the electorate would reject it. The Liberals believed that they were the likely beneficiaries of polarization over the FTA and so wanted to make the agreement the central issue. The last thing they wanted was for the FTA to become law; this would raise the stakes in campaigning against it and might, if enough time passed, even make the issue disappear. The Conservatives were content to make the impasse the occasion for a dissolution: the government party led in the polls.

SETTING THE STAGE

By September 1988 the Conservative party was the choice of 40 to 45 percent of respondents in most published surveys. The Liberal party, which had led most polls since mid-1985, had slipped to under 35 percent. The NDP was threatening to displace the Liberals as the second-place party and official opposition. In a parliamentary system, the real currency is seats, not votes; votes are important pri-

Figure 1-1
Will the Conservatives Get a Majority?

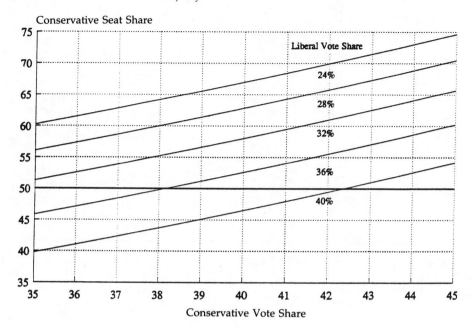

marily as a means to gaining seats. And the poll results indicated that the Conservatives were poised to be returned as a majority government.

These judgments reflect the logic of how Canada's electoral system translates votes into seats, as depicted in Figures 1-1 and 1-2.[1] Figure 1-1 focuses on how the Conservatives obtain a parliamentary majority. To read it, first find the Conservative vote share on the horizontal axis. Then move vertically to the line which corresponds to the Liberal vote share in question. Finally, look horizontally left to read off the predicted Conservative seat share on the vertical axis. For instance, if the Conservatives get 40 percent of the popular vote and the Liberals get 32 percent, the Conservative seat share should be between 55 and 60 percent. If the Conservatives get 40 percent and the Liberals also get 40 percent then the Conservatives should get between 45 and 50 percent of the seats, a plurality but less than a majority.

In Figure 1-1 the NDP is, in effect, a constraint on the Liberals. If the NDP gets 20 percent of the vote, its typical share in recent elections,[2] then the Liberals cannot get more than 80 percent minus whatever percentage the Conservatives get. If the Conservatives get

Figure 1-2
Who Forms the Opposition? Liberal and NDP Seat Shares

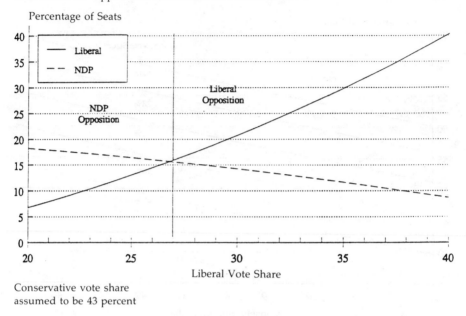

Percentage of Seats

Liberal Vote Share

Conservative vote share
assumed to be 43 percent

40 percent the Liberals cannot realistically get more than 40; they
may get less.

   The primary lesson of Figure 1-1 is that the strategic challenge
facing the Conservatives in 1988 was not that daunting. To get a
parliamentary majority they needed a vote share at most in the low
40s. Under certain circumstances they could win an outright majority
with less than 40 percent of the vote. This latter scenario was not
merely possible; on the eve of the 1988 campaign it was highly
plausible. For a Liberal share in the low 30s, the Conservatives could
get an outright majority with as little as 35 percent of the vote. Even
with the Liberal share at 36 percent, the Conservatives could form
a majority government with 39 percent of the vote.[3] The Liberal-
Conservative standing at dissolution on 1 September 1988 would
have given the Conservatives around 55 percent of the House.

   The Liberals were at serious risk of ceasing to be the official opposition. Figure 1-2 is based on the assumption that the Conservative vote share was 43 percent; this was their typical standing in
late September polls and it was also the party's share on election
day, 21 November. On this assumption, Liberal and NDP seat share
lines intersect at a Liberal vote share of 27 percent. If only three
parties capture votes, this threshold implies an NDP vote share of

30 percent. Minor-party percentages in 1988 hovered around 3 percent, though, and so the threshold of seat equality was also, practically speaking, the point at which the Liberals and NDP had the
same vote share. At that point each opposition party would control
just over 15 percent of the House. And, obviously, if the Liberals
dropped below 27 percent they themselves would cease to be the
official opposition.[4]

The strength of the Conservatives and the weakness of the Liberals
represented departures both from the historical norm and from the
pattern of the preceding three years. The last time the Conservatives
had returned consecutive majority governments was in 1891. The
1984–8 Conservative government had been deeply unpopular; the
recovery of its position had occurred only in the three months just
before the election. The historically dominant party and the one
which had led most polls since 1985 was the Liberal party. The NDP
had become a serious political force over the preceding three decades
but it had never been a serious contender federally to form the
opposition, much less the government. Its electoral power had been
negative: to frustrate the ambitions of the other parties.

How, then, had the stage for the 1988 campaign been set? The
answer seemed to lie in a combination of the issue over which Parliament was dissolved – the Canada-US free trade agreement – and
leadership.

The FTA was strategically ambiguous. Support for the agreement
seemed soft, but published polls indicated that it was more popular
with the public than were the Conservatives themselves. Emphasis
on the issue thus looked like a promising lever for ratcheting that
party's vote back up. Figure 1-1 reminds us that the Conservatives
did not need a majority, or even a plurality, of Canadians to support
the FTA. As long as the pro-FTA share was a large minority, or as
long as the pro-FTA camp could be supplemented by a modest number of voters who found the Liberal alternative no longer acceptable,
the Conservatives ought to sail home with at least a modest parliamentary majority. They needed to energize the FTA as an issue to
force its supporters into the party's camp. But they did *not* want to
energize it too much, to induce a serious shift in opinion on the deal
or to produce too great a consolidation of anti-FTA voters into the
Liberal camp. The government, accordingly, approached the issue
gingerly. It sought to bring other issues into high relief as well. Some
of these, such as a proposed child care program, seemed calculated
to calm jitters that the FTA would make such social policies impossible. Most of all, though, the government wanted the election to
turn on a comparison with the partisan alternatives.

The comparison seemed especially favourable, ironically, with the Liberals, the traditional party of government. Few Liberal veterans had survived the 1984 election and almost none wanted to return to elective politics. Since 1984 the Liberal party had been consumed by internal factional struggle. Occasionally the struggle was over real issues. More often it was over whether John Turner was up to his job as leader. Mr Turner had had to survive a challenge at the party's 1986 convention. The failure of that challenge did not prevent others; one occurred as recently as April 1988. Among the most conspicuous dissidents in these events were some of the party's best-known members. The Liberals, in sum, could not say much about their attributes as a team; they weren't, after all, much of one.

If the Liberals were to be saved, two themes had to be linked and made central in voters' minds. One theme was the FTA itself. Even if the agreement were not to prove a big enough club to beat the Tories, it was still the biggest one available. The other theme was the untrustworthiness of the prime minister. Although the government enjoyed a considerable advantage from its attributes as a team, that did not seem to rub off on the captain: Mr Mulroney seemed to be a liability. His reputation was a problem for his government *qua* government: whatever else may be at stake, Canadian elections turn inevitably on the question of who shall form the government. But Brian Mulroney was also a liability for his major policy initiative, the FTA. The agreement was so complex and so subject to uncertainties that it naturally invited voters to assess it in terms of the trustworthiness of its negotiator. It did not help that in 1983 Mr Mulroney had opposed the very sort of agreement he now had to defend.[5]

The NDP also made much of the FTA, but not nearly as much as the Liberals. Instead, the NDP tried to advertise its long-standing role as an advocate for social policy and for environmental consciousness, as well as its right to be taken seriously as a government-in-waiting. Significantly, the NDP campaign was set to open in Saint-Basile-le-Grand, Quebec, the site of a PCB leak that marked a turning point in that province's environmental politics; the party seemed to take both the issue and the province seriously. New Democrats also played to what seemed to be a another strength, the popularity of their leader, Ed Broadbent. Campaign-eve polls encouraged the NDP to look as much like a major party as possible, a party able to address a wide a range of issues, a party capable of brokerage.

At the same time the NDP reckoned that, although emphasis on the FTA might help bring the government down, the beneficiaries

Figure 1-3
Liberal (Frontrunner) Share in the Gallup Poll: Selected Post-War Campaigns

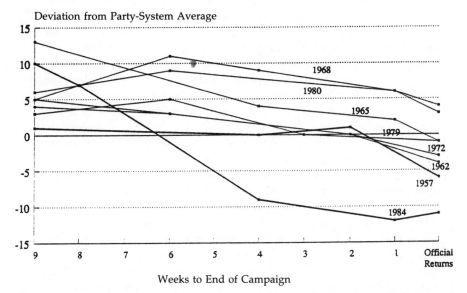

would not be themselves but the Liberals, because of lingering doubts about the NDP's ability to handle economic issues.[6] The NDP's own history and its principal supporters dictated that the party oppose the FTA. But they had as much reason as the Conservatives to fear *over*energization of the FTA. They, like the Conservatives, were set to mount a frontrunner's campaign.

How complacent could a frontrunner afford to be? The record of recent campaigns was not reassuring, although a Conservative frontrunner might be less daunted by it than a Liberal. The fact that the Gallup organization has been polling since the mid-1940s allows us to reconstruct the gross features of each campaign since 1945. Of the fourteen campaigns from 1945 to 1984, eight exhibited notable shifts, all against the pre-campaign frontrunner. These eight appear in Figure 1-3.[7]

The largest shifts occurred, in descending order, in 1984, 1965, 1962, and 1957. In each of the eight the frontrunner, always the Liberal party, lost ground. On six of the eight occasions, the election clearly was called at a time of the frontrunner's chosing, as the frontrunner was the government. Only once, in 1962, did the trailing party choose the moment. In five of the eight cases (1957, 1962, 1965, 1972, and 1984), a parliamentary majority was clearly lost.[8] In 1968 and 1980 the Liberals lost ground but still returned a seat majority.

Three times (1957, 1962, and 1984) the pre-campaign majority yielded to an outright loss. Twice (1965 and 1972) majorities became pluralities.

Seven of the eight significant campaign periods occurred since 1960. The one pre-1960 campaign that did matter, that in 1957, brought a long period of electoral stability to an end, as chapter 2 will show. Not only did campaign periods matter more after 1960 than before, but they have generally become the dominant type: seven of nine from 1962 to 1984 made a difference to the outcome.

Does this mean that campaigns as such – the active choices that parties make, as opposed to the mere passage of time and the overall heightening of the political sound level – have more often than not become critical factors in the ultimate result? The evidence in Figure 1-3 is mixed. The typical effect of a campaign period has been to bring the Liberal share not just downward but closer to the long-term average. Even where the Liberal share was ultimately below the average, it was closer to that mark than the pre-campaign share had been.[9] Much of the time, then, the campaign could be characterized less as a disruptive force than as a conservative one: it helped rebuild the coalitions that typified an electoral period.

One reading of this evidence is that party strategists – Liberal ones, at least – often react to information which is misleading. The information could be misleading simply from sampling error. In this case, even where voters' preferences do not change from the weeks before the campaign to election day itself, the record of preferences revealed in published polls will not be so stable. The more deviant the reading in any given poll, the greater tends to be the correction – the regression effect – that follows. Campaign strategists might be tempted to advise a dissolution on the basis of an adventitiously favourable poll. The campaign which ensues may just pick up the unfolding of the regression effect. In fact, the actual path of campaign effects is hard to square with this account. The overall movement is greater than we would expect from sampling error associated with samples such as Gallup's. Moreover, where regression effects associated with deviant samples ought to be immediate, the shifts in Figure 1-3 are not always immediate; often they come only after some weeks have passed and after other samples substantially confirm the pre-campaign poll.

There may be another, more plausible way in which pre-election polls are misleading. Vote intentions expressed outside the campaign period are not the same thing as the vote itself.[10] They may be subject to all sorts of influences, influences which do not count when the chips are down on election day. All that the heat of the campaign may do is burn these influences off, not because of parties' strategic and tactical moves and counter-moves, but just because the overall sound level is raised and voters are finally awakened to the fundamentals of the choice. Whatever those fundamentals are, they are in place long before the campaign begins. In this respect, note that, with two exceptions, the official returns in Figure 1-3 are not just lower on average than earlier poll readings, they are also more tightly packed around their mean value.[11] One reading of this is that election-day outcomes, the ones that matter, are determined by a small set of forces; conversely, the forces that operate on the response to sample surveys between elections may be more complex, but their complexity is largely irrelevant to real election outcomes.

Two campaigns stand out as exceptions to this conservative pattern: 1957 and 1984. In each of those years, the Liberals ended up *further* away from the baseline than they began – and much below it. The 1984 campaign opened with a post-convention boomlet that made the Liberal party appear to enjoy a ten-point margin over the baseline. On election day the Liberals ended up eleven points *below* the 1963–80 norm. In 1957 the Liberals entered the campaign with a share right on their average for the previous two decades.[12] They ended up six points below it.

Whatever the source of the decline, the narrative record indicates that campaign managers did not (at least not always) expect it to occur. For instance, the 1965 miscalculation was a grievous blow to the career of Walter Gordon, who had advised Liberal Prime Minister Lester Pearson to seize the day and go for the majority that the poll indicated would be his. The 1962 reverse indicated Mr Pearson's own weakness as a campaigner.[13] The 1972 result was a stunning reverse and ushered in a memorable parliamentary period.

In any case, the source of the shift may not matter much to the frontrunner: the simple fact was that the party in front at the start of a campaign seemed at serious risk of losing ground. The 1988 campaign was the first since 1960 that the Conservatives entered as the party to beat. Would they, unlike the Liberals, be immune to change over the course of the campaign? Or had they just replaced the Liberals as the party with the most to lose?

FIRST ACT: GETTING TO 23 OCTOBER

The first three weeks of the 1988 campaign seemed to compound the initial pattern of advantage and disadvantage: it brought an unbroken string of Liberal reverses. One high-profile actor, Keith Penner, an incumbent MP from northwestern Ontario and author

Table 1-1
Chronology of Events

October

1	– Parliament dissolved; commencement of campaign.
5	– prominent Liberal MP Keith Penner announces that he will not run again; Liberal hopeful William Dery attempts to disrupt Turner's announcement of child care policy in Montreal; Turner and aides revealed as not understanding the policy.
17	– Turner unilaterally announces an abortion policy; adverse reaction in the ranks.
19	– CBC national news reports on a failed Liberal leadership coup.
22	– nominations close.
23	– party advertising allowed to begin.
24	– leaders' debate in French.
25	– leaders' debate in English.
27	– Gallup poll sample indicates that Turner perceived as winner of debates; the Canadian dollar loses .36¢ US.
28	– Environics poll confirms Gallup on popular perceptions of the leaders' debates.
29	– first post-debates publication of polls on party standing; prospect of Conservative majority recedes.
31	– the Canadian dollar loses a further 1.46¢.

November

3	– Emmett Hall denies that medicare at risk under the FTA.
4	– Brian Mulroney calls John Turner a liar for the first time; Quebec NDP candidates assert priority of linguistic protection over Charter of Rights guarantees.
7	– Gallup poll indicates that Liberals would form a majority government; Canadian dollar drops again; TSE 300 composite also drops.
9	– Environics poll is the first to contradict Gallup.
10	– Michael Wilson lays out costs of Liberal campaign promises; Broadbent confronted with contradictions over language policy.
16	– Robert Bourassa supports FTA in the National Assembly.
17	– Ronald Reagan praises FTA.
18	– Margaret Thatcher praises FTA.
19	– last day for party advertising; three polls indicate that Conservative majority restored.

---

of a celebrated report on aboriginal self-government, announced his decision not to seek renomination. The same day, a storm broke over someone who actually did want to run; William Dery had been working for the nomination in the Quebec riding of Saint-Laurent for some time, only to be told that the seat was being held in reserve for a candidate with a higher profile. He protested his treatment by disrupting his own leader's announcement, in Montreal, of the Liberal policy on child care. The child care announcement would have

Figure 1-4
Party Shares

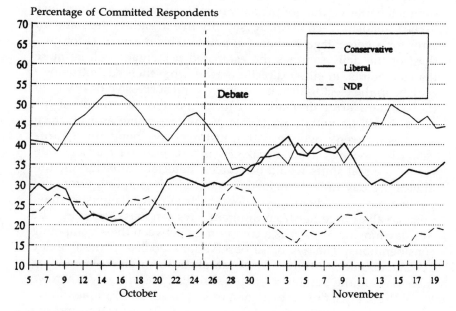

Percentage of Committed Respondents

5-day moving average

been a fiasco anyway: the press conference revealed that neither Mr Turner nor his aides understood their own policy (Fraser, 1989, pp. 165, 206ff).

Two weeks later the Liberal campaign hit bottom. On 17 October Mr Turner announced the party's policy on abortion. Apparently, he had consulted none of his candidates beforehand. The issue had been divisive and many in the party had wished that no collective position be taken. Many candidates felt that Mr Turner's announcement cut the ground out from under them.

This set the stage for a report on the CBC's "The National" news program on the 19th that Liberal senior executives and advisors had tried to get Mr Turner to step down. The story seemed so important and so sensitive that "The National"'s usual anchor, Peter Mansbridge, yielded the chair and delivered the story himself. The story was pursued at length the next day in the country's highest-profile newspaper, the Toronto *Globe and Mail*.[14]

How voters responded to these events appears in Figure 1-4. The figure gives the five-day (the current day, the two days before, and the two days following) moving average for each party's share of vote intentions.[15] The smoothed data are almost certainly closer to the truth for any given day than is the reading from only that day's completed interviews. For the daily number of completed interviews in the Canadian Election Study, seventy-five to eighty, the standard error for a percentage is about six points. This means that for one-third of the daily samples the estimated percentage will lie more than six points, in either direction, away from their day's true percentage in the electorate at large. By pooling successive days we cut the standard error dramatically, to 2.6 points. Two-thirds of the samples will lie within 2.6 points of the true value and nineteen samples in twenty will lie within just over five points of the true value. By pooling days we make Figures such as 1-4 readable; otherwise the real shifts would be scarcely detectable through the uninteresting day-to-day fluctuation induced by sampling error. But pooling has a disadvantage: where the true percentage is shifting, mixing values together from different days can mask the shift. The five-day moving average is a compromise between these competing considerations. The 375 or so observations pooled in the five-day average do not constitute a large sample in themselves, but adding more days to the moving average seems ill-advised. Only when we break the sample down, by region or language, for example, do we extend the moving average to seven days. By using the moving average, as opposed to some predetermined breakdown of time, we allow the campaign chronology to speak for itself.[16]

In the first two weeks the Conservatives surged at the Liberals' expense. The most plausible reading of this surge is that it reflected the bad press that the Liberals received. No early trend was visible for the NDP. Notwithstanding the Liberal reverses on and after 17 October, the third week of the campaign brought what looks like a correction to the Conservatives' original surge and the Liberals' initial decline. Although we cannot dismiss the possibility that the shifts in this period were the product only of sampling error, the range over which both old parties' moving averages tracked was greater than the confidence interval for 375 observations, the typical number pooled in the five-day moving average. This suggests that the movement requires a substantive explanation.[17]

For all that, the Conservative position in week three was comfortable. By our reckoning, the Conservative share for that week oscillated around 45 percent. The Liberals had a 30 percent share and the NDP about 25 percent.[18] This distribution would have produced a comfortable Conservative majority. The NDP, too, had reason to be satisfied; with 25 percent in the polls, they were five points ahead of their best election return and were breathing down the

Liberals' necks. For the Liberals, for John Turner in particular, the prospect was ignominious; it presaged near certainty of a second lopsided defeat and the distinct possibility of finishing third.

THE SECOND ACT: 23 OCTOBER TO 10 NOVEMBER

By 23 October the campaign was ready to shift into higher gear. On the ground, in the constituencies, all candidates were now in place. In the air, the leaders' tours were converging on Ottawa for televised debates. The most visible indicator of heightened intensity was the appearance, on the 23rd, of the first party advertisements. Before this date advertising was prohibited.

Who stood to benefit from the onset of party advertising? One possibility is a party whose leader's tour has gone – or has been reported – badly. Advertisements under the party's direct, unmediated control might begin to redress the imbalance. Another possibility is that the appearance of advertisements only reinforces the advantages already enjoyed by the party in power: the formula for allocating paid television time gave the Conservatives more minutes than the Liberals and NDP combined.[19] The two parties whose shares seemed to grow just as advertising began were the parties which fit each of these models, the Liberals and the Conservatives. Any such scenario encounters two problems, however. First, these movements predated the official beginning of the advertising period, and secondly, no sooner had advertising begun than another pair of events came along to disturb the campaign.

These were the leaders' debates, on 24 and 25 October. The timing and format of the debates had been under intense negotiation. At the Conservatives' insistence, the debates came nearly a full four weeks before election day, so that any damage might be repaired. The debate in French came first, on the 24th. Mr Turner performed relatively well and Mr Broadbent relatively badly. Most accounts have emphasized the English debate on the 25th, however.[20] The critical moment seems to have been a riveting Turner-Mulroney exchange over the FTA; at one point the two were shouting at each other. The theme of the exchange was precisely the one that the Liberal campaign had been trying to implant in voters' minds – Brian Mulroney's trustworthiness. Mr Turner got off a phrase that summarized the Liberal message: "I happen to believe that you have sold us out."

The tracking bears out the emphasis on the English debate. After the 25th, the Conservative share dropped like a rock: some thirteen to fourteen points in three days, to bottom out on 28 October between 34 and 35 percent. Both other parties surged, by our reckoning. Of the two, the Liberals experienced the less dramatic immediate effect. Their share did move up slightly, but the truly dramatic Liberal surge came *after* 28 October. More stunning in the short run was the NDP surge. This may have been a sampling fluke, as we could have underestimated the NDP share on the eve of the debates. The share that we impute to the NDP after the debates was not strikingly larger than the NDP norm for the campaign's first two and a half weeks. Whether the NDP actually surged or merely held their own, the party's continuing strength at this point is worth emphasizing.[21]

But after the 28th or 29th, a familiar pattern of Canadian politics re-emerged: only the Liberals and the Conservatives were seriously in the race: the NDP share dropped some ten points in about four days, never really to recover. The Conservatives did begin to recover from their fall, but only fitfully; by 10 November, their share appeared to have moved from the mid- to the upper-thirties. The Liberal surge peaked by the end of the first week in November. No decay in the Liberal share occurred, however; it seemed to oscillate at roughly the same level as the Conservative share. The NDP by this time was down around 20 percent.

In terms of the real stakes, seats, the Conservative gamble appeared to have failed. With both parties at roughly 38 percent in the popular vote, the Conservatives would win no more than about 45 percent of the seats and might lose their majority. That the Liberals would probably win fewer seats was small consolation. Party polarization over the FTA was such that a Conservative minority government would almost certainly fall right after the election. And the campaign's surface appearances suggested that the Liberals were going from strength to strength. The high point came with the Gallup poll, released on Monday, 7 November, which indicated that a Liberal parliamentary majority was now likely.[22] A fair degree of scepticism could be detected in reactions to the poll, but accounts also suggested that its immediate impact on Conservative morale was devastating.[23]

The poll also devastated the markets. The Canadian dollar dropped another two-thirds of a cent in that day's trading. The Toronto Stock Exchange 300 Composite Index dropped dramatically on the 7th and dropped further, although at a slower pace, over the next few days. These falls were widely interpreted as adverse reaction to the possible non-ratification of the FTA. The reactions could equally have been to other probable characteristics of a Liberal government, such as a relatively high tolerance for deficit financing.[24]

The counter-attack began within a week of the debates. As early as Monday, 31 October, Mr Mulroney's speeches began to focus on Mr Turner. The real turning point seemed to be Thursday, 3 November. Up to that time the opposition's most telling point against the FTA had been that it threatened Canada's social programs. Among these was the publicly financed health care system, whose blueprint had been a royal commission chaired, over two decades earlier, by Mr Justice Emmett Hall. On the 3rd, the same Mr Justice Hall denied opposition claims that the health care system was at risk under the FTA. On the same day the first major non-party pro-FTA advertisement, a four-page newspaper insert placed by the Canadian Alliance for Jobs and Opportunities, appeared. This day also marked the appearance of the first negative Conservative party advertisement, in which John Turner was accused of lying. Lying was also the central theme of Mr Mulroney's 4 November speech in Winnipeg. One expression bears repeating: "..to nail the lies down and pin them right on John Turner's forehead." Attacks on various facets of Mr Turner's credibility dominated speeches and advertisements for the next two weeks.[25]

THE THIRD ACT: 11–20 NOVEMBER

In the final week the anti-Liberal heat was turned up even more. The Conservatives were alleged to have budgeted $2 million for advertising in that week alone, and they were expected to run twice as many advertisements as the Liberals and NDP combined.[26] Non-party advertising also stepped up and became especially important in the last two days of the campaign, when party advertising was banned. Non-party advertisements tilted overwhelmingly in favour of the FTA and, thus, in favour of the Conservatives.[27] And in the Quebec National Assembly on the 16th, Premier Bourassa reminded Quebeckers of the benefits of the agreement.[28]

Figure 1-4 makes clear that in the last ten days, *something* happened and that it happened quickly, between 9 and 12 (or 14) November. The Liberals dropped and the Conservatives gained about ten points in four days, and perhaps another five points over the next two days. On each side, the impulse then decayed: the Conservatives fell back about five points and the Liberals recovered about five points. This left the Conservatives some eight to ten points above and the Liberals some five points below their post-debates level.

When the dust settled, the Conservatives had recovered their parliamentary majority. The moving-average reading for the last day gave the Conservatives about 45 percent and the Liberals 35 percent of vote intentions. This would have yielded a Conservative seat share of 61 percent. On election day, the Conservatives and Liberals won, respectively, 43 and 32 percent of the popular vote and 57[29] and 28 percent of the seats. The NDP was still locked in at 20 percent of the vote and 15 percent of the seats.

TWO ELECTORATES?

Canadian campaigns are run in parallel. For the most part this reflects simple, practical considerations: three voters in four speak English, one in four speaks French. Materials must be prepared in both languages. Parties cannot realistically plan on a single leaders' debate; they must think in multiples of two. Any party which is serious about forming the government must mount a credible campaign everywhere in the country, including Quebec. For linguistic reasons alone, the Quebec campaign cannot just be an extension of the campaign in the rest of the country.

Apart from these simple facts, the folk wisdom of Canadian elections suggests that francophones in Quebec respond to the party system in a distinct way. Awkwardly, Quebec is sometimes thought to be distinct in not one way but two, and these two partly contradict each other.

In one account, Quebec is said to hew to one party only, come what may. In doing so, it sets the terms of the parliamentary game by guaranteeing its preferred party a place in the final choice that *English* Canadians make. Left to its own devices, English Canada may have dealt the party in question out of the game long ago. For most of Canada's history this party has been the Liberals. After 1984, it may have been the Conservatives. The second account says that Quebec francophones monitor English Canadians and follow them. As a national minority living under a Westminster-style single-party majority-government system, francophone Québécois cannot afford the luxury of being in opposition. They must identify the party most likely to form the government and support it. Sometimes their support can make the difference between a minority and a majority government.

Neither account has been substantiated. Each argues that the Quebec electorate (sometimes, the francophone electorate within Quebec) should be examined separately. Figures 1-5 and 1-6 give the daily tracking for the two electorates. As these are subsamples, daily entries are for the seven-day moving average. The figures suggest that *both* renderings of the folk wisdom are true and yet that Quebec voters can also respond to events much as voters elsewhere in the country do.

Figure 1-5
Party Shares in Quebec

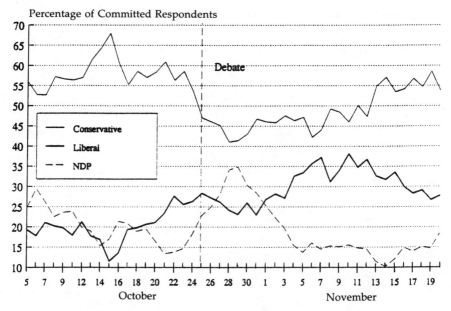

Percentage of Committed Respondents

7-day moving average

At every point in the campaign, Quebec voters in Figure 1-5 were more onesidedly Conservative than were the rest of the electorate. Towards the beginning, the difference was about twenty points. At the end it was fifteen points. To be sure, Figure 1-6, for the rest of Canada, masks important regional variation. Alberta, for instance, was as onesidedly Conservative as Quebec. But Alberta was the only place outside Quebec to fit this description. The figures also indicate that Quebec did not contradict the rest of Canada: the Conservatives returned a plurality of votes in both places. But the plurality outside Quebec was tiny, not enough to yield a majority of seats. In Quebec the Conservatives gained an outright majority in the popular vote, which in turn yielded the party almost all of the province's seats. And Quebec seats alone constitute one-quarter of the House of Commons. All this is consistent with an emphasis on Quebec as the agenda-setter.

Quebec voters were not impervious to the campaign. Indeed, in the immediate aftermath of the leaders' debates, Quebec voters were, dynamically speaking, indistinguishable from voters across the rest of the country. The flight from the Conservatives seemed

Figure 1-6
Party Shares Outside Quebec

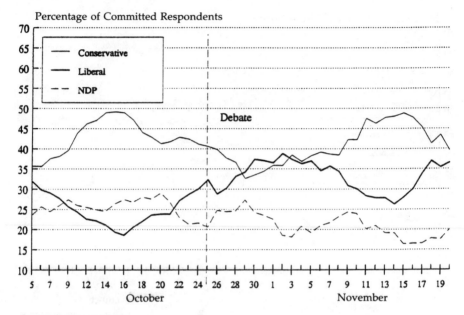

Percentage of Committed Respondents

7-day moving average

even more dramatic in Quebec than in the rest of Canada. That flight ended in Quebec and in the rest of Canada on the same day, 28 October. Also as in rest of Canada, Quebec's shift away from the NDP was delayed. In both subsamples the short-run effect of the debates seemed to be to rehabilitate the NDP. This part of the account suggests that Quebec and the rest of Canada are one seamless electorate.

After the 28th, Quebec and the rest of Canada diverged. The Liberal surge started later and continued longer in Quebec than elsewhere. Outside Quebec the Liberals began to slip towards the end of the first week in November; the turning point may have been Emmett Hall's dramatic intervention. In Quebec the Liberal share continued to move up for another week; the total Liberal gain was roughly twice as great in Quebec as in the rest of the country. Further, the Conservative recovery in Quebec was delayed. Outside Quebec the Conservative share began to move up right after it hit bottom, on 28 October. The Conservatives had regained some five points, half of the ultimate recovery, by 9 November. In Quebec the record is a bit murkier, because of higher sampling variance, but the trend line plotted on the raw daily numbers from 28 October to 9 November is essentially flat.[30]

Quebec voters could thus be said to be playing the same game as voters elsewhere and yet not quite doing so. Quebec voters responded to the debates much as did voters in the rest of Canada. The relatively large post-debates drop of the NDP in Quebec may have reflected nothing more than the historically exceptional height to which the NDP had risen before the debates. The same logic may explain the Liberals' relatively large post-debates gain.

But the Quebec status quo ante that the late campaign restored was unique to that province: a weak NDP share and dominance by one – and only one – of the old parties. The restoration of that status quo ante was hesitant, delayed. Part of the Quebec electorate may have been waiting to see which way the rest of Canada would turn.

WHERE DOES THIS LEAVE US?

On the face of it, did the 1988 campaign matter? The chronology does not yield a simple answer. On one hand, the campaign took the electorate in two directions – first away from the Conservatives and then back. Such two-way movement was unprecedented in the history of Canadian campaigns, at least since the beginning of the Gallup poll record. It is not possible for both these movements to stem from the mere passage of time or from the mere heightening of the sound level. The shifts, when they came, were abrupt. This adds to the impression of externally-induced impact.

Also weighing on the side of real campaign effects are the Liberal and Conservative trajectories after the debates. If the debates had only a transitory impact, the impulse that they had imparted would have begun to decay immediately. Only for the Conservatives did the reversal begin as soon as the bottom was reached. But if the debates were truly ephemera, the Conservative recovery would have been rapid in its early stages and would have slowed down thereafter. The opposite was true: the recovery was slow, fitful, and inadequate for nearly two weeks. For the Liberals, the story is inconsistent in every respect with an impulse-decay model. Liberal gains were not as immediate as Conservative losses. And Liberal gains continued for nearly two weeks, in Quebec at least. Ultimately, the Liberals were undone. But the events or circumstances that undid them cannot be described as just a waning of the debate impulse. To all appearances, the Conservatives had to win the election back: had the pattern of the fortnight following the debates carried throught to election day, the result would have been a standoff.

Of course, the final result was not a standoff. The strongest evidence against the thesis that the campaign mattered was the final party standings. The party that led at the beginning won in the end and by almost the exactly the margin it began with. The party that finished second, the Liberals, did gain a permanent advantage over the course of the campaign. But that advantage was one they had enjoyed for many years. The anomaly was the early campaign strength of the NDP; perhaps this was fated to evaporate, come what may.

To resolve the confusion requires more than simple chronology. The campaign has to be taken apart before it can be put back together. The place to start is with the historical legacy.

2 The Electoral Background: History and Geography

The 1988 election brought the Canadian party system and the Canadian people nearly full circle. The modern era of Canadian party politics began in 1878 in an election fought on commercial policy. The Conservative party won in 1878 but on a platform diametrically opposed to their 1988 one: in 1878 they championed protection; in 1988 they opposed it. Until 1988 no attempt to undo the results of 1878 succeeded; indeed, after 1911 none was even ventured. The 1988 election thus defied at least three long-standing norms of Canadian electoral politics: that no party would dare to propose commercial union with the United States; that any party doing so would lose; and that the Conservative party would be the last one even to consider such a proposal.

The Conservative party which did so was in power and seemed to have a realistic prospect of staying there. This too represented a departure from the historical norm. The ministry formed in 1984 was only the second Conservative majority government since 1930 and only the fourth since 1891. In most elections between 1878 and 1984 the dominant force was the Liberal party. This domination persisted through three distinct party systems. The transition between each system was marked by a Conservative landslide but the government formed by each landslide was short-lived. Each period in power left the Conservative party worse off in at least one key particular. One possible reading of electoral history, then, is that the 1984 landslide was just another occasion for the Liberal party to regroup and for the Conservatives to alienate yet another part of the electorate.

But the electoral record admitted an alternative reading. At each realignment of the party system at least one important element in its social base shifted profoundly. Two shifts are especially critical for this book. By 1984 the alignment of groups with a stake in commercial policy – with tariffs in particular – had rotated 180 degrees: the cleavages of 1878 had been reversed. In 1984 another group appeared to have rotated 360 degrees: Quebec francophones. In 1878 this group lay at the heart of the then dominant Conservative coalition. The Liberals supplanted the Conservatives in great part by detaching Quebec from them. If the Conservative party has ended the Liberal century, the final step in its doing so was taking Quebec back.

At each realignment in this century, the Liberals' support shrank. In the third system, Liberal governments were narrowly grounded in the electorate and often weak in Parliament. There was, then, no mistaking the trajectory the Liberals were riding. On this reading, 1984 heralded not just a short-lived censure of the natural party of government but a wholly new alignment of electoral forces – forces that promised to make the Conservatives the dominant party.

This chapter fleshes out these propositions. It draws lessons from a century of elections for the events of the later 1980s. It makes the point that many features of the party system are, by the standards of representative democracies, of ancient vintage. Special attention is paid, though, to the transformations that set the stage for 1988's peculiar dynamics: changes in commercial policy and in the role of Quebec.

Emphasis in this chapter is on the mass electorate, on one hand, and the policy and personal appeals that parties made to that electorate, on the other. It argues that each transition signalled a change in the party-electorate nexus. The chapter does not dwell on party organization and finance or on how campaigns were organized. But each of these areas also changed as one party system yielded to the next. These changes are reviewed in outline in two other places, by Carty (1988) and Smith (1985). This chapter should be read as a complement to those pieces.

THE ADVERSARIES AND THE STAKES

The Canadian electorate has been polarized along three basic dimensions, much as other representative democracies are (Lipset and Rokkan, 1967). One dimension, itself really several dimensions, is *ethno-religious*. Electoral cleavages in this realm tend to be peculiar to each country, reflecting the configuration of religious groups and nationalities that happens, often accidentally, to get enclosed by a juridical boundary. Here we must resort to some historical narrative. The outstanding group for this account is French Canada, one of the key coalitional elements in setting 1988 up. The second dimension is *urban-rural*. For the Canadian case, the central cleavage is between export-oriented agriculture and the rest, and the issue is precisely the one that dominated 1988: commercial policy. The third dimension is *class*. As a practical matter, the operative definition of the class cleavage is the union movement versus the rest. This cleavage too is implicated in the debate over commercial policy. The order in which the cleavages were just enumerated is the order in which they appeared in historical time.

Ethno-religious Divisions

Cultural divisions have persisted from the beginnings of Canadian politics. The main antagonists have been Catholics and Protestants, although the most visible expression of this cleavage has often been linguistic, French versus English. More recently, groups which stand outside the old religious-cum-linguistic division were added to the mix; typically the new groups allied with Catholics and the French.

Only some of the time were the stakes specifically religious or linguistic. Indeed, religion dominated as a policy question only at the Liberal century's beginning: the Liberal party's rise was attended by conflict over the place of the Catholic church in the emergent Canadian nationality. Language policy dominated only towards its end, in the third party system.[1] Neither religious nor linguistic conflict promised easy returns for any party; indeed, both conflicts divided each party against itself, partly as a reflection of the awkward fit between the geography of group membership and the location of provincial boundaries. The parties sometimes changed their positions on the divisive issues, as they sought tactical advantage, or as their own makeup shifted. Sometimes the parties' leaders colluded to keep the issues off the agenda.

For most of the past century, however, the ethno-religious division has been over something else entirely: over the moral and symbolic claims of the British connection. Down to 1945 (and perhaps 1962), the problem was mainly one of external policy, of how much Canada collectively and Canadians individually owed the Empire. This was not just a disagreement over sentiment. At least until the 1920s, Canada arguably needed the diplomatic weight of the Empire to counter the claims of the United States. But British diplomatic support carried a price; it required Canadian participation in overseas wars, in South Africa and in the First and Second World Wars. What one thought possible, or even desirable, in external relations depended on the price one was willing to pay and thus on how aggressively one was prepared to force the question of the Canadian nationality's essential character. The nationalism of the years before 1920 was commonly linked to imperialism; with resistance to imperialism also went resistance to assertive definitions of the national interest, in either economic or military policy. After 1920 rival versions of nationalism competed. For some, the imperialistic version was still the only realistic one; the continuation of the Empire as a diplomatic unit was deemed essential for the realization of Canada's own goals. For others, imperialism and nationalism seemed antithetical: Canadian interests had to be expressed in their own right, were little served by combining diplomatic forces with the Empire, and, indeed, could often be blocked by conformity to an imperial line. After 1960 nationalism was stripped of its British content; there was no longer an empire for Canada to be a part of.

As long as the British connection was viable, English Canadians were naturally more enthusiastic about both its internal and external aspects than were French Canadians. Within English Canada, Protestants were palpably more sympathetic to the moral claims of the Empire and to the symbolic appeal of a British definition of the polity than were Catholics. Non-Christian groups, Jews at first and later other groups as well, gained demographic weight and tended to side with Catholics. On the place of Canada in the Empire and of the Empire in Canada, the two parties have differed profoundly and consistently over the entire period under consideration. The Conservative party championed the British connection. Although not all Conservatives sought a closer integration of Canada into the Empire, almost everyone who sought such integration was perforce a Conservative. The Liberal party resisted the pull of empire. Not all Liberals opposed the connection; but most of its opponents were forced, sooner or later, into the Liberal camp. As long as questions were defined in terms of the British connection, the various lines of force in the country's ethno-religious structure tended to cumulate and the cleavage that divided Catholics and Protestants, Liberals and Conservatives, tended to be wide but simple.

Farmers versus All Others

Farmers producing for the world market found themselves at odds with the major thrust of national commercial policy – protective tariffs. As the prairie west filled up in this century's first decade, export-oriented agriculture gained political weight. In due course, grain producers shifted their attention from tariffs to other targets. In particular, they sought government intervention in key markets, for credit and, most importantly, for the commodities themselves. These demands were pressed all the more strongly as the agricultural sector as a whole shrank relative to the rest of the economy. Farmers producing for domestic consumption also pressed for government intervention.

While the Liberal party may not always have been the farmers' friend, the Conservative party before 1957 was always their foe. The "National Policy" of tariff protection, railway subsidies, and dominion lands (Mackintosh, 1964) was *their* policy. For Conservatives it was justified not just on economic grounds but also as an expression of mutually reinforcing national and imperial interests: creating a transcontinental polity and economy secured an "All Red Route to India." An attack on the National Policy was vulnerable to being treated as an attack on the nationality, at least in its British definition, and as a thinly veiled plot to deliver Canada to the American enemy.

Since 1957 the Conservative party has moved away from this position. In part this reflected a profound realignment in its geographic base. Export-oriented farmers shifted into the Conservative coalition. In doing so they helped prepare the way for the 1988 version of the politics of free trade. Also preparing the way was the disappearance of the Empire; Conservatives' evaluation of commercial policy now had to be detached from imperial considerations. As the Conservative party moved away from protectionism, the Liberal party moved towards the Conservatives' former ground and came to share it with the NDP.

The Union Movement

A second economic division has gradually become more important. The growth of the labour movement has injected labour-management issues more centrally into the national agenda, as well as into the agendas of most provincial governments. Provinces have the principal responsibility for labour law, but they act in an economic context in which the most important Canadian governmental actor remains Ottawa. Moreover, labour law in most provinces is modelled on federal examples (Gunderson and Riddell, 1988).

Organized labour roughly trebled its share of the labour force between the onset of the Second World War and the mid-1950s. The unionized share grew still more over the 1960s and 1970s. Now about 35 percent of the labour force is unionized – not a large share by the

Figure 2-1
National Popular Vote Share, 1878–1984, Liberal Party

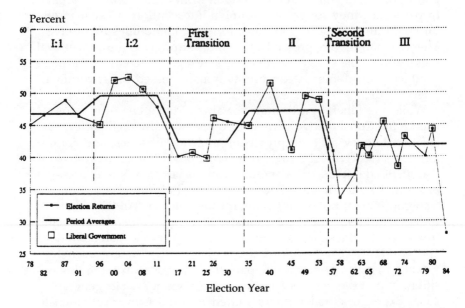

standard of many European countries but about twice the unionized share in the United States. No less important than the growth of the labour movement has been its consolidation, at least in English Canada. The creation of the Canadian Labour Congress in 1956 removed the major barrier to official links between the English-Canadian labour movement and a political party (Horowitz, 1968). The link was consummated, after a fashion, in 1961, with the founding of the New Democratic Party (NDP).

The interplay of these adversaries and stakes defined the temporal boundaries in the history of the party system. The passages that follow identify the factors which dominated each system and which seemed to bear most specifically on each transition between systems. Special attention is paid to ethno-religious factors, mainly but not exclusively as they affected voting in Quebec, and to shifts in commercial policy.

THE FIRST PARTY SYSTEM

Figures 2-1 and 2-2 track Liberal and Conservative shares, respectively, of the national popular vote from 1878 to 1984. The first year of the series, 1878, marked a key institutional boundary for Canadian

Figure 2-2
National Popular Vote Share, 1878–1984, Conservatives

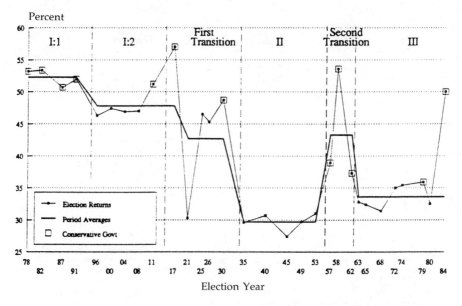

elections. It was the first election in which a secret ballot was employed and only the second in which virtually all writs were issued
on the same day (Qualter, 1970). Imposed on the election-by-election
tracking are means for each party system and for each transitional
period. Figure 2-3 tracks the combined share for all other parties
over the 1878–1984 period. It also isolates the only enduring third
party, the Cooperative Commonwealth Federation and its offspring,
the New Democratic Party, for 1935–84.

The Liberals became the natural party of government in and after
1896. Their base grew, if rather fitfully, over the 1880s and 1890s
and peaked in 1904. Although the Liberals lost office in 1911, their
1911 share exceeded that for every election but one (1887) before
1900. The Conservative record (Figure 2-2) in the first system largely
mirrored the Liberal one. Usually, when the Liberals gained, the
Conservatives lost and vice versa.

Temporal boundaries in the first system were a bit ambiguous.
Popular vote movements in 1880s foreshadowed the system to come.
But the full flowering of the changes had to await 1896. Thus the
system is split into its Conservative and Liberal periods at that year.
The last election fought clearly under first-system rules was the 1911
one. Although the dominance of the two old parties continued, in

Figure 2-3
National Popular Vote Shares, 1878–1984, Other Parties

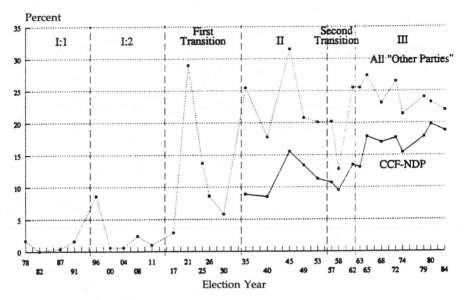

CCF/NDP included in 1935-84 "Other Parties" total

a manner of speaking, through 1917, the parties which contested the 1917 election were not quite what they had been before: what we record as the Conservative share really belonged to the Unionist coalition, formed by Conservatives and English-speaking Liberals and dedicated to, among other things, conscription for overseas service in the First World War; the Liberal party was reduced to a preponderantly French and Catholic rump.

The sectional foundations of the two 1878–1911 subsystems are contrasted in Figures 2-4 and 2-5. Each figure gives Liberal and Conservative vote shares averaged, province by province, over several elections. Provinces are ordered from west to east, to emphasize the party system's geography. Two contrasts dominate the transition between the two subsystems.

The first is in the place of Quebec, on one hand, and Ontario and Manitoba, on the other. Before 1896 Quebec was in the Conservative camp. After 1896 it was in the Liberal camp. In the popular vote the swing was not dramatic, a net shift of some ten points. In seats, the significance of this swing was much greater. We return to the special place of Quebec seats in the parliamentary game below, when we consider Figure 2-12.

Figure 2-4
The First Party System 1: Conservative Party Dominant, 1878–91

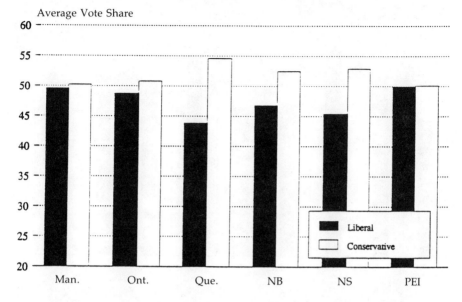

The second contrast is in the sheer number of provinces: it grew, effectively, by three. British Columbia did not really engage in party politics before 1896. And Manitoba's pre-1896 appearance in Figure 2-4 is something of a courtesy: the province was much more important after 1896. But if Manitoba and British Columbia grew in importance, Alberta and Saskatchewan fairly exploded. They did not acquire provincial status until 1905 and their demographic growth from 1896 to 1911 was nothing short of astounding. By 1911 Saskatchewan was the third most populous province in the dominion.[2] And Saskatchewan, like Alberta, was squarely in the Liberal camp.

How the Liberals supplanted the Conservatives is still a subject for scholarly investigation. The Liberals were clearly on the rise over the 1880s. Their growth was probably a compound of the Conservative government's own senescence, of economic distress, and of careful linguistic and sectarian tactics on the Liberals' part. The Conservative government was old: eighteen uninterrupted years to 1896 and twenty-four of the twenty-nine years after 1867. By the 1890s the Conservative organization was corrupt and rotting. The 1880s and early 1890s were also a period of intense economic distress. The price level in 1896 was well below that of 1873. The country experienced severe net outmigration. In the ethno-religious game, the

Figure 2-5
The First Party System 2: Liberal Party Dominant, 1896-1911

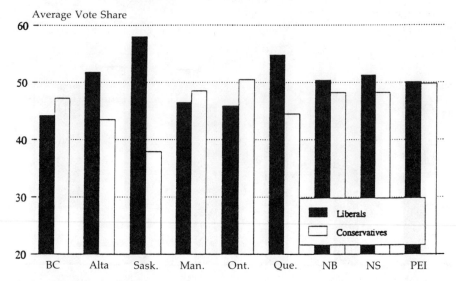

Saskatchewan and Alberta,
average for 1908–11 elections only

Liberals held a trump in Quebec: Wilfrid Laurier, the first Catholic francophone to lead a national party.

The dawn of the Liberal era in 1896 was accompanied by a minor party surge (Figure 2-3) that was rich in anticipation if not in result. Minor-party and independent candidacies in the 1890s reflected agrarian discontent and labour insurgency, in reaction to the persistent economic adversity. Disturbances in the Canadian system were, if anything, pale by comparison with American populism in this period and they abated after 1896. But they anticipated later disruptions, including the ones which brought the first system to an end.

Notwithstanding these tensions, the parliamentary character of the first system was simple and quite stable. Figure 2-6 plots seat shares for the two old parties combined and for the winning party. Down to and including 1917 virtually every seat was held by one of the major parties. Governments were always returned with a majority and always by about the same margin.[3] For instance, when the Laurier government fell in 1911 the Borden government which replaced it had almost exactly the same number of seats as the Liberals had won in 1908. In no year did the government utterly

Figure 2-6
Seat Shares, 1878–1984, Election Returns and Period Averages

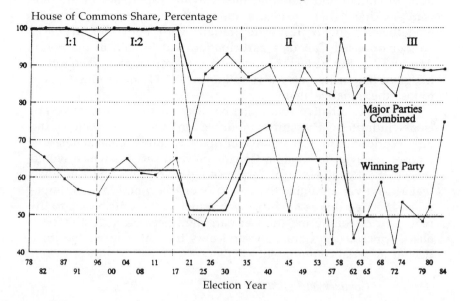

swamp the opposition, yet in no year was the government's majority razor-thin.

Ethno-religious Divisions

One thread running through the geography of the post-1896 Liberal coalition was religion. Liberals tended to be strong where Catholics were numerous and vice versa. The Liberal base was not just in Quebec but in the heavily Catholic Maritime provinces as well. Ontario, Manitoba, and British Columbia were, conversely, the heartlands of Anglo-Protestant triumphalism. It bears emphasis that this relationship was *not* the product of a close identification of the Liberal party with the Catholic project for church and state – that is, the defence of the separate school system in Manitoba, the extension of separate schools in Ontario and the Northwest Territories (later Saskatchewan and Alberta), and the settlement of the Jesuit Estates in Quebec. Collectively, the Liberal party was ambivalent about the place of Catholicism, just as the Conservative party was. They may have been helped by being *out* of power in Ottawa for the most critical years.

The issues Liberals were forced to manage once in power tended to be outward-looking, to be about Canada's place in the Empire.

This allowed a simpler coalitional strategy than the internal questions of church and state and the growing importance of the outward-looking issues explains much of the post-1896 pattern. Nonetheless, the issues were fraught with peril. For instance, Laurier opposed Canada's participation with Britain in the South African War. But he lost the initiative and Protestant opinion forced his government into an active military role. He determined never to lose the initiative again.[4]

Taking the initiative could also be risky, as the next imperial episode indicated. Pressures mounted in the years before the First World War for Canada to contribute to imperial naval defence. Laurier resolved to create a Canadian naval service, which would relieve the Royal Navy of responsibility for protecting Canadian waters and yet minimize the risk of overseas complications. Imperialists decried this as too little, as not materially contributing to the real need of countering the German High Seas Fleet. Anti-imperialists opposed the Canadian service as the entering wedge for a deeper imperial commitment.

Commercial Policy

Canadian commercial policy has traditionally been embodied in the National Policy on which the 1878 election was fought. The National Policy was designed to create a transcontinental nation and was the Conservative party's legacy to that nation. The policy traditionally had three elements: railway subsidies, virtually free access to dominion-controlled western lands, and protective tariffs. Abolition of those tariffs lay at the heart of the 1988 free trade agreement.

The National Policy created its own coalition. A manufacturing sector emerged as a political interest in its own right. For most of the last century, labour and capital saw their interests as allied on the National Policy, much as international trade theory would predict. Both capital and labour were in short supply and thus were highly priced in this period – in contrast with land – and so ought to have been net beneficiaries of protection.[5] Allied with them traditionally have been the railways, for which manufactures from Ontario and Quebec provided the westbound freight. In the earlier period the policy was not merely National; it was also Imperial. The policy's first decade coincided with a renewed interest by Britain in its empire and with a growing desire in many English Canadians for a larger place in the imperial sun, as indicated by the enthusiasm to support Britain in the South African war. Between its enactment in 1879 and its effective repeal in 1988, the National Policy was challenged twice. Each time it survived.

The first challenge came in 1891. In that year, the Liberal party committed itself to "Unrestricted Reciprocity" with the United States. The Conservative party responded with the slogan "the Old Flag, the Old Policy, the Old Leader" and produced the downturn in the Liberal share which is shown on Figure 2-1 as putting a brake on the trend that ultimately put that party in power.[6]

The Liberal government finally formed in 1896 appeared to have learned its lesson. The principal commercial-policy initiative of its first fourteen years of office was a brilliant tactical coup: imperial preference. By reducing tariffs on British manufactures,[7] the party genuflected towards its free trade roots. By confining preference to imperial production, it neutralized arguments that the Liberal party was disloyal to the British connection. The timing was brilliant: the policy came into force in 1897, Queen Victoria's Diamond Jubilee year.

These lessons seemed to be forgotten in 1911, the year of the second challenge to the National Policy. In 1910 the Laurier government won an agreement for reciprocal free trade in natural products from the Taft administration.[8] Canada enjoyed comparative advantage in most natural products. To wheat, the most important product of all, the agreement was essentially irrelevant; America and Canada were both exporters, principally to the European market. The agreement seemed politically unassailable, in that it left protection for manufacturing essentially untouched. These considerations did not carry the day. The principal argument against the agreement spoke of the "thin edge of the wedge": the agreement was cast as the harbinger of a more comprehensive trade liberalization. The latter threatened the British connection as well as the domestic interests that the National Policy had created. This time the slogan was "No Truck or Trade with the Yankees."

The Liberal defeat in 1911 may not have been quite the product of miscalculation that this barebones narrative suggests. Like the Conservatives in 1896, the Liberals in 1911 had been long in office and were unpopular. Figure 2-1 records that their vote share in 1908 was markedly lower than it had been in 1904. The naval controversy, mentioned above, peaked in 1910. It threatened to eat into Liberal support in Quebec, which, given the importance of secondary manufacturing to the province, could also be expected to oppose reciprocity. The Liberals may still have reckoned that Quebec voters would not desert them for the arch-imperialist Conservatives, whatever the trade issue.[9] Outside Quebec, the same imperialists who opposed the Naval Bill as doing too little for imperial defence also opposed reciprocity; it is not clear, then, that the cumulative effect of the two controversies was to increase the total weight of opposition to the government. Canada was still overwhelmingly agrarian, after all, and the prairie region's electoral weight (Figure 2-5) reinforced the Liberals' traditional agrarian base in Ontario. The free trade commitment may thus have offset losses that the government would otherwise have incurred in English Canada.[10] Still, the most straightforward lesson of 1911, as of 1891, seemed to be that free trade was electorally too risky.

THE FIRST TRANSITION

The 1911 election result, although a reverse for the Liberals, was hardly a cataclysm. But it set the stage for a truly profound realignment, which began in 1917 and took until 1935 to be realized fully. In 1917 the Liberals' share dropped to 40.1 percent and it barely changed in 1921 and 1925. In these three elections, the party pulled in nearly 10 percentage points less than its average share from 1896 to 1911.

Where 1917 was the year the Liberal share collapsed, 1921 brought retribution to the Conservatives. It was frightful: in 1921, the party lost nearly 27 percentage points, almost half its 1917 share. To be sure, that 1917 share did not fairly represent the pre-1921 Conservative base; but the 1921 result was stunning by almost any standard. Taken against the Conservative average share over the 1896–1911 period, the 1921 vote represented a drop of nearly 17 to 18 percentage points.[11] The Conservative decline in 1921 was two to three times as large, depending on how one counts, as the Liberal drop in 1917.

The avenging angel was the Progressive party, an agrarian movement. Figure 2-3 indicates that the combined minor-party vote in that year reached 29 percent, almost all of it for Progressive candidates. The Progressive breakthrough weakened both old parties: the 1921 election brought the first hung Parliament since Confederation, as the Liberals won only 41 percent of the vote (slightly more than in 1917) and 49 percent of the seats. Although the Progressives themselves were destined to disappear, both they and candidates with labour-cum-socialist allegiances anticipated the CCF, a party which was destined to survive.

Figure 2-7 gives the geography of old-party collapse and third-party insurgency. For clarity, old parties appear above the zero percent line and new parties below it. For both old parties, support outside Quebec took on a rough east-west gradient. The Liberals maintained a beachhead in Saskatchewan and the Conservatives one in British Columbia. In Alberta and Manitoba the Liberals were weaker than both the Conservatives and the new parties. Conser-

Figure 2-7
The First Transition, 1921–30

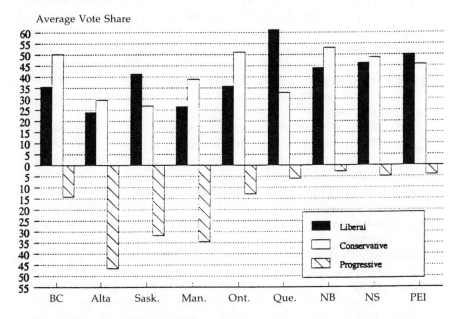

Average Vote Share

vatives were weaker than the new parties in Alberta and Saskatchewan. In each prairie province new parties controlled either the
largest or the second-largest share. A new-party bloc was also visible
in both British Columbia and Ontario. In the Atlantic provinces and
Quebec, third-party voting was of virtually no significance.

Thanks to their sectional concentration, the new parties made a
beachhead in Parliament. Since 1921 parties other than the Liberals
and Conservatives have occupied, on average, 14 percent of the
seats, according to Figure 2-6. Although their biggest share came in
1921 and the next three elections saw a restoration of much of the
old major-party joint parliamentary share, the third-party presence
weakened governments appreciably. Before 1921 the party in government typically controlled just over 60 percent of the House; from
1921 to 1930 the winner's parliamentary share averaged just over 50
percent. From 1921 to 1926 no single party had a majority and neither
the 1926 nor the 1930 majorities approached the pre-1917 norm.

Ethno-religious Divisions

The transition between the first and second party systems pushed
ethno-religious differences to the limit. This is implicit in the geo-

graphic pattern captured by Figure 2-7. In 1917 the Liberals collapsed outside Quebec; in Quebec they surged. The Conservatives, leading a coalition with English Liberals and calling themselves Unionists, surged outside Quebec but collapsed inside that province. Although Figure 2-7 concentrates on 1921–30, for the contrast between Quebec and the rest it also gives a good reading for 1917. Compare the sharp differences between Quebec and the rest with the modest vote differences that prevailed in either part of the first party system (Figures 2-4 and 2-5).

Both the cause and the pattern of the Liberals' collapse outside Quebec was foreshadowed by the geography of prewar party choice. The 1896–1911 regional differences in Figure 2-5 corresponded closely to the most powerful imaginable indicator of 1914–18 commitment to the Empire: the rate of voluntary enlistment. Overseas service was proportionally highest by a wide margin in Manitoba and British Columbia and third-highest in Ontario; apart from Quebec, the lowest rates were in the maritime provinces and Saskatchewan and Alberta. [12] The 1917 crisis was brought on by the Unionist government's desire to go beyond voluntary enlistment, to bring in conscription.

If the 1917 crisis sharpened one element in the prewar geographic pattern, it shattered the other one. In the first system, the attachment of Alberta and Saskatchewan to the Liberals, like their low Great War enlistment rates, reflected not just ethno-religious considerations but also the dominance of their economies by wheat production. The last election under the old dispensation, 1911, turned in great part on this polarization. But in 1917 the opposition of some Liberals to conscription and the disappearance of the rest into a Conservative-dominated coalition discredited the party for many prairie westerners.

One result was an agrarian insurgency, the Progressives. The insurgency picked up threads from 1896. In doing so, it combined two elements of Canadian third-party activity which after 1935 were to be separated. One part was protest against some facet of politics-as-usual; an element in this was distaste for party politics as such, a theme which had surfaced in 1896 and which continues to recur. This distaste has been a theme in agrarian insurgency in America as well as in Canada. [13] It reflected an individualistic model of society which was congenial to farmers, especially on the wheat-producing frontier, as they saw themselves on the defensive against urbanization and industrialization.

If one part of the Progressives' appeal looked back, the other part foreshadowed issues that were both new and destined to endure.

The Progressive movement and the other political tendencies which sprang up in the early 1920s were also outlets for impulses originating in cities and in the ranks of English Canada's intelligentsia. A new cultural nationalism had emerged from the crucible of the Great War. Intellectual leaders in the universities and the Protestant churches had hoped that the war would produce an enlarged sense of citizenship and an end to sectarianism. For this reason many supported the Unionist government; its commitment to conscription seemed consistent with the call to civic duty and it did embrace more than one party. But the government disappointed them and the war purged the intelligentsia's nationalism of much of its overt Britishness and jingoism. [14]

Commercial Policy

On economic policy as well, the Progressive movement embodied both old and new thinking. The old thinking was on the tariff. The 1920s saw an exception which proved the rule that the tariff was too dangerous politically for any party to handle: tariffs on agricultural implements went down. Most tariffs deliver benefits to a concentrated set of producers and impose costs on a dispersed and politically ineffective mass of consumers. Tariffs thus are politically difficult to overturn. But tariffs on implements impose costs on a specific producer group. The group in question, farmers, increased their political power dramatically with the postwar Progressive surge. In consequence, implement tariffs went down in 1919, 1922, and 1925. The Progressives' disappearance in the late 1920s facilitated implement (and other) tariff increases in the next decade.

But the Progressive insurgency also led to the articulation of a wholly new agrarian program. The circumstances which produced the Progressive movement challenged the very individualism that seemed to infuse the party's style. During the war demand for wheat had been buoyant; after the war the wheat economy collapsed. Wartime demand coincided with centralized management of the crop; the postwar collapse coincided with the termination of that system. Farmers drew the obvious moral: centralized management would give them monopoly power and should, thus, supplant the open market. Where in 1911 the central agrarian demand had been for an implicit *reduction* of the government's role in commercial policy, 1921 saw the first focused demand for an *increased* role in the management of commodity markets. [15] But the late 1920s recovery in the grain market, a major factor in the Progressives' disappearance, made this demand less pressing.

THE SECOND PARTY SYSTEM

By 1930 the Progressive impulse was spent and the onset of the Depression led voters to the Conservative party for the first time since 1917. In Quebec the Conservatives won 45 percent of the vote and 37 percent of the seats – totals commensurate with their performance in Quebec in the first party system. The 1930 election, then, seemed to signal the triumph of the old alignment, a return to the balanced two-party competition of the first system.

Nothing was further from the truth, as 1935 ushered in a new alignment. The old rural-urban dichotomy took new forms and a new cleavage, based on class conflict and the experience of the Depression, struggled to emerge. Despite these new forces, the Liberal vote share was hardly touched. The Conservatives, in contrast, met catastrophe: a drop of about nineteen points, which left the party at an even lower level than in 1921. This time the Conservatives did not recover; their 1935 share was virtually identical to the party's average for the next two decades, 29.7 percent, a remarkably feeble share for a system's second major party and official opposition.

The rest of the vote went to third parties, whose collective share rivalled that of 1921. This time, however, the minor-party vote was split three ways. One minor party, the Reconstruction party, attracted votes from a base which was wide but not deep. Reconstruction won only one seat and disappeared in 1940. A second party, Social Credit, had the opposite profile: a narrow base but a deep one, primarily in Alberta. This made it an instant parliamentary presence and helped it survive for the entire span of the second party system. Long-lived though it may have been, Social Credit, like the Progressives, was a vehicle for anti-party sentiment.

The third party was the Cooperative Commonwealth Federation, or CCF. The CCF staked a serious claim from the outset. It articulated a program which combined agrarian, labour, and socialist elements. Protest voting was one factor in the party's early success. But the CCF set out to govern – or at least to affect how other parties governed – and to claim a long-term place in the political order. The CCF did *not* embody antipathy to parties as such, despite its occasional spasm of ritual self-purification.[16] Its members tended to accept that party action is necessary for the achievement of collectivist objectives. By the same token, the CCF was commonly sympathetic to executive prerogatives; executives, after all, actually perform the tasks that social democrats wish upon the state. And CCF MPs tended to be masters of the parliamentary game. If the Progressives were fated to disappear from their internal contradictions, the same could not be said of that part of their legacy which emerged as the CCF.

Figure 2-8
The Second Party System, 1935–53

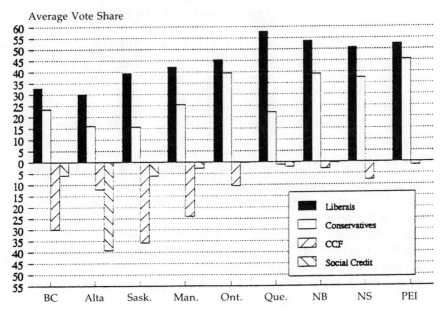

The geographic basis of the second party system appears in Figure 2-8. In the five easternmost provinces, continuities with the first party system were obvious. The Liberal party remained strongest in Quebec and retained a comfortable plurality in the maritime provinces. As in the first system, Ontario remained the weak link in the Liberals' eastern chain. In the east, the Conservatives simply mirrored the Liberals. But the Conservative base in each eastern province was markedly lower than in the first system. Where the Liberal advantage in Quebec under the first system had been substantial but reversible, in the second system it verged on hegemonic. Even in the Tories' places of relative strength, Liberals typically returned pluralities.

Conservative first-system weakness in Alberta and Saskatchewan was converted into virtual nonexistence. Even in Manitoba and British Columbia, erstwhile bases for the Conservative party, the Tory vote had eroded. The slack was picked up by parties indigenous to the region, heirs to the Progressive movement. The CCF was the most important, rivalling the Liberals in Saskatchewan and British Columbia. In Manitoba and Alberta they did only a little worse than the Conservatives. Social Credit was a party almost purely of Alberta, where it typically won pluralities.

Where the 1921 insurgency produced a hung parliament, its 1935 counterpart produced a smashing victory for the Liberals. This came to typify the second party system. According to Figure 2-6, the 1935 Liberal seat majority was the largest in Canadian history to that date. The majority only increased in 1940. The government barely survived in 1945 but came back in 1949 with a majority larger than in 1935 and almost as large as in 1940. The majority was cut in 1953 but was still above the pre-1917 norm. No less striking than the parliamentary strength of the government was the feebleness of the offical opposition: the average Conservative seat share was only 18.9 percent.

Yet Figure 2-1 reminds us that the 1935 Liberal share of *votes* was slightly lower than in 1930. The 1935 outcome set the pattern for the next two decades. Although later elections returned the Liberal vote share to levels akin to those in the 1880s and 1890s, it never reached the level of the early 1900s. The one-sided Liberal parliamentary majorities that typified the second party system were largely artifacts of the electoral system: as Figure 2-8 indicates, the Liberals enjoyed pluralities – sometimes quite narrow ones – in eight of nine provinces.

Ethno-religious Divisions

Just as the Conservatives overplayed the imperial hand in 1917, they continued to do so over the next several decades. Where the country's mood was isolationist in the 1920s and 1930s and diffidently internationalist in the 1940s and 1950s, the Conservatives continued to emphasize the diplomatic unity of Empire and Commonwealth. For instance, when the report of the 1929 Commonwealth Conference which recommended the outlines of the Statute of Westminster, the legal affirmation of Canada's sovereign status, was presented to the House of Commons, Conservative frontbencher C.H. Cahan summed up the essentially negative reaction of his party: "I am persuaded that it is in the best interests of Canada that the British commonwealth of nations, which is commonly known as the British Empire, should remain a subsisting political unit, and not merely a free association of independent states."[17]

In 1938 Sir Arthur Meighen, sometime Conservative leader, tried to rally English-speaking delegates to that year's leadership convention to a military commitment to the Empire. The failure of the attempt alienated some of the party's traditional supporters even as it reminded others of the continued presence of imperialist tendencies in the party. During the Second World War, Conservatives pressed for a forward policy and called repeatedly for the formation of a National Government, a reminder of 1917. An even more chilling reminder was their call for conscription.[18] Even in the 1950s the party's external affairs spokesman, Howard Green, speaking in opposition to the Canadian role in the Suez crisis that brought Lester Pearson a Nobel Peace Prize, could link nostalgia for the Empire to antipathy to the United States.[19]

Commercial Policy

The biggest story of 1930–5 was economic: the Conservatives had the misfortune of being in power for the worst years of the Depression. Their early response to the event was instinctual: a raising of tariff barriers and a renewed emphasis on imperial economic consolidation. Only at the end, with the "Bennett New Deal," did they attempt anything innovative. Few of their enemies were persuaded that this was anything other than a deathbed repentance.[20] Tory times came to be seen as hard times. In this respect 1935 reinforced the lessons of 1896 and 1921. This helps explain the Conservative retreat in the country as a whole. It also helps explain part of the geographic differentiation in that retreat: the Depression hit the grain-exporting prairie provinces hardest of all.[21] The west thus once again became the heartland of insurgency. This time the insurgents persisted: agrarian politics seemed to have come of age.

The agrarian politics case should not be overstated. The only unequivocally agrarian party was Social Credit, a party which was confined to one province and which had little in the way of a program. The CCF had a broader sectional base because it was not, in the end, much of a farmers' party. Only in Saskatchewan could it claim to represent farmers. Elsewhere, and most notably in its other bastion, British Columbia, the party had no agrarian pretensions at all. The claim the CCF could assert everywhere was to represent the organized working class. To this extent the party represented the emergence of an urban class cleavage. In some ways, the party of farmers, workers, and Canadians of all sorts was still the Liberal party. It was strong in each eastern province. Even though indigenous parties flourished in the west at the expense of both old parties, the Liberals were still the plurality party in most of the region. As a party in Parliament, the Liberals were broadly based.

And the Liberals seemed to have learned the lesson of 1911. After that year no government dared submit free trade with the United States to the electorate for another seventy-seven years. The most venturesome gesture by the Liberals after 1935 was to undo tariff increases made by the Conservatives in 1932. In 1948 the Liberal government contemplated accepting an American offer of complete reciprocity but recoiled before the electoral implications. For the most part, Canadian governments were prepared to shoulder the political risks of general tariff reduction only in a multilateral context, the General Agreement on Tariffs and Trade (GATT).

At the same time, direct support for farmers was an inadmissible issue. One part of the agrarian program that emerged in the 1920s did get embodied in policy: the Canadian Wheat Board was reinstated in 1935. Governments did spend money on field rehabilitation as well. But beyond this neither party, even the Liberal party, was prepared to go.[22] Both parties seemed to regard direct cash support for the sector as verging on immoral. In effect, they tacitly adopted a gag rule.

In the second system the old parties' economic policy positions could be stylized as in Figure 2-9. The vertical axis could be defined as willingness to truck or trade with America, to paraphrase an earlier Conservative slogan. On this the parties had different locations partly because of their legacies: *all* tariff reductions mentioned above had been made, even if grudgingly, by Liberal governments. The positioning also reflected abiding non-tariff differences in attitudes towards markets: Conservatives expressed unease about American direct investment while Liberal governments acted to facilitate it. Otherwise there was little to choose. The horizontal axis concerned willingness to extend direct aid to the primary sector, especially agriculture. This axis was effectively suppressed by the parties' identical positions on it.

Two things emerged in the 1950s to upset this equilibrium. First, the grain export sector was plunged into crisis by an international glut. Secondly, the Conservative party, almost in spite of itself, chose a leader who understood and sympathized with farmers and other primary producers: John Diefenbaker.

THE SECOND TRANSITION

In 1957 the Liberal party's overwhelming parliamentary majority collapsed. In the popular vote, the Liberals lost eight points from 1953 to 1957. The Conservatives, now led by John Diefenbaker, gained a like amount. Although the Liberals still outpolled the Conservatives by two percentage points in 1957, they won fewer seats and were forced to surrender office. This paved the way for the smashing Conservative victory of 1958: the second-largest major-party vote surge, 14.7 points,[23] and the second-largest popular vote share, 54 percent,[24] in Canadian electoral history.

Figure 2-9
The Commercial-Policy Basis of the Realignment

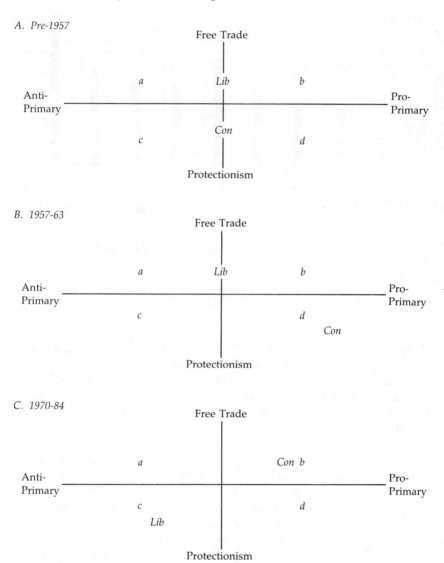

A. *Pre-1957*

B. *1957-63*

C. *1970-84*

Some of this second surge came at Liberals' expense, as that party lost seven more points in 1958. The total drop in Liberal share from 1953 to 1958, fifteen points, was one and a half times as large as their drop from 1911 to 1917. Never before had the Liberal share of the national popular vote fallen below 40 percent. The 1958 Liberal

Figure 2-10
The Second Transition, 1957–62

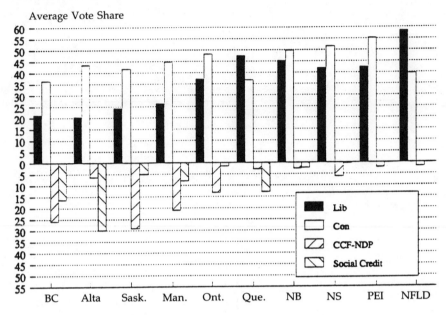

Average Vote Share

share, 34 percent, was not much larger than the average Conservative share had been in its weakest period, 1935–53. If the Liberals suffered, so, according to Figure 2-3, did the smaller parties. Where virtually all of the Conservatives' 1957 net gain had come from the Liberals, in 1958 over half the gain came from third parties, especially Social Credit.

The geography of the second transition appears in Figure 2-10. The most striking thing about the Conservatives' transitional geography was its *uniformity*. Their growth was greatest where they had thitherto been weakest, most notably in the west. This was even true in Quebec, especially in 1958. In that year Mr Diefenbaker assembled a coalition whose sectional makeup was just as diverse as any the Liberals had built in the second party system. The Liberals, for their part, now had a profile similar to that visited on the Conservatives in the second system: a sharply differentiated one. Now it was the Liberals whose western vote shares were derisory.

Commercial Policy

On commercial policy, John Diefenbaker upped the stakes dramatically. Beginning in 1957–8, the government supported nine commodity prices at 80 percent of their preceding ten-year average; credit facilities were greatly expanded; the Wheat Board began advance payments on the crop; and it sold the crop aggressively.[25] Altogether, direct transfers to western wheat producers increased more than sevenfold in constant dollars between 1957–8 and 1961–2 and accounted for *all* the Agriculture Department's budget growth. Payments fell back to nil in 1965–6,[26] by which date, significantly, the government was once again Liberal.

Support also went to non-agricultural parts of the primary sector, especially to oil and gas producers. To protect the industry from imports of cheaper oil from Venezuela and the Middle East, the government reserved the bulk of the Ontario market for the high-cost Alberta product. For the first time central Canadian consumers were forced to subsidize a western industry which seemed to have no realistic prospect of comparative advantage in the world market.

As a party now committed to defending the primary sector, the Conservatives had moved dramatically rightwards on the pro/anti-primary axis of Figure 2-9. Note, though, that the figure does not portray the Conservatives as also moving to the free trade position; the party did not abandon its commitment to the National Policy and to the ethos that supported it. John Diefenbaker was no more inclined towards closer ties with the United States than was the man with whose shade he seemed to be in constant contact, Sir John A. Macdonald. A compelling example was his refusal to countenance export of electricity generated on the Columbia River. Instead, Mr Diefenbaker committed his party to protection all around, squarely into Figure 2-9's quadrant *d*. But the sectional and sectoral reorientation that Mr Diefenbaker had effected, for exquisitely protectionist reasons, prepared his party to abandon the National Policy.

THE THIRD PARTY SYSTEM

The Tory millennium was not to be: the Conservatives proceeded to dissipate most of their gains. Where their 1957–8 popular vote gain was the second-largest to that point by any party in Canadian history, their 1958–62 drop of 16.3 points was the third-largest.[27] Some of the rest of the 1958 margin was squandered in 1963. For all that, Mr Diefenbaker left his party better off than when he found it. The Conservative vote share from 1963 to 1980 averaged 33.6 percent, about four points higher than the party's average from 1935 to 1953.

The modesty of the Conservatives' net gain from the second system to the third masked its significance. The Conservative base was

Figure 2-11
The Third Party System, 1963–80

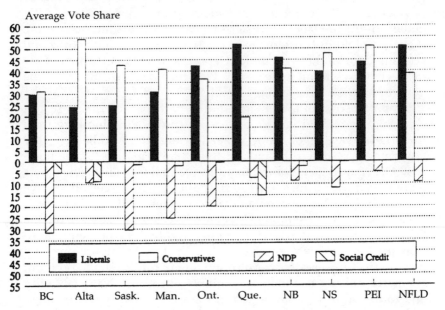

Average Vote Share

| | Liberals | | Conservatives | | NDP | | Social Credit |

BC Alta Sask. Man. Ont. Que. NB NS PEI NFLD

not just widened, it was reshaped, as Figure 2-11 indicates. Now it was the Conservatives who played the ends against the middle: their support was greatest in the maritime and prairie provinces. From 1962 to 1980 the Conservatives were the dominant party in Prince Edward Island and Nova Scotia. Conservative margins there were typically rather narrow, however, and their strength in the region was a legacy as much of Robert Stanfield of Nova Scotia, Conservative leader from 1967 to 1976, as of Mr Diefenbaker.

The truly dramatic contrasts with the second party system were in the three prairie provinces. Alberta, Saskatchewan, and Manitoba did not desert the Conservatives in 1962–3. Over the 1962–80 period Manitoba and Saskatchewan gave the Conservatives only a slightly smaller share than did Nova Scotia and Prince Edward Island. This support commonly netted the Conservatives a plurality.[28] Alberta, which under the first two party systems had been a Conservative graveyard, became by far the most one-sidedly Conservative place in the country.

The Conservative party now often enjoyed pluralities in six provinces: British Columbia (from 1972 on), Alberta, Saskatchewan (especially in the early years), Manitoba, Nova Scotia, and Prince Edward Island. These were, to be sure, provinces of only medium to small weight. But that the Conservatives could return a plurality in *any* province was a significant shift from the second party system. And the Conservatives remained competitive in Ontario. Thus, even though popular vote gains outside Quebec were offset by losses in Quebec and the net shift made to seem small, Conservative vote gains and losses were efficiently distributed and the party made a significant net gain in seats. While in the second system the Conservatives typically won less than 20 percent of House seats, in the third system their usual seat share was 30 to 35 percent.

The history of the Liberal party in this period was one of recovery, although an exceedingly fitful one. The party's average vote share over the 1962, 1963, and 1965 elections was 39.7 percent. In the two minority victories of 1963 and 1965 the share barely cleared 40 percent. Only with Pierre Trudeau's accession to leadership did the Liberal popular vote bring the party in range of parliamentary majorities. In Mr Trudeau's five elections the Liberal share averaged 42.3 percent. His very best outing was his first, in which the party pulled in 45.5 percent. Contrast this with Liberal shares before 1957: down to that year there were only four (out of nineteen) elections in which the Liberal share was lower than the party's *average* share under Mr Trudeau.[29]

As the Liberal base shrank overall, relative to the second party system, so did it contract geographically. As was true in the second party system, Liberal support followed an east-west gradient. But west of Ontario the gradient was now very steep indeed, just as steep as in the 1957–62 transition. The Liberal drop was especially marked in Manitoba and Saskatchewan.[30] In the third system the Liberals held pluralities, typically, in only four provinces: Newfoundland and the three contiguous provinces of New Brunswick, Ontario, and Quebec. In the third party system, the Liberal party made its stand in its traditional core, a zone which might be thought of as Catholic Canada. Fortunately for the Liberals, this zone continued to be the country's demographic centre of gravity.

In part, then, the narrowing of the Liberal base complemented the modest broadening of the Conservative one that was Mr Diefenbaker's legacy. But Liberal weakness also reflected the strength of two new-old political forces, one a temporary rival, the other a more serious long-term threat. The short-term problem was Social Credit, the long-term one the NDP.

Social Credit recovered in 1962. But its recovery took place in Quebec, the very heartland of the Liberal party. Thanks to Quebec, Social Credit's national share grew to 11.7 percent. It edged up a little further in 1963 but then began an inexorable decline. By 1968

Social Credit had, to all intents and purposes, disappeared outside Quebec. By 1980 the party was effectively wiped off the map inside that province. As long as it lasted, Social Credit was a reminder that the Liberal base in Quebec could not be taken for granted. Merely by existing, Social Credit inhibited the Liberal recovery from the 1958 débâcle. The weakness of Liberal governments before 1968 was partly a result of the Social Credit presence. The strength (by comparison with 1963–5) of the Liberals under Mr Trudeau was mainly the result Social Credit's marginalization.

The NDP, formed in 1961 out of the remains of the CCF, could not be marginalized. The contrast between the NDP and the CCF is instructive. The CCF's impact was limited; indeed its primary effect may have been to inflate the Liberals' seat share. Apart from the surge in 1945, the party's vote share never got above the low teens. Although 1957 and 1958 were poor years for the CCF, they were not much worse than 1953 had been. The NDP was a significant player from the very beginning of the third system. The 1962 election brought the highest CCF/NDP share, apart from 1945, to that date. The NDP stepped up about another four points in 1965 and stayed at the new level (17–18 percent) until 1972. The 1974 election brought a reverse, which was more than made up in 1979, and 1980 brought the party close to the 20 percent level. This was nearly twice the average CCF share. Figure 2-3 also drives home that the variation in this share was mainly in the form of a gradual positive trend. The NDP share was resilient: not likely to surge much, perhaps, but not likely to decline much either. The NDP reached this eminence in spite of the single-member-plurality electoral system's powerful pressures to the contrary.

The NDP base grew by both broadening and deepening. Figure 2-11 indicates that in the third party system the NDP was a stronger competitor than the CCF in two provinces, Manitoba and British Columbia, and remained strong in the CCF's bastion, Saskatchewan. By 1980 the NDP had become the Conservatives' main rival in the west.

Although the NDP fills up much more of the space in the west than the CCF did, it is not as peculiarly a party of that region. For the CCF and NDP, the other important shift from the second to the third party system was NDP strength in Ontario. Before 1957 Ontario returned, on average, a smaller CCF share than Alberta. In the third system, in contrast, Ontario gave the NDP around one vote in five, close to the national average share. And even if this share was only two-thirds of the typical Saskatchewan or British Columbia share, the raw number of votes represented by Ontario was enormous.

The NDP's new-found strength in Ontario (and British Columbia, for that matter) represented the injection of class politics into the third party system. Neither of the old parties could readily displace the NDP's connection to the union movement.[31] At the same time, in spite of the NDP's attempt to stake a pan-regional claim, the party was still concentrated disproportionately in the west. But the new geography meant that the NDP could convert votes into seats. Indeed, now it did so much more efficiently than in the second system.

Thus the third system was characterized by competition that seemed close but, for all that, was futile. It was close by comparison with the second system, where only the Liberal party could claim to be a national party. The Liberals won every election hands down and faced only a weak opposition. In the third system, *no* party was truly national. The Liberal party could no longer command regular pluralities virtually anywhere outside Quebec. But by comparison with the first system, the competition was futile. Although the Liberals dominated the first system, the Conservatives were never far behind. If the third system saw the Conservatives edge closer to the Liberals than they had been in the second system, they were still much further back than they had been in the first system. The Conservatives had become the dominant party in English Canada again, but their ability to generate support in Quebec declined in 1962 and diminished still more as the third system matured. The Conservatives thus were still only barely feasible as a single-party government.

Figure 2-12 brings out the sectional foundations of the impasse. It illustrates the critical role of Quebec in forming governments. In recent decades Quebec seats have constituted about 25 percent of the House. In earlier years the share was closer to 30 percent. If a party could control nearly all of Quebec's seats it would already be halfway to a parliamentary majority. Figure 2-12 indicates that whenever Quebec Liberals make up 18 percent or more of the House, the Liberals form the government; the one exception to this rule is 1979. As it happens, Quebec seats have tended to come en bloc. The secret for Quebec has not been that all Quebeckers vote the same way. It is true that there have been periods in which Quebec vote distributions were very skewed and the later years of the third system happened to be one such period. But the Liberals' first-system bloc in Quebec was based on quite a narrow popular majority in the province, as Figure 2-5 indicated. Modest though the vote swing was, Figure 2-12 makes clear that it accounted for almost all of the seat gains the Liberals made in the 1880s and 1890s. Only later did English Canada swing towards the Liberals, mainly through the

Figure 2-12
Quebec in the Liberal Coalition

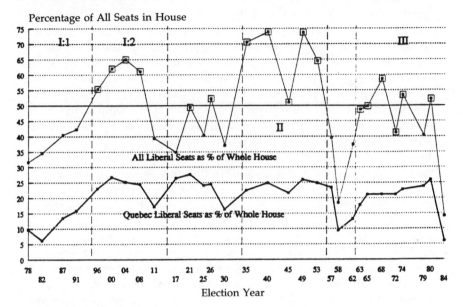

Boxed election years returned
Liberal seat pluralities or majorities

addition of western seats to the Liberal total. For most of this century Quebec seats have gone almost exclusively to Liberals. This has been so even in the face of fluctuations in the Liberal vote share in that province. For instance, the Quebec landslides in and after 1917 did not net the party many more seats than it had already locked up with the modest majorities of the first system. Quebec was not always the numerically preponderant element in the Liberal party; in the second system the Liberal coalition was remarkably broad. But Quebec was the insurance policy: even when the Liberal party suffered sharp reverses in English Canada, its Quebec bloc maintained the party as a serious player in the parliamentary game. In the 1920s Quebec seats made up a good half of the Liberal total. This was commonly true once again in the third system.

   For the Conservatives to form even a minority government, the popular reaction in English Canada against the Liberals had to be extraordinarily intense and a very big fraction of any anti-Liberal swing had to go exclusively to the Tories. But limiting the Conservatives' growth was the NDP. Although the NDP was never feasible in this period as a government, it became steadily more important in a negative sense. It almost always barred the Conservatives' way to pluralities and it often blocked the Liberals from majorities.

Thus, although the Liberals were almost always in government over this period, they were so on a kind of sufferance. Thanks to Conservative renewal and NDP growth, Liberal governments were denied the vote and seat margins typical of earlier periods. Three of their six victories and seven of their roughly twenty years in government were as a minority. Each election in which the Liberals gained votes was followed by an election in which they lost votes (except for the similarly feeble 1963 and 1965 pluralities). No Liberal seat majority was followed by another Liberal majority. As Figure 2-6 shows, governments in the 1960s and 1970s were even more weakly based than those in the transitional period of the 1920s. What was a symptom of crisis in the 1920s was, in the 1970s, politics as usual.

Ethno-religious Divisions

One element in the geography of the third system Conservative vote was John Diefenbaker's populism. This allowed the Conservative party to preempt the populist impulses that had earlier threatened the two-party alignment. But the legacy, in common with earlier manifestations of populism, was ethnically and religiously narrow.

Before John Diefenbaker, populism and the Conservative party were antithetical. A party of eastern business could hardly be expected to espouse the interests – not to mention the sentiments – of small producers on the resource frontier. Given this mutual antipathy in economics, a pan-regional coalition could appear only in moments of extreme stress, as happened, for example, in 1917. By 1960, however, stress was mounting and the situation was ripe for change. The relative shrinkage of the agricultural sector made it tactically ripe for a focused appeal to its interests. It seems to be true as a generalization that farmers do not really become powerful until they are about to disappear.[32] By giving resource producers most of what they wanted, Mr Diefenbaker abolished the antipathy in economics at a stroke.

At the same time, the Anglo-Protestant definition of the country was increasingly on the defensive. In the 1920s, notwithstanding the emergence of a new, non-imperialist form of nationalism, most politically active Protestant Canadians agreed that the country was British, somehow. Similarly, even if they might disagree over just how much Canada owed the Empire, none seriously believed that Canada's and the Empire's interests would actually clash. By 1960 this consensus had been shattered. Internally, the country was awakening to its growing diversity, and the strongest challenge to the British definition of the country came from Quebec. Externally, the Suez crisis seems to have been a watershed. Many in English Canada were stunned when their government sided with America against Britain and when their prime minister, a francophone Catholic, referred pejoratively to Britain and France as "the supermen of Europe."[33]

Practically speaking, such pro-British sentiment may have been unsustainable nostalgia. Whereas in 1911 the Empire was a living entity, in the 1950s the influence of its successor, the Commonwealth, was clearly waning, and by the 1970s the old imperialism was only a memory, for many an embarrassing one. But nostalgia did help to broaden the Conservative base, not just in the wake of 1956 but in reaction to Liberal initiatives after 1963. The Conservative party gathered to itself the agrarian and anti-party sentiment that earlier had fuelled third-party movements. Ironically, the Conservatives moved themselves closer to power by preempting the agenda of those who feared power the most and who saw parties as vehicles by which minorities combined to frustrate the wishes of natural majorities.

The Liberal recovery from the débâcle of 1958 was engineered by a group of middle-class reformers, mainly from Toronto. They moved the party to the left on social and economic policy and tailored its appeal to a more specifically urban clientele. They centralized the party's operations by creating direct links between the constituencies and the leader and national office; squeezed out were provincial notables, the people who had traditionally been the party's brokers.[34]

The Liberals also grasped the nettle of an issue which was awakening, the place of French Canada in the larger national scheme. As the third party system matured, the Liberal party chose a specific path in addressing this issue, a path which eventually created an opening for the Conservative party. But that is matter for a later section of this chapter. For most of the third party system only the Liberals succeeded in doing anything creative in relation to French Canada. The Liberals also set out to reshape the symbolism of the polity. The British features of public life were downplayed and emphasis fell instead on ethnic diversity as a value in its own right. Bilingual and multicultural emphases suited the Liberal party's traditional ethnic bases well. But it alienated many others who in earlier years had supported the Liberal party for lack of an alternative.

Commercial Policy

John Diefenbaker's other legacy was his reorientation of commercial policy. The third party system saw the final moves in that reorientation, moves that anticipated the Canada–United States free trade agreement.

As the party of government, the Liberals made the first post-1963 move. They preempted the Conservatives' traditional control of the nationalist pole. Liberal nationalism advanced on two fronts: an increased commitment to protection for secondary industry, and an attack on the primary sector. In terms of Figure 2-9, they moved significantly south and west. One front, investment policy, looked to the enemy without. Now it was the Liberals, not the Conservatives, who worried publicly about the weight of (mainly) American investment. As the government, Liberals were in a position to act on the concern, with the establishment in 1974 of the Foreign Investment Review Agency (FIRA), with a mandate to review foreign takeovers of Canadian firms. The other front was internal, pitting energy producers against energy consumers. In the 1960s energy producers were grateful for the protection, in maintained prices and reserved markets, that Mr Diefenbaker had given them. In the 1970s the protection no longer seemed necessary. Indeed, the policy instruments created to provide it were now turned against the sector in a bitter struggle over rent created by the oil price increases.[35] This culminated in the National Energy Program (NEP) of 1980, which sought to reduce foreign ownership in the oil and gas sector and to increase the federal government's share of energy rents.

Conservatives opposed all of this and so moved towards, and perhaps into, quadrant *b* of Figure 2-9. They promised to loosen FIRA regulations and did so once in power.[36] They fought the NEP in Parliament and through their control of the key energy province, Alberta. At one point in 1982 they brought Parliament to a halt. In power, they abrogated the NEP's most objectionable features. But they remained silent on free trade. Protection of manufactures had, after all, been *their* policy, one of the party's constitutive values. It had derived warrant not just on economic grounds but also as an expression of mutually reinforcing national and imperial interests. An attack on the National Policy could be construed as an attack on the British definition of the nationality and on the connection which sustained it. But there lay the rub: the Empire had disappeared. Conservatives' evaluation of commercial policy now had to be detached from imperial considerations. The remaining considerations

that the party found congenial argued against protection. The party
was poised to shift. Only tactical considerations held it in check: the
party remembered 1911.

THE 1984 ELECTION

In some respects the 1984 election was *déjà vu*, a re-enactment of
1958. The Conservative share surged 17.5 points, slightly larger than
the 1957–8 swing but smaller than the total 1953–8 shift. Once again,
the gain in seats was spectacular, as the Conservatives more than
doubled their parliamentary share. In absolute numbers the 1984
majority was the largest in Canadian history; in relative terms it was
second only to the Conservative share in 1958. To all appearances,
the Conservatives had gathered together the accumulated discon-
tents of more than two decades of Liberal rule and administered this
generation's punishment for Liberal hubris.

For the Liberals, 1984 was not just a recapitulation of earlier reverses. First, the sheer magnitude of the fall in their share was
unprecedented: it dropped sixteen points in one outing. Recall that
the drop from 1911 to 1917 was only eight points and that the total
drop from 1953 to 1958 was fifteen points and required two elections
to be realized. Secondly, in 1984 the cliff edge over which the Liberals
stumbled was already some four to five points nearer bottom than
it had been in either 1917 or 1957–8. The Liberals' 1917 share, 40.1
percent, would typically have given the Liberals a minority government in the third party system. Even their 1958 share, 33.6 percent,
was close to the typical Conservative share after 1963. The 1984
Liberal share, 28 percent, was the second lowest major-party share
in Canadian history.[37]

Liberal losses were greatest at the very core of the party's coalition.
According to Figure 2-13, the 1980–4 swing (defined as the difference
between the 1984 and 1980 percentages of the province's popular
vote) was smallest in the westernmost and easternmost regions.
Shifts were modest in Prince Edward Island and Nova Scotia, at one
geographic extreme, and in Manitoba, Saskatchewan, and British
Columbia, at the other. Of the provinces outside the core, only
Alberta fled the Liberals at a notable rate.

In Newfoundland, New Brunswick, Ontario, and, most dramatically, Quebec, the Liberal share collapsed. Although the 1984 Quebec Liberal share was still larger than in all but two other provinces,
it represented the worst Liberal performance in Quebec history.
Only once before (1962) had the Liberals received less than 40 percent

Figure 2-13
Swing in Popular Vote, 1980–84

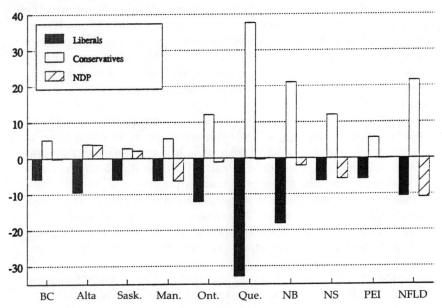

of the Quebec vote and even then they managed to win nearly half the seats in the province. Figure 2-12 indicates that the 1984 Liberal collapse in Quebec turned what would have been a sharp reverse into a rout.

Conservative gains were even more sharply differentiated than Liberal losses. The Conservatives made virtually all their popular vote gains in the four provinces that had been the Liberal core. While Conservative gains in Newfoundland, New Brunswick, and Ontario were striking, in Quebec they defied belief. The 1984 Conservative share in Quebec was roughly four times that for 1980. The Conservative breakthrough in Quebec averted the nightmare of a parliamentary majority based solely in English Canada: the Conservatives won 153 seats outside Quebec, 54 percent of the whole House, as comfortable a margin as the Liberals enjoyed in 1974 and 1980.

The 1984 result showed the resilience of the NDP. Only in Newfoundland did the party lose more than seven percentage points. In Saskatchewan and Alberta the party actually registered small gains; in Ontario and British Columbia its losses were tiny. In both popular vote and parliamentary seats, the NDP was figuratively breathing down the Liberal party's neck.

1984 AND THE BURDEN OF HISTORY

The Liberal party dominated three electoral alignments and was the presumptive party of government for nearly a century, an extraordinary record of longevity. Over the entire period the Conservative party was the only serious alternative. The Canadian system thus was the only nineteenth-century one, apart from the American party system, to survive into the late twentieth century with its major features more or less intact.

But the Conservative position often seemed tenuous. As parliamentary oppositions go, it has been weak. It never came close to victory from 1896 to 1908 and from 1935 to 1953. Between 1963 and 1984 it held power for less than a year.[38] Conservative breakthroughs tended to come only at the punctuation points between party systems. Their success reflected accumulated grievances and their electoral coalitions were never sustainable. Two episodes of power (1911–21 and 1930–5) left them much worse off. Only one (1957–63) left them better off. Even after 1963 the party did not seem poised to form the government.

Although Liberals dominated the entire period, each transition weakened their base. The shrinkage over the first transition ultimately was small and was more than compensated for by the fractionalization of the rest of the popular vote. But it hinted at shifts to come. The second transition had a major impact on the Liberals' base. And in the third system the Liberal share was typically smaller than the opposition share had been in the first system. The Liberal share was usually just large enough to ensure a parliamentary plurality or majority, but not enough to generate the overwhelming Liberal majorities that had typified the second system.

Each transition brought permanent third-party gains. The key to this permanence was the appearance of a party of the left, first the CCF, later the NDP. The CCF and NDP aside, third-party activity was episodic; it was often an expression of distaste for the party battle itself and for the grubby compromises of government, and was commonly linked to agrarian discontent.

In the first system the foundation of Liberal dominance was a combination of Quebec, Catholics outside Quebec, and (towards the end) the two new wheat-producing provinces of Alberta and Saskatchewan. The second system was more complex and more polarized. Quebec became more thoroughly Liberal while the Liberal share in the prairie west shrank modestly. That the Liberals could retreat in the popular vote outside Quebec and yet add to their seats was testimony to the Conservatives' abject weakness: the Tory vote collapsed in both Quebec and the west. The vacuum in the west was filled by new parties, the CCF and Social Credit. The second party system thus brought a sharpening of divisions along the lines which, in a modest way, had controlled choice in the first system: between Catholics (including the French) and Protestants; and between wheat-producing and manufacturing regions. The third system raised electoral polarization to a new level. This polarization produced an endemic parliamentary weakness for all parties. The Liberal party retained and even strengthened its domination of Quebec while the western part of its coalition evaporated. Its inheritors were the Conservatives and the NDP. Now *no* party straddled Canada's traditional cultural and economic boundaries very well. In addition, the third system brought a third cleavage: a union/non-union division. Growth of the NDP was tied in part to the increased importance of this division. When the NDP articulates a class perspective, it must be taken seriously. [39] The same could rarely be said of the CCF.

Confined socially and geographically though they now were, the Liberals could still govern. The provinces in which they remained strong were the demographically dominant ones. If the Liberal base outside Quebec was now more than ever confined to Catholics and to new Canadians, these groups were bigger than ever. The Conservatives dominated the largest (even if shrinking) groups in English Canada. The narrowing of the Liberal base outside Quebec did mean that the party had lost most of its cushion against an electoral reverse. A small popular vote swing would sharply reduce its modest share of seats in English Canada, as happened in 1972 and 1979 (Figure 2-12). But such a shift would still not give the Conservatives a majority. The Liberals held a trump: Quebec.

Underneath all of this were shifts fraught with implications for the years after 1984. Obviously, one set of shifts was in commercial policy. The Conservative party captured western resource producers, traditionally a pro-free trade group. Once this group joined the Conservative coalition, other elements in that coalition began to move towards the free trade position. Among these was the business community. As chapter 5 will describe, the business community became increasingly concerned about *United States* protectionism; a free trade pact could be construed as insurance against US trade policy. And, of course, commercial policy no longer raised imperial questions. The Conservatives, thus, were poised to abandon one central part of their history.

Another group poised to abandon an historical antipathy to free trade was francophone Quebec. Quebec francophones had, for purely economic reasons, traditionally been protectionist. But for cultural reasons they had shunned the natural party of protectionism, the Conservative party. Instead, Quebec support for Liberals had restrained the free trade impulses which surfaced from time to time in that party. It was a double irony, then, that just as Quebec francophones were about to find the Conservative party congenial, that party was poised to abandon its protectionist tradition. But so, it seemed, was francophone Quebec. The conversion is commonly laid at the door of a post-1960s surge in cultural and economic confidence among francophone Quebecois. Not all the facts square with this explanation and the conversion remains something of a mystery. But occur it did. This meant that to Quebec, the newest building block in the Conservative coalition, a free trade agreement would be quite congenial.

Why were Quebec francophones drawn to Mr Mulroney's Conservatives? Part of the answer directly parallels the realignment of 1896: in 1984 Mr Mulroney was the only party leader from Quebec, as was Wilfrid Laurier in the earlier period. For 1984 this explanation may suffice, but longer-run tendencies were at work as well. Even if they were only part of the 1984 story, they were critical to the years immediately following. Over the 1970s the Conservative party supplanted the Liberals as the party of provincial rights. Earlier, Conservatives had commonly championed a centralized view of the nation, one which hardly accommodated the claims of French Canada at all. This centralism was an expression of the nationalism which for Conservatives had been the other side of imperialism. As the Conservative party became less nationalist in economic policy and less interventionist overall, it could comfortably side with provincial governments, many of which it controlled anyway. This created an opening for a special accommodation with Quebec, for the Liberal party under Pierre Trudeau had pursued the interests of French Canada aggressively but along a path at variance with the position of political élites in Quebec. If the Conservatives could craft an appeal to local-majoritarian impulses in Quebec, they could reconstitute much of Sir John A. Macdonald's coalition. But in doing so, they would introduce a new incoherence into their ranks.

Indeed, the Conservatives would come to match the Liberals for coalitional incoherence, though the new Conservative variant would be different. The Liberals embraced groups with both federalist and centralist conceptions of the constitution: minorities who needed a strong central government to defend them against local majorities and Quebeckers who wanted, if anything, a weaker central government. Sentimentally, though, the Liberal coalition was at one:

French Canada, inside and outside Quebec, has a moral unity on many questions and the non-francophone elements shared with francophones an aversion to British conceptions of the nationality. Constitutionally, the emerging Conservative coalition is coherent: a general preference for a relatively decentralized federation in which local majorities dominate. But sentimentally the Conservatives would be incoherent, divided between francophones and franco-phobes. But incoherence has always been the price of successful brokerage. The 1984 landslide gave Conservatives the chance to work this brokerage out. If they succeeded they could displace the Liberals as the natural party of government.

1984–88: A THIRD TRANSITION?

Did the Tory millennium arrive this time? Or were the Liberals bound, after a decent interval, to profit from this generation's draw-ing of the usual lesson from experience with a Conservative gov-ernment? The record of polls between 1984 and 1988 was as ambiguous as it could possibly be. There was evidence for a true realignment with the Conservatives as the dominant party, for a reassertion of the third-system pattern of Liberal dominance, and for a wholly new alignment in which the NDP was a key actor.

For over a year after the Mulroney government was formed, ac-cording to Figure 2-14, the Conservatives maintained a healthy lead in the Gallup poll. The trend over that year was mainly negative, although the government still seemed to be holding its ground in the summer of 1985. In the autumn of that year, though, the rot began. September 1985 came to be called "Black September." Scan-dals and a bank failure forced two resignations and embarrassed the whole cabinet. Other scandals and some unpopular policy initiatives littered subsequent months. By the beginning of 1986 the Conser-vatives had completely dissipated their lead.

For most of 1986 party preferences seemed to revert to the third-system norm. The Liberals typically won 40 to 45 percent of Gallup respondents, the Conservatives 30 to 35 percent, and the NDP 20 to 25 percent. By early 1987, however, the NDP had supplanted the Conservatives in second place. In the summer of that year the NDP and the Liberals were effectively tied for first place; a wholly new alignment seemed foreshadowed.

After October 1987 the system began to revert to the older pattern, as the Conservatives gained at the NDP's expense. Thus far, one long-standing verity was being reaffirmed: the NDP was being dealt out of the government-formation game. The Conservative recovery

Figure 2-14
Party Support, 1985–88, Gallup Poll

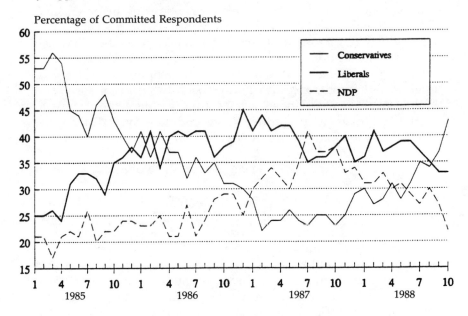

Percentage of Committed Respondents

slowed down in early 1988 and the Liberals held their position in
the high 30s. By the seat-vote estimations in Figure 1-1, standings
in the June 1988 Gallup poll would have produced a relatively strong
Liberal minority, 46 percent of House seats. The Conservatives'
worst nightmare still threatened to come true: a predicted seat share
of only 25 percent, possibly even behind the NDP.

July brought a marked Conservative jump. That month brought
the Tories their first Gallup share of at least 35 percent since September 1986. The Liberals began to slide, and in September the
Conservative and Liberal lines had finally crossed: the Conservatives
returned their first Gallup plurality since March 1986. The next Gallup poll (the last one in Figure 2-14 and the poll alluded to at the
beginning of chapter 1) indicated a clear Conservative parliamentary
majority: according to Figure 1-1, a prospective seat share of 60
percent. The Liberals, who had enjoyed Gallup pluralities in twenty-
six of the preceding twenty-nine months and who had led every
monthly Gallup poll for nearly a year, now faced another Parliament
in opposition, with a likely seat share of only 26 percent. The Gallup
record was confirmed in its essentials by other September polls.

Perhaps the 1984–8 shifts meant nothing, or less than they
seemed. It is striking just how closely the September 1988 standings

corresponded to the situation that seemed to have settled in by mid-1985, at the end of the Mulroney government's honeymoon.[40] One tempting interpretation is that 1984–8 simply exhibited an inevitable cycle of unpopularity, one which all governments experience. Governments do their least popular things first, reap a short-term whirlwind, and then restore their favour later in the cycle. Unfortunately for this interpretation, there is no suggestion from earlier inter-election periods that anything like this (apart from the appearance and decay of the post-election honeymoon) happens regularly in Canada.[41]

Perhaps economics drove the government's standing. In other countries, government popularity follows key macroeconomic indicators.[42] The track of Liberal popularity from 1980 to 1983 followed the path of unemployment and inflation (Johnston, 1986). Outside this period, however, the evidence is mixed. Monroe and Erickson (1986) make a strong case that the macroeconomy has no effect. Nadeau (1987) does find some effect, but the pattern shifts from decade to decade. In any case, none of these controversies really apply here: the economy moved steadily *upward* in the months of the Mulroney government's deepest unpopularity.

Commercial Policy 1984–8

One thing the polls did seem to be interacting with was the negotiation, which spanned much of this period, of the Canada-us free trade agreement. Critical points in the negotiations coincided with shifts or turning points in the government's popularity. And the government's weak poll standing may have helped drive the negotiations themselves.

Even as the Conservative government was being formed in 1984, circumstances favouring a free trade agreement were emerging.[43] The previous Liberal government, notwithstanding its nationalist orientation, had initiated discussion about sectoral free trade. These came to nought, however. It was increasingly clear that if an agreement were to be pursued, it would have to be comprehensive, with tradeoffs between sectors.

If in the past such an agreement was shunned, rising protectionism in the United States forced the issue. Although the American target typically had not been Canada, Canada often seemed to get caught in the backwash. The momentum that the protectionist omnibus trade bill seemed to be gathering in Congress was especially ominous. And one important dispute, over softwood lumber, did have Canada as its specific target. An earlier attempt to have the us

International Trade Commission impose a countervailing tariff on Canadian softwood imports had failed; the ITC had found the claim to be without merit. To Canadians little in the specifically economic realm seemed to have changed since that earlier dispute; yet this time the countervail bid succeeded. That an American tariff was ultimately replaced by a Canadian export tax (and thus that the imputed rent remained in Canada) did not mollify Canadian opinion. The dispute suggested that trade politics in the United States were shifting to a new level of toughness. Many Canadians concluded that Canada had better try to insure itself against the worst.

At the same time, a case for a US-Canada agreement emerged from an independent source. On 5 September 1985 the Royal Commission on the Economic Union and Development Prospects for Canada, also known as the Macdonald Commission, delivered its report. The commission was a creature of the previous Liberal government and originally seemed tainted by that paternity. Despite early difficulties, the commission was able to establish its seriousness and legitimacy. Although Mr Mulroney had apparently intended to shut it down, he had been dissuaded. Indeed, the commission's suspect origins worked to his political advantage. The commission, whose chairman had been an architect of the Liberal government's nationalist policies in the 1970s, came out strongly for free trade. Its proposal was quite concrete and supplied a basis for the government to proceed. Official notice of intention to negotiate was given on 26 September 1985.

This brings us to a central question: were these external events so compelling that *any* government, not just a Conservative one, would have yielded to them? The fact that even the Liberals had begun sectoral discussions is awkward. We are sceptical, though, that a Liberal government, with the electoral coalition it had assembled, could have stomached the comprehensive agreement that seemed to be the only alternative to no agreement at all. Evidence in chapters 3 and 5 confirm this scepticism. For Conservatives, pressures to reach an agreement were not uncongenial, even if acceding to them was risky. And the risks arguably came to be overshadowed by the possible benefits. The month in which the government declared its intent to negotiate was the aforementioned "Black September." Subsequent months brought the government so low that free trade could pose no further risks. Pursuit of an agreement at least gave the government the appearance of purpose and of political courage; these were electoral assets in their own right. If an agreement could be reached, Conservatives might hope, given the basic coalitional structure of Canadian elections, that its usual supporters would have no choice but to vote for them.[44]

But were the Conservatives' usual supporters sufficiently numerous in their own right? Was the lesson of the three party systems indeed that the Liberal century was fated to end and that the Conservatives had assembled a coalition sufficiently broad to make them the presumptive party of government? Or was the lesson that each transitional period would bring a rejuvenated Liberal party back to power? For that matter, could any party really count on much in the way of long-standing support? The 1984–8 Gallup record was perfectly ambiguous: the swings for and against each party were remarkable but the pattern which finally emerged looked familiar. The record of earlier survey-based work on Canadians' party commitments is similarly ambiguous. It is time, then, to turn to the record of individuals' party identification in the 1988 survey.

3 The Background of the Party System: Party Identification, Social Structure, and Sentiment

The history of Canadian elections left us with contradictory readings of its 1984 instalment. The Conservative landslide in that year may have been just another chastening of the natural party of government, the Liberals, or it may have signalled the end of the Liberal century and the beginning of a new alignment of parties.

Which interpretation is correct? A standard way of understanding changes in partisan alignment is to look for changes in the *deus ex machina* of voting studies – party identification (Campbell et al., 1960). If Conservative identifiers now outnumber Liberal ones, some would argue that a realignment has occurred. Others, LeDuc (1984) for instance, argue that the notion of realignment is inappropriate for understanding Canadian elections and that party identifications – at least not abiding ones – are not the Canadian norm.

Both views seem flawed to us. Canadians do exhibit abiding identification with parties; so, it is useful to count heads, to see if one party has supplanted the other as the dominant one. But realignment involves more than just arithmetic. Also critical is how the parties fit into the social structure and where they are located on the fundamental dimensions of policy and sentiment. To locate the parties is to explore the bounds of the possible.

The 1988 election affords an opportunity to explore how parties square their historical legacies with their desire to win. For some time, the study of party choice has been influenced by a model, associated with Downs (1957), which makes a strong prediction that parties' policies will converge on the preferences of the median voter.

These predictions are hard to reconcile with the existence of party identification: Why would individuals identify with parties that are as mobile as this model implies, especially if they use their mobility to deny voters a choice? Wouldn't rational voters soon discard partisan identities in a system where parties gathered together at the median? Yet the logic of Downs's model seems compelling.

It is so compelling that one wonders why party identifications even exist. Such identifications might result when parties grow from small, coherent, and well-disciplined factions in legislatures or parliaments, or when social movements – the trade union or environmental movements, for instance – form parties. But these explanations tell us why identifications might form in the first place, not why they continue. Persistence may be explained by party leaders with ideological as well as electoral goals. Yet is this enough to explain the persistence of party identifications in highly competitive single-member plurality systems where ideological fancies carry the risk of extinction? We propose than another mechanism is at work here. Because citizens are notoriously inattentive to politics, they must be mobilized anew every election. The most effective way to do this is to employ issues that appeal to their basic values and commitments. In this chapter we show that Canadian parties have at their disposal a small number of issues that can appeal to the most basic identities in the electorate.

This chapter uses the language of spatial modelling to elucidate the Canadian case. It also uses the Canadian case to elucidate the spatial theories and party identification. So far there has been little empirical flesh on multidimensional models of party choice, and few attempts to incorporate party identification into such models. This chapter aims to do so by showing that elections feature a dynamic tension: parties are pulled towards their respective bases by a need to mobilize them; yet they also feel centripetal tugs towards the median voter, the pivot for a popular majority.

The chapter opens by accounting for parties' core support. First we claim that many Canadians do indeed have abiding party commitments; the challenge is to measure them correctly. Earlier attempts seemed to fail and observers were tempted to conclude that the effort was misconceived. We propose a new, more resilient, measure. Then we ask: How big was each party's electoral base? How did the base fit into the Canadian social structure? How much of the party system's history can we recognize in its 1988 manifestation? What did this history portend for the 1988 campaign? Analysis must proceed in tandem: Quebec is an electorate in its own right. On each track – Quebec and the rest of Canada – analysis

begins with the social structural foundations of individuals' identification with parties. This is followed by an account of the basic
policy commitments that help explain the social structural pattern.
This requires us to identify the basic axes of party choice and then
to locate parties – as organizations and as bodies of supporters – on
the axes. From this will come a sense of the alternative possible
agendas for the 1988 campaign.

MEASURING PARTISAN COMMITMENT

By 1988 the Conservatives had strengthened their base in the electorate: more people thought of themselves as Conservatives than as
Liberals. But the Conservatives' margin over the Liberals was small.
And the century of politics before 1984, especially the delicate lay-
ering of cultural commitments, was still clearly visible in the parties'
coalitions.

This chapter employs an indicator of party support commonly
referred to as a measure of party identification. It is commonly argued that party identification has little relevance in the Canadian
case; indeed, it is thought by many to have little relevance outside
the United States. Canadians are unlikely, we believe, to identify
with parties in the same way that Americans do, given critical institutional and cultural differences between the two countries. But
we also believe that the difference between the two countries is
overdrawn.

Some argue that what Canadian survey respondents claim as a
long-standing party commitment is little more than the current voting intention. One highly plausible ground for such a contention
lies in the countries' differing electoral systems. American voters
face an inherently more difficult task than Canadians do. Some
Americans get to make as many choices in one election as most
Canadians make in a lifetime. The American voter's party commitment may thus play a special role in anchoring some of these choices,
especially the more obscure ones towards the bottom of the ticket.
Americans are also quite capable of departing from the party commitment for highly visible national races. This combination of party
loyalty low on the ticket and independence of spirit higher up may
give American partisanship a peculiar flavour. Canadians may usually be more tied to specific parties than Americans, but when forced
to switch they do not have Americans' luxury of making a partial
and modulated shift; they must shift *tout court*. In this Canadians
are like the rest of the world and Americans are truly exceptional.

The presence of a distinct, spatially compact sub-electorate – Quebec – may also distinguish Canadians from Americans. Chapter 2 yields a mixed record for Quebec: a pivotal role and some propensity to swing electorally, but also an abiding affinity for the Liberal party. But in this respect is Quebec so different from the American South?

Canadian parties themselves have been alleged to discourage voters from feeling much commitment to any one of them, except perhaps to the NDP. Canadian parties *do* engage in brokerage and their policy reversals have been spectacular; these were emphasized in chapter 2. But Canadian parties are hardly peculiar for either brokerage or for reversals. The very image of the brokerage party is, after all, American in origin. Downs's prediction for convergence at the median is a stylization of brokerage. And reversals are the staple of social choice theory (Arrow, 1951; Black, 1958; Riker, 1982). In their insistence that Canadian parties are peculiarly indistinct from each other and peculiarly given to reversals, students of Canadian elections may have been speaking the universalistic language of Downs and Riker, rather as the Bourgeois Gentilhomme spoke prose.

For all that, Canadian parties are not always indistinct. The old parties may not have been driven by ideology, but they have certainly been vehicles for powerful and divisive sentiments, as Siegfried (1907) recognized early on. These differences are not just residues of a clash of empires; they are proxies for contrasting ideas about the essential character of the nationality. Disputes over national questions are not, moreover, a peculiarly Canadian vice. They are an inevitable concomitant of nation-building.

Parties' reversals have not occurred at random. The commercial-policy shifts, for instance, required several steps, each of which followed its own logic. The response that parties made to the new challenges of the 1960s was generally consistent with their respective ethno-religious legacies. The continuities are just as notable as the discontinuities.

If Canadian history and Canadian parties are not so unique, why is it alleged that Canadian voters act so peculiarly? Why do they seem so fickle in their party allegiances, by comparison, for example, with Americans? The answer is they are not so different in fact.

A Canadian-American difference in the way party identification is measured has been fatal to the validity of substantive comparisons to date. The party identification item in American studies has always contained a non-partisan option; US respondents are given "independent" as an alternative to "Democrat" and "Republican." Before

Table 3-1
Trends in Party Identification, 1965–88

	Conservative %	Liberal %	NDP %	Other/None %	N
1965	26	37	10	27	2,118
1968	24	46	9	21	2,767
1974	22	46	9	23	2,562
1979	26	39	11	24	2,761
1980	26	42	13	19	1,731
1984	37	28	13	22	3,377
1988	29	24	11	35	3,478

the 1988 study, the Canadian party identification item did not contain such an option. As a consequence, more Canadian than American non-partisans were induced to give what appeared to be a party
commitment. This inflated the percentage appearing to identify with
some party and made the identifier group appear quite unstable
over repeated measurements.[1] In the 1988 study this item was made
more comparable to the American original. Comparability was
achieved not by a straight borrowing of the peculiarly American
word, "independent," but by adding the culturally neutral expression, "none of these."[2]

The 1965–88 party identification series appears in Table 3-1. The
first thing to note is that from 1965 to 1984 the "other/none" percentage averaged 22 to 23 percent; for all but 1984 this slightly
*over*states measured non-partisanship as Social Credit identifiers
were also included in this group. In 1988 non-partisans made up
35 percent of the sample, not because their numbers grew but simply
because they were, so to speak, encouraged to come out of the closet.
The 35 percent rate is very close to the non-partisan (that is, "independent") rate in the United States.

The surplus partisans did not distribute themselves at random
across the other party alternatives; instead, they gravitated to winners. From 1965 to 1980 the ratio of Liberal to Conservative identification shares varied from 1.4 to 2.1. Then in 1984 it abruptly flipped.
Did this signal a realignment? It may well have, but not on the scale
that the numbers imply. Only in 1968 did the Liberal-Conservative
vote-share ratio approach even the lower bound of the 1965–80 iden-
tification-share ratios. The 1965–80 surveys clearly overcounted Liberal identifiers and did so by about the same margin that those
surveys arguably undercounted non-partisans.[3] We must assume

Figure 3-1
Party Identification by Day

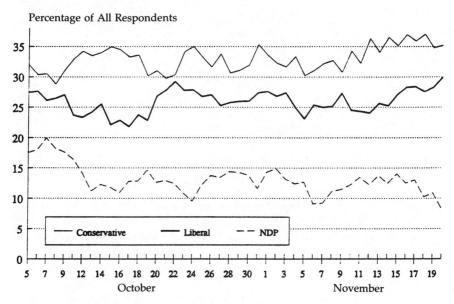

Percentage of All Respondents

5-day moving average
Non-partisans included in calculation

that the same logic produced an overestimation of the Conservative share in 1984.

All this said, the true Conservative share was still probably larger in 1984 than before, although it is not possible to say just how much larger. By 1988, if not before, the Conservatives had gained the plurality among identifiers. What is more, this plurality was one the Conservative party could count on, according to Figure 3-1. The figure has the same basic layout as Figure 1-4, the five-day moving average. As with the earlier figure, the daily sampling fluctuation is mostly smoothed away; no interpretable fluctuation remains. Virtually no trend, linear or curvilinear, is discernible for Liberal and Conservative identification. The Conservative share seems higher at the end than at the beginning, but this may be an endpoint illusion: the party's closing share was not strikingly different from its share in mid-October. For Liberals there was simply no trend at all; there was a slight hint of defection in mid-October, but that was all. Only for the NDP was there any serious suggestion of a decline in identifications. As with the Conservative share, though, much of this drop occurred at the very beginning, in a period

Table 3-2
The Regional Base of Party Identification, 1988

	Conservative %	Liberal %	NDP %	None %	N
Atlantic	32	28	5	35	273
Quebec	21	30	7	42	921
Ontario	30	26	11	34	1,331
Prairies	39	16	13	32	574
BC	27	17	23	33	380

in which the NDP vote share was not dropping. For no party is there any impact from the forces that swept through vote intentions at mid-campaign.[4]

We appear, then, to have come up with a workable representation of each party's core clientele. Equally importantly, we can say that such clienteles actually exist, that the electorate is not an undifferentiated mass.[5] Yet 35 percent of the electorate did not identify themselves with a party. This leaves ample scope for massive shifts.

A FOURTH PARTY SYSTEM?

If it is clear from Table 3-1 and Figure 3-1 that the Conservatives were no longer the subordinate actor in the system, so also is it clear that no party held a commanding share. The Conservatives enjoyed support from about 29 percent of the sample, while the Liberals could count on about 24 percent. The two old parties controlled larger shares of party identifiers than the NDP, but neither decisively outnumbered the other. The plurality rested with those who refused to make a party commitment. The rehabilitation of the Conservative party in 1984 made the third party system's standoff, if anything, even more complete.

The regional pattern of post-1984 identifications had a very familiar look. According to Table 3-2 the Conservatives continued to play the ends against the middle. Most notably, they continued to trail the Liberals in Quebec. The Liberals and the NDP still had complementary east-west patterns.

Table 3-2 also brings out the special position of Quebec, a distinctness that the rest of this chapter will respect. Even as Quebec respondents continued to show the residual effect of a century of Liberal dominance of the province, they also exhibited the highest rate of non-partisanship in the country (a pattern which also held, despite measurement differences, in earlier election surveys). Where

Table 3-3
Religious and Ethnic Differences

	Conservative %	Liberal %	NDP %	None %	N
A: Religious Denomination					
Protestant	**40**	18	11	31	1,216
Catholic	24	**32**	11	33	797
Other	20	25	16	**39**	194
None	27	12	19	**42**	313
B: Ethnic Group					
British	**35**	20	13	32	1,265
N. Europe	**39**	15	13	33	311
E. Europe	**34**	19	14	33	194
French	20	**32**	15	33	193
S. Europe	21	**39**	12	28	121
Other	22	28	14	**37**	302
None	29	23	8	**41**	172

Quebec respondents excluded

outside Quebec about one respondent in three was not identified with a party, the proportion for Quebec was over two in five. In 1984 the Conservatives profited from the existence of this non-partisan pool. By 1988 they appeared to have won converts, but their base was still smaller than that held by the Liberals.

CLEAVAGES OUTSIDE QUEBEC

Ethno-religious Divisions

Table 3-3 explores the religious and ethnic basis of party identification outside Quebec. Religious affiliation is compressed into four categories, "Protestant," "Catholic," "Other," and "None." For our purposes the violence this does to the complexity of Canadian religious life is small. Although the major Canadian Protestant denominations once differed politically among themselves, they no longer do so. Smaller denominations, especially fundamentalist ones, do tend to be distinct, but they carry little weight in a national sample.[6] That adherents of small sects are highly mobilized is not an issue here; the religious basis of the Canadian party system lies not primarily in faith or morals, but in denominationally differentiated conceptions of the nationality. An individual's degree of religious commitment is important primarily as an indicator of integration into the social life of group.[7] The emphasis, then, is on nominal identification with a big denomination. In Canada the big Protestant battalions are in the Anglican and United Churches (Presbyterians, most of whose adherents were absorbed into the United Church, remain as a flying column), which have long since ceased to differ politically. Similar considerations apply to the group that we have cavalierly labelled "Other." This group includes religions from all over the globe, some of which have been here almost as long as any Protestant denomination, others of which arrived, at least in politically significant numbers, only in the last few decades. What all these other religions hold in common for our purposes is that their ethnic associations are neither British nor French. Canadians who can muster no religious commitment are included in the analysis to make a point about secularization and the left.[8] In other countries, parties on the left have profited from and have encouraged a general secularization of society. They inherit the red side of the confrontation between red and black. To what extent is this true of the NDP?

The Catholic-Protestant cleavage persisted in 1988, according to Table 3-3, and was as large as any major-party regional contrast in Table 3-2. The bold figures are the largest in each row. They show that Protestants tended to be Conservatives and Catholics tended to be Liberals. A Catholic was nearly twice as likely as a Protestant to be a Liberal. A Protestant was 1.7 times as likely as a Catholic to be a Conservative. Only 11 percent of Protestants or Catholics chose to be New Democrats. Those of "other" religions and of no religion tended not to choose a party at all.

The NDP did tap a religiously differentiated base, but in its own distinct way. It received its smallest share from Protestants and Catholics, a four to five point larger share of those with "other" religious identifications,[9] and its greatest support from the "no religion" group. A Canadian of no religion was nearly twice as likely as either a Protestant or a Catholic to be a New Democrat. This lends support to notion that parties of the left draw disproportionately from the "secularized" portions of the population.

The "no religion" group was the least partisan overall. This reflects a process completely different from the secularization argument for NDP identification among those with no religion. For some, lack of religious identification is the end point of an act of conscious rejection. This rejection can be a step on the road to NDP identification, as it has been for labour and social democratic parties in other countries. For others, lack of a religious identification and lack of a party identification are just alternative indicators of a many sided disconnection from the country's social and institutional life.

Table 3-4
Religion and Ethnicity, Joint Effects

	Prot	Cath	Diff	Prot	Cath	Diff
	Conservative %			Liberal %		
Ethnic Group						
British	40	27	+13	19	34	−15
	(796)	(247)				
N. Europe	47	28	+19	11	24	−13
	(170)	(69)				
E. Europe	35	39	+ 4	12	22	−10
	(53)	(82)				
Other	35	13	+22	25	34	− 9
	(80)	(85)				

Quebec respondents excluded

Table 3-3 also breaks party identification down by ethnicity. Again the composition of the population is radically simplified for expository purposes; just seven categories appear.[10] This categorization makes a powerful point: the Conservative party continued to attract disproportionate support from backgrounds that correspond to English Canada's traditional ethnic core – in other words, voters with backgrounds in the British Isles or in the Protestant monarchies of northern Europe. Also in the Conservative camp were voters of eastern European origin. On the other side were Canadians of French, southern European, and "other" origin. A southern European, for instance, was only about half as likely as a northern European to support the Conservatives. A roughly complementary polarization underlay Liberal support. Here, the northern-southern European contrast was even more marked: a southern European was nearly three times as likely as a northern European to be a Liberal. The NDP was, to all intents and purposes, not implicated in the ethnic contrast. It got 12 to 13 percent support in each ethnic group.

It would be tempting to explain away the religious cleavage by reference to the ethnic divisions. The polarization seemed about as sharp in the ethnic breakdown as in the religious one and the sharpest contrast of all involved a group, southern Europeans, which is almost entirely Catholic. But for denominationally heterogeneous ethnic groups, religion cut through ethnicity. This is the lesson in Table 3-4, which controls religion and ethnicity simultaneously. In this table the entries in the first two columns are the percentages of Conservatives within the group defined by ethnicity (rows) and religion (columns). The first entry, 40 percent, is the Conservative share among Protestants of British extraction. The difference between the Protestant and Catholic columns shows how much difference religion makes in party identification once ethnicity is controlled. The right side of the table presents a corresponding analysis for Liberals.

In Liberal support the widest religious difference was in the largest group, that of British origin. This was not a disguised Irish/non-Irish contrast. A majority of the Irish in the sample (as in the population; see Akenson, 1984) are Protestants. Catholics in turn make up a significant fraction of those who give Great Britain proper as their own or their family's place of origin.[11] Similarly, the substantial fraction of Dutch and German Canadians who are Catholic were significantly more likely than Protestants of the same background to be Liberal and less likely to be Conservative.[12]

Farmers

One key difference between the second and third party systems was the place of farmers. In the second system no single party seemed to represent them and the Liberals could make as strong a claim as any party. In the third system, farmers shifted decisively to the Conservatives. Table 3-5 indicates the farm/non-farm cleavage in 1988. A farm family was nineteen points more likely than a non-farm family to support the Conservatives. Note, however, that the difference for the NDP and Liberals was small. Conservative strength on the farm was at the expense of non-partisanship: farm families were markedly more mobilized than non-farm ones, as only about one in five claimed no party tie.

The farm-Conservative link helps explain the political distinctiveness of the prairie west. To show this, Table 3-5 also gives the farm/non-farm cleavage within the prairies and Ontario.[13] Farm families had the same likelihood in each region of supporting the Conservatives: about one in two. Part of the story, then, is compositional: the relatively pro-Conservative farm group makes up a bigger fraction of the prairie than of the non-prairie electorate. The rest of the story is one of true structural differences. The non-farm Conservative share was close to ten points larger in the west than in Ontario; and the Liberal share among farmers was about ten points larger in Ontario than in the west, where the Liberal slack was taken up by the NDP. But it is also true that Table 3-5 understates farmers' importance in the political order. The farm category here includes only families on the land. Many respondents that we have classified as

Table 3-5
Party Identification by Farm/Non-Farm Status

	Conservative %	Liberal %	NDP %	None %	N
Farm	50	20	9	23	124
Non-farm	31	23	13	34	2,434
Ontario					
Farm	49	25	0	26	48
Non-farm	29	28	12	31	1,283
Prairies					
Farm	49	16	14	21	65
Non-farm	37	16	13	34	510

Quebec respondents excluded

non-farm are dependent on the farm economy, especially in the prairie west. Some of the prairie-Ontario difference in the non-farm category undoubtedly reflects this difference.

Unions

Another important shift from the second to the third system was in the place of the union movement. The English-Canadian labour movement formalized its link to the party system through the NDP. The NDP in turn became a markedly more important party than its predecessor, the CCF, and it tended to be most successful where its ties to the union movement were closest (Archer, 1985).

The basic union/non-union cleavage appears in Table 3-6. A union family was about eight points more likely than a non-union one to support the NDP. The absolute difference was not huge, but the ratio was large: about 1.8:1. Over half the respondents supporting the NDP were from union families. If the NDP was one pole of this axis, the other was the Conservative party; the difference in Conservative support was fully as great, but in the opposite direction, as that of the NDP.

To present only the total non-Quebec union/non-union cleavage would be misleading, however. The division was both more and less important than the top part of Table 3-6 makes it seem. In the Atlantic provinces, as the bottom part of the table indicates, the difference was, to all intents and purposes, non-existent. In Ontario and the prairies the cleavage was close to the non-Quebec average

Table 3-6
Party Identification by Union Membership

	Conservative %	Liberal %	NDP %	None %	N
A. Total Sample (Excluding Quebec)					
Union	26	20	**18**	36	804
Non-Union	**34**	23	10	33	1,709

B. Within Regions	Union	Non-U	Diff	Union	Non-U	Diff
		NDP			Conservatives	
Atlantic	5	4	+ 1	33	32	+ 1
	(80)	(185)				
Ontario	16	9	+ 7	25	32	− 7
	(422)	(878)				
Prairies	18	11	+ 7	34	40	− 6
	(158)	(411)				
BC	31	18	+13	17	33	−16
	(143)	(235)				

(for the NDP, at least). But in British Columbia, the cleavage between union and non-union families was as wide as any we have discussed in this chapter. In that province class drives the party system more decisively than does religion or culture.

CLEAVAGES WITHIN QUEBEC

Do the same kinds of social identifications underpin partisanship in Quebec? The place to start is obvious: with language. Language, even more than religion or ethnicity, is an everyday social identification. Moreover, in Quebec, language differences are reinforced by ethnic and, to some extent, religious differences. Of those who speak French, over 90 percent are Catholic and almost three-quarters identify their ancestors as French. Those who speak English are more variegated: 40 percent say their ancestors came from the British Isles and only 13 percent describe their ancestors as French. About one-quarter are Protestant.

Table 3-7 divides the Quebec sample into its francophone and non-francophone parts. The Liberal party held a plurality in both camps, although its edge among francophones was modest. Among non-francophones, it verged on hegemonic; it had over three times

Table 3-7
Party Identification by Language, Quebec Only

	French %	English %
Conservative	22	15
Liberal	27	**49**
NDP	7	9
None	**44**	27
N	696	106

as large a share as for the next largest party and about two-thirds of all partisans. Moreover, partisans formed a bigger fraction of the non-francophone group than of francophones. Indeed, Quebec's linguistic minority exhibited a degree of partisan mobilization which rivalled that of farmers and which certainly exceeded the norm elsewhere in English Canada.

The social divisions within the province's francophones were few in number and weak in effect. Only two bear close scrutiny: church attendance, and age. Table 3-8 looks at both.

The primary church-going boundary fell between weekly communicants and all the rest. For a Catholic population, this is precisely where canon law says the boundary should be. Weekly communicants were about one-half again as likely as all others to be Liberals. Conservative support was undifferentiated by church attendance, and NDP support was highest amongst those who claimed never to assist at mass. The NDP aside, the religiously differentiated alternative to Liberal support was support for no party at all. Weekly communicants reported a non-partisan rate, 36 percent, rather like the norm outside Quebec. The non-partisan rate among all others averaged 46 percent.[14]

The pattern for age resembled that for church attendance fairly closely.[15] Younger respondents were less likely to report a Liberal identification. The age pattern was not so much a gradient as two discontinuities: Liberal support remained in the low 40 percent range for respondents over sixty, whereas for those aged fifty-one to sixty the Liberal share was in the mid-30s, and for those fifty and younger the Liberal share was in the low 20s. The discontinuities thus were roughly before versus after the Second World War and before versus after the Quiet Revolution.

Once again, the Conservative party was not the only beneficiary of Liberal weakness. Rather, the Conservative share tended to be

Table 3-8
Party Identification by Church Attendance and Age, Quebec Francophones

	Conservative %	Liberal %	NDP %	None %	N
A. *Frequency of Attendance*					
Never	21	27	12	**41**	81
1-2/Year	24	23	7	**46**	169
Often	25	24	3	**48**	231
Weekly	20	**37**	7	36	167
B. *Age*					
Under 30	18	23	10	**49**	200
31-40	23	20	8	**49**	170
41-50	24	24	4	**48**	146
51-60	21	36	2	**41**	103
61-70	33	**44**	6	18	54
Over 70	23	**43**	2	32	23

in the low 20s in every age group. The NDP did do better in younger groups than in older ones. But the real winner in the retreat from the Liberal party was, again, no party; the non-partisan share was over half again as large in the post-Quiet Revolution cohorts as in the pre-Second World War ones.

The social structural pattern of federal party support was strikingly similar to the provincial pattern identified by Blais and Nadeau (1984). With the disappearance of Pierre Trudeau from the federal scene and with the rehabilitation of the Conservative party in the province, the federal Liberal base of the late 1980s came to be rooted in the older and more religious sectors of the electorate. This was also the clientele of the provincial Liberals and of the "No" forces in the 1980 referendum.[16] The other side of the electorate did not simply mirror the Parti québécois base, however. The Conservative party was not peculiarly the party of the young and the secularized. The antithesis to the Liberal party was not any specific party so much as the *refus global,* so to speak, to the entire system.

Party identification in Canada is rooted in religious, ethnic, and occupational identities. Individuals' party ties reflect the subtle geology of the historical episodes discussed in chapter 2. But neither geological formations nor party identifications are immutable. Both can change slowly over time. by erosion. But both can also change suddenly; along the fault lines, earthquakes can occur, all the more ferociously the longer the energy is stored up. The rest of this chapter is a search for the fault lines.

ATTITUDINAL FOUNDATIONS OUTSIDE QUEBEC

Are partisan identities related to political issues? They might not be. If party identification is like religion or nationality, then differences in party identification might persist in groups even after the issues or events that created the identifications become irrelevant. Party identification might be passed from one generation to the next with little policy content. This would be consistent with a "socialization" theory of party identification and alignment (Campbell et al., 1960, chapters 6 and 7; Beck, 1974). If this is so, issues such as commercial policy, the place of French Canada, or the role of the union movement might, notwithstanding their historical importance, play little or no role today.

A rival view (Fiorina, 1977) holds that current party identification summarizes the voter's evaluations of parties' performance as evidence accumulates over the voter's life. In this view, party identification is at least partly the creature of issue positions and is continuously modified. This second view, we believe, is a good deal of the story. As Franklin (1984, p. 475) argues:

In the traditional view, the early development and great stability [of party identification] implied that partisanship could lose touch with politics. Shifts in party behavior would not be reflected in identifications. In contrast, the revised [notion of] partisanship is intimately connected with politics, and the politics of the day rather than of the last realignment. The revised view sees party identification as a central, summary judgment of the parties, informed by policy preference and performance.

This view has been influential all along in the study of Canadian elections; a particularly pointed statement is Jenson (1975). Our sense, though, is that Jenson and others want to assert that the model which suits Canada also distinguishes Canada from the United States. If Fiorina and Franklin are right, though, partisanship ought to be very much alike in the two countries.

But they would resemble each other along lines altogether different from those implied by the older, socialization theory. Which theory is correct has implications for the dynamics of election campaigns. If the socialization theory is correct and party identification has no ongoing relationship to issues, then campaigns too should have little to do with issues. Such dynamics as campaigns exhibit should consist largely of identifiers homing in on their respective parties, of the rebuilding of long-standing coalitions. If the summary judgment model is correct and partisan identification does have a strong relationship to issues, then campaigns will probably be fought over them and party strategies will matter.

This section will show that party identification is strongly linked to issues. But the issue-based model of party identification says nothing about what kind of issues will dominate. In the model, new issues are just as likely to be energized as old ones; the agenda is wide open and parties are potentially as mobile as Downs posits them to be. Historically pivotal issues – Canada's ties with the United States, the role of French Canada, and the place of labour unions, for example – seem to be on an equal footing with new issues, such as abortion or the size of the government. Alternatively, if the agenda is stable for any length of time, this is not because social forces dictate that it be so. Rather it represents a deliberate manipulation by the parties (or their clients) which have been the prime beneficiaries of that stability. Brodie and Jenson (1980, p. 1), for instance, see

... parties less as aggregators of individual voters' preferences and more as actual creators of the pattern of those preferences ... They identify which among a broad range of social differences and tensions will be raised and debated in elections, and they nurture and sustain the criteria by which an electorate will divide against itself in a more or less stable system of partisan alignments.

Our own view lies somewhere between these poles. Brodie and Jenson are right to inject the idea of agenda control into the study of Canadian elections. A party concerned with its own survival *should* work to make elections turn on the considerations that favour it strategically. The Darwinian logic of politics makes it overwhelmingly likely that parties and politicians that behave otherwise will disappear. But to say this is to bring voters' own preferences, often derived independently of the machinations of parties, back in. Parties may select strategies, but they do not create the preference distributions that argue for and against particular strategies as readily as Brodie and Jenson imply. Nor can they, in a country as geopolitically and economically marginal as Canada, select the problems that the external world imposes. Parties are intensely strategic, but they do not choose the terrain for their strategy.

To make this point, we start with every issue that seemed to have campaign potential in the summer of 1988. What was their structure? To answer this question, we use factor analysis (McDonald, 1985), from which will emerge the three-dimensional structure described in chapter 2. Which factors, if any, drove party identification outside Quebec? This question is best answered with discriminant analysis.

What Issues Might Matter?

The operative word in this question is "might." Before the campaign began it was not entirely clear just how dominant the issue which occasioned the House-Senate impasse, the Canada-United States free trade agreement, would actually be. The campaign wave of the 1988 CES survey included an item on each issue which we could identify in advance as holding strategic promise for at least one party. The wave also contained an item on each issue which some non-party group was striving to place on the agenda (abortion is the best example). Finally, the campaign wave included a battery of questions about basic Canadian institutions and groups – objects that strategic politicians might seek to associate, positively or negatively, with key policy questions.

The following thirteen[17] elements made up the group and issue pool for factor analysis:

- *The Place of French Canada* (h1a): Should more or less be done to promote the French language in Canada?
- *Canada–USA Ties* (h2a): Should Canada have closer or more distant relations with the United States?
- *Union Power* (h3): Should Canada have stronger or weaker unions?
- *The Size of Government* (h4a): Should the level of taxes and services be higher or lower? (This question was designed to force respondents to accept higher taxes if they wanted more services and to advocate lower taxes only if they were willing to cut services.)
- *Free Trade with the United States* (I2): Does the respondent support or oppose the FTA?
- *NATO* (I3): Should Canada stay in NATO or get out of the alliance?
- *Meech Lake Accord* (I4): Does the respondent support or oppose the accord?
- *Immigration* (I5): Should Canada admit more immigrants or fewer immigrants than at present?
- *Abortion* (I6): Should abortion be a woman's personal choice, permitted only after need is established, or never be permitted?
- *Privatization* (I7): Does the respondent favour or oppose the privatization of Air Canada?
- *Official Languages Act* (I8): Does the respondent favour or oppose the recent extension of services for francophones outside Quebec and anglophones inside Quebec?

– *Nuclear Submarines* (l9): Should the government buy nuclear submarines for the navy?
– *Child Care* (l14): Should the government provide financial help to
day care centres, should it help parents pay for child care, or
should parents pay for child care themselves?

Some of these questions are obvious candidates for inclusion, either
because they are manifestly about the concerns in chapter 2 or because hindsight indicates that they were important in 1988. What
about the others? All of these were *potential* issues in mid-1988.

Some issues were potentially embarrassing for at least one party.
The nuclear submarine program looked to be a target for both opposition parties, an $8 billion gift that they could promise to spend
on something else. Leaving NATO was an albatross for the NDP:
would Mr Broadbent go along with his party policy – recently reaffirmed in convention – and thus betray our allies? Or would he
support our allies and thus betray his party?

The Meech Lake Accord represented a very different dynamic.
Each party had taken a clear position on the accord – the same one.
The government appeared to have identified the dominant solution
in at least the electoral part of the constitution game, if the speed
with which both opposition parties converged on it was any indication. The logic of Figure 2-12 seemed to lurk in the background.
But the accord was already stirring up opposition in the country at
large and the politics around the proposal were to intensify dramatically only a month after election day. Each party was divided
internally over the accord; the leadership had simply overridden the
divisions. Could they keep the lid on?

At least the parties were clear in their support of the Meech Lake
Accord. On other issues they tried to avoid taking a position. Abortion was probably the best example. The NDP position was clear and
was not hard to square with the party's secular base (Table 3-3). The
Conservatives and Liberals were both divided. Recall from chapter
1 that Mr Turner's maladroit move on the issue occasioned his worst
week of the campaign. If these two parties strove most of the time
to suppress the issue, actors outside the party system tried to get it
on the agenda. The run-up to the campaign had featured nomination
battles in which pro-life and pro-choice forces were mobilized and
individual MPs were being targeted.

Underlying Dimensions

How, if at all, do these issues fit together? Factor analysis allows us
to identify the master ideas or sentiments that underlie response to

Table 3-9
The Structure of Issue Opinion outside Quebec

	Commercial Policy	National Question	Foreign Policy	Class	Communality
A. Factor Loading					
Close tie to USA	**0.66**	−0.07	−0.03	−0.04	0.46
FTA	**0.77**	0.00	−0.01	−0.03	0.61
Pro-French	0.02	**0.63**	−0.15	0.26	0.56
Official Languages	−0.06	**0.64**	0.11	−0.06	0.41
More immigration	−0.01	**0.23**	−0.18	−0.02	0.08
Submarines	0.18	−0.04	**0.34**	−0.02	0.17
NATO	0.10	0.07	**0.28**	−0.15	0.14
Union power	0.04	−0.02	−0.03	**0.51**	0.24
Air Canada Privatization	0.16	0.13	0.18	**−0.36**	0.26
Parents pay child care	0.08	−0.13	−0.05	**−0.24**	0.11
Abortion	0.04	0.03	−0.16	0.01	0.03
Meech Lake	0.18	0.21	0.27	0.08	0.17
Lower taxes	−0.09	0.10	0.15	0.15	0.08

B. Correlations among factors	Commercial Policy	Nationality	Foreign Policy
National	0.02		
Foreign policy	0.19	0.05	
Class	−0.44	0.26	−0.09

Method: Maximum likelihood factor analysis with oblimin rotation

the policy items, to look for a set of underlying dimensions. How much an individual item is related to a given factor is indicated by its "factor loading"; the loading is like a regression coefficient, but standardized to run between −1 and +1. Values near zero indicate that there is no relationship between the item and the factor. Values near +1 indicate a strong positive relationship, and values near −1 indicate a strong negative relationship.

Table 3-9 gives loadings for a four-dimensional factor solution. Items which have loadings near +1 or −1 on one dimension and near zero on all the others can be interpreted very simply as good exemplars of the dimension. For example, "Close ties to the USA" and FTA opinion have large factor loadings (0.66 and 0.77 respectively) on the first dimension and nearly zero on all others. Because these two items are the only one to have large loadings on this factor, we call the factor *Commercial Policy*. Similarly, two items load heavily on the second factor and not on any other. These items, support for French and for official languages, along with a smaller but suggestive loading from the immigration item, lead us to name the second factor after the *National Question*. Finally, the items about unions and privatization of Air Canada load heavily – and oppositely – on the fourth factor, along with a third item involving support for child care. We call this a *Class* dimension.

Other items do not work so neatly. Two foreign policy or cold war items, support for nuclear submarines and support for NATO, load together, but their loadings are relatively small. Three items do not have very high loadings at all. The abortion and size of government items seem to have no relationship to the others. Meech Lake is somewhat of a surprise, but its failure to load on the nationality factor probably reflects the fact that our item was as complex as the accord itself. We manipulated the question experimentally, with four different treatments: one group was asked about the Meech Lake Accord with no elaboration, another was told that the accord strengthened the position of the provinces, a third group that under the accord Quebec would ratify the constitution as had the nine other provinces, and a fourth that the accord recognized Quebec as a "distinct society." When the factor analysis is restricted to this fourth group, the Meech Lake item has a loading of 0.41 on the nationality factor and essentially zero loadings on all other factors. But the polyvalent representation of the issue seems to be the right one for 1988: the ethno-linguistic spin on the accord still lay in the future; and treating the four campaign-wave versions of the item as one item does a good job of predicting response to a repetition of the no-elaboration version in the post-election wave of the survey.

Canadians outside Quebec organize a substantial part of their political thinking around the three dimensions identified in chapter 2:

– *Commercial Policy:* The items on ties with the United States and the FTA tap what was always in the background of attitudes to the British Empire: the behemoth to the south. In the campaigns of 1891 and 1911 the United States moved to the foreground. As the Empire receded, Canada's ties to America became more central as the organizing focus for opinion on external policy. Chapter 2 showed how resources and investment policy came to be caught up in anti-American sentiment in the 1970s and the early 1980s. The FTA placed Canadian-American relations squarely at the centre of the 1988 election.
– *Nationality:* The items on the place of French Canada and on the Official Languages Act represent the most continuously contentious element on the ethno-religious agenda since 1960. Since 1965 attitudes to immigration have also become, we believe, an avenue

for expressing discontent over the ethno-religious agenda and this is reflected in the loading for the immigration question. Note, though, that immigration attitudes are less central to the factor than French-English ones.

- *Class:* The items on unions, privatization, and, to a smaller extent, child care, represent issues of class. We argued in the last chapter that one distinguishing feature of the third party system was the enhanced role of the union movement. The movement's growth in the 1960s, especially in the public sector, and its ties to the NDP, make it a prime candidate for controlling responses to the party system as a whole.

The weakness of the rest of the factor solution also validates the emphasis in chapter 2. Foreign policy, detached from specifically British or American connections, and other policy questions, such as abortion or even the size of government, should have little connection to the core issues and they should be so precisely because they are *not* centrally engaged in the party battle. And this is what we find: the two foreign policy items have relatively low loadings even on the factor that can be best said to characterize them; abortion loads nowhere; and Meech Lake loads weakly on three factors. These questions also have weak communalities – which measure how much variance in the item is explained by all the factors on which it loads – compared to items on the other three dimensions (Meech Lake is something of an exception).

Finally, the oblique rotation allows us to see how much the factors overlap. All the overlap is in one place: between class and commercial policy. This should come as no surprise, in that the labour movement has historically had a stake in Canada–United States trade relations. Much of the movement's strength has been in import-substitution manufacturing. The class dimension, as we measure it, is not just a matter of organized labour, of course. It taps a general orientation to the market, including the market for child care. As the FTA promised a stiff injection of market principles into the Canadian political economy, the class-commercial policy association is only to be expected.

How Much Do These Dimensions Matter?

For this question we employ discriminant analysis, which looks for those predictors that do the best job of, literally, discriminating among groups. Consider, for example, two issues – abortion, and support for the union movement. The mean value for the three-point abortion question (+1 indicates that abortion is a "woman's personal choice" and −1 indicates that it should "never be permitted") are +0.33 for the Liberals, +0.35 for the Tories, and +0.50 for the NDP. The standard deviations for each group are approximately equal at 0.66. Hence, the *largest* difference between parties (0.17, between Liberal and NDP identifiers) is about 26 percent of the standard deviation. Compare this with group means for support of unions, (where +1 indicates that unions should have "much more" power and −1 indicates that they should have "much less"), and we find −0.14 for Liberals, −0.32 for Tories, and +0.06 for the NDP. Standard deviations for each group are approximately equal at 0.48. Hence, the *smallest* difference between parties (0.18, between Liberals and Conservatives) is about 38 percent of the standard deviation and the largest is about 79 percent of the standard deviation. Clearly, the question on union power does a better job of discriminating among parties. Discriminant analysis formalizes the approach suggested by this example by considering all issues at once.[18]

Discriminant analysis says nothing about causation. A respondent's positions on a group of issues may predict his or her partisanship, but it does not mean that these opinions produced attachment to the party. Causation can flow in either direction, as one factor which helps Canadians form opinions is the very party they identify with. Here we are concerned to find which issues are related to party identification. Later in the book we show not only how party cues can help shift respondents' positions on issues, but also how issues can cut across partisanship and open up new coalitional possibilities.

Using all the questions listed above, except the one on Meech Lake, a discriminant analysis of all those outside Quebec correctly classified 62 percent of the cases, much better than the 33 percent that would be correctly classified by chance alone.[19]

A discriminant analysis with just the five best predictors (FTA, union power, NATO, French Canada, closeness to the United States) produces almost as good a fit as one using all the items. The five best items cover the four dimensions identified by the factor analysis. The other items add virtually nothing. This does not imply that all of these items are irrelevant to party identification. For example, since privatization of Air Canada is highly correlated with attitude to union power and since support for the Official Languages Act is highly correlated with the support for French Canada, these are important predictors of party identification in their own right when taken alone; they are just not important once the initial five items are in the analysis.

Where does this leave us? The three basic dimensions of commercial policy, nationality, and class seem to structure political be-

Table 3-10
Percent of Party Identifications Correctly Predicted by Discriminant Analysis Using
Respondents' Positions on Various Combinations of Factors

	Opinion Variables in Discriminant Equation						
Ties to US							
Free Trade Agreement (I2)	yes	no	yes	yes	no	no	yes
Closeness to US (h2a)	yes	no	yes	yes	no	no	yes
French Canada							
Official Languages Act (I8)	yes	yes	no	yes	no	yes	no
Pro-French (h1a)	yes	yes	no	yes	no	yes	no
Class							
Privatization (I7)	yes	yes	yes	no	yes	no	no
Union Power (h3)	yes	yes	yes	no	yes	no	no
Percent							
Correctly Predicted	63	50	60	58	49	46	54

liefs and they are strong predictors of partisanship. One item from
another much weaker dimension on the factor analysis, NATO, also
helps predict partisanship, but its companion item, nuclear submarines, provides absolutely no help. We suspect that NATO's importance reflects efforts by Liberals and Conservatives to embarrass
Ed Broadbent. In any case, when the NATO item is dropped from
the five-item pool prediction, the percentage correctly predicted
drops by little more than 1 percent, to about 61 percent.

What remains are the three dimensions defined in chapter 2. How
well do these predict partisanship, relative to each other? Table 3-
10 shows the percentage of cases correctly predicted for models with
the six basic indicators for the three dimensions. The table indicates
that the incremental impact of the nationality measures is about
4 percent, of the class measures about 5 percent, and of the commercial policy measures about 12 percent.[20]

ATTITUDINAL FOUNDATIONS: QUEBEC

Do the same dimensions matter in Quebec? We can profit from what
we have learned for the rest of Canada to be short and to the point
for that province. We begin with the same attitudes set as outside
Quebec, with one crucial substitution. The Meech Lake Accord could
hardly have figured in the structure of sentiment within Quebec:
support for the accord was virtually unanimous. Instead, Quebec
respondents differ over a federalist-sovereigntist axis. The axis was
tapped by an item, put only to Quebec respondents, which asked,

"What is your opinion on Quebec independence? Do you ..." and then supplied four response alternatives.[21]

Quebec respondents exhibited a structure similar to that outside the province. Two dimensions are clear parallels: commercial policy, defined by the ties with United States and free trade items (loadings of 0.67 and 0.63, respectively) and the national question, defined by the sovereignty item (0.55) and support for French Canada (0.57).[22] The Official Languages item performs differently in Quebec than elsewhere. The response it evokes is not connected to generalized support for French aspirations. Rather, in three- and four-dimensional solutions it forms its own, fairly strong factor: a generalized willingness to concede official language minority rights within provinces. This factor is *not* correlated with the nationality dimension. For many Quebec respondents the vital thing about the Official Languages Act is not that it extends services to francophones outside Quebec but that it extends them to anglophones inside Quebec. The sharpest contrast, though, between Quebec and the rest is over class; in Quebec there was no such dimension.[23] In terms of the structure identified above, the simplest representation of the Quebec case is two-dimensional.

Discriminant analysis reinforces the two-dimensional interpretation. When all thirteen items are entered in a discriminant analysis, the three most powerful predictors are the FTA, sovereignty, and French Canada items. The item on general ties with the United States enters much later, but only because free trade is an excellent proxy for it. An analysis with the four core items predicts just over 1 percent fewer of the cases (62 percent versus just over 63 percent) than an analysis with all thirteen variables. The two dimensions were of roughly equal weight and are almost perfectly independent of each other. Commercial policy items alone correctly predict 46 percent of the cases (mostly Conservative and NDP identifiers); nationality items alone predict only 49 percent (mostly Liberal and NDP identifiers). Commercial policy items thus produce a 13 percent gain over chance prediction, nationality items yield a 16 percent gain, and their joint gain over the chance prediction is the sum of their separate contributions, 29 percent.[24]

THE PARTIES IN DIMENSIONLAND

Now we map the strategic terrain for 1988. Figures 3-2 and 3-3 take dimensions in pairs and on these dimensions locate parties and various subsets of the electorate. Figure 3-2 gives locations on the commercial policy and national question dimensions. Figure 3-3 gives them for commercial policy and class. Each dimension is rep-

Figure 3-2
Voters and Parties in the Ties to us-French Canada Space

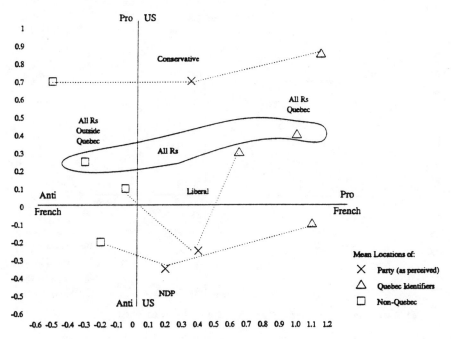

Dotted lines link party identification groups to their party's perceived location

resented by its most convenient single indicator, the five-point scale on closeness to the United States, the place of French Canada, and union power. Scales are centred on zero and range from −2 to +2.

The measures in this particular set are maximally comparable. As they were all in the same battery and used a similar format, respondents could implicitly compare responses between items. Two items, French Canada and union power, used identical responses: "much more" to "much less." The United States item was only slightly different: "much closer" to "much more distant." All three questions had a clear status quo option in the middle of the scale. Respondents were asked to make two relatively easy decisions: first, choose between the status quo and more or less of something, and then choose how much more or how much less. It seems reasonable to suppose, then, that respondents could make psychologically equivalent judgments across questions. Another critical consideration is that on two of the three items, French Canada and the United States, respondents were also asked to place each party on the same

Figure 3-3
Voters and Parties in the Ties to US-Union Power Space

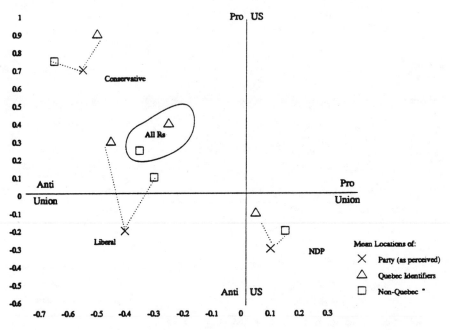

Dotted lines link party identification groups to their party's perceived location

scale. This was not asked for union power, and so placements on that dimension are average values for each party's identifiers.

In 1988 French and English Canada differed far more over the ethnic character of the nationality than over Canada's ties to the United States. This point is made by the serpentine shape on Figure 3-2, which encloses the locations of the average respondent in three electorates – all of Canada (the location denoted "All Rs"), Quebec, and outside Quebec – jointly on the two dimensions. The serpentine's orientation is almost perfectly horizontal: its span – the Quebec/non-Quebec difference of means – takes up over one-quarter of the total possible horizontal (national question) distance but virtually none of the vertical (commercial policy) distance. Where on commercial policy the Quebec/other gap is only about 0.15 units, on nationality the divergence is about 1.3 units. This was not because Canadians as a whole differed less over commercial policy than over defining the nationality: the standard deviation of 1.29 on the French Canada item is not strikingly larger than the 1.04 for the United States item. Figure 3-3 shows that smallest French-English gap was over union power (again despite the fact that the whole-sample standard deviation was almost as large at 1.01 for union power as for the other questions).

If French and English Canadian respondents were far apart on the national question but close on commercial policy, the reverse was true for parties, at least as they were perceived. Average placements are indicated by Xs. On Figure 3-2 almost all the party distance is vertical; the NDP are perceived to be a little less oriented toward promoting French-Canadian interests than the other parties, but the Liberal and Conservative placements are almost indistinguishable. In contrast, the vertical range is a full point; the parties are seen to be almost as far apart on commercial policy as Quebec and non-Quebec respondents themselves were on the national question. Respondents who could locate the parties[25] were not confused on the matter; standard deviations ranged from 0.39 for the Conservative placement on the United States item to 0.50 for NDP placement on the French Canada item. Quebec and non-Quebec respondents hardly differed over party perceptions.[26]

Figure 3-2 embodies the culmination of the reversals chronicled in chapter 2. The Conservatives, once reflexively opposed to all trucking with America for fear of its impact on the British connection, now had become the party of, so to speak, the American connection. New Democrats and Liberals occupied the opposite pole. The lack of difference over the nationality item reflects the other reversal – the Conservative party's success in taking Quebec back. There is only the merest perceptual hint (the Liberal placement is slightly closer to the pro-French pole in Figure 3-2) of the traditional Liberal domination of the francophone electorate. We simply cannot believe that such a result would have emerged in, say, 1980.

Figure 3-2 makes clear why parties might choose to divide over commercial policy but not over nationality. First consider what it takes to win a parliamentary majority. Recall that Figure 2-12 showed how hard it is to form a government without Quebec. But that figure also showed that, by themselves, Quebec seats do not suffice; also required is at least a significant minority of seats elsewhere in Canada. Now look at how hard it is for a party to pull Quebec and non-Quebec voters together. For the NDP and the Conservative identifiers, the Quebec/non-Quebec gap is enormous; for Conservative identifiers the gap, about 1.7 points, is wider even than in the electorate as a whole. The Liberals mobilize a sentimentally more coherent base (for them the Quebec/non-Quebec gap is about 0.7 points) than either of the other parties but even its base is more divided over the national question than over commercial policy.

In 1988 all three parties entertained thoughts of forming a government. For the NDP, the government in question may have been one or two elections away, but they clearly saw themselves as moving into the parliamentary big time. If all three parties seek to form a government and if doing so involves spanning French and English Canada, then all three parties should converge on the same location in the policy space. The Conservatives probably supplied the location by engineering the Meech Lake Accord. The parties' perpendicular line-up on Figure 3-2 is a classic case of tacit agreement not to open an issue. The dangers in opening up the national question, which have become all too apparent since the 1988 election, are also visible in our data. Recall that the Meech Lake item is a composite of four alternative versions. One version supplied the fact that the accord recognized Quebec as a distinct society; this aroused national question passions. Mention of the distinct society clause reduced anglophone support for the accord dramatically but increased its support among francophones: an English-French cleavage of 14 percent when no information was supplied became a 39 point rift when the clause was mentioned. The lesson was clear: the national question arouses divisive sentiments. Collusion was an easy way out.

If parties collude, where should they do it? In the spatial models of party competition that began with Downs – that is, models with one dimension and two competitors – parties typically are predicted to offer identical policies. When there are three parties and multiple dimensions, the situation is more complicated (Shepsle, 1991). It can be rational for parties to differ and for parties to offer combinations of various extremes. But if parties do agree on an issue, then the point of agreement is usually a middling one. This minimizes internal divisions, even though the minimum can still be pretty divisive. Collusion at an extreme position might make voters on the other side fertile ground for a protest party. Alternatively, one of the colluding parties may be tempted to defect. In short, choosing the middle ground is a risk-averse strategy for party leaders. In abstract models, though, the collusive mid-point is the preference of either the median or the average voter. In 1988 the Canadian parties lined up on the Quebec side of both the median and the average on the national question (the "All Rs" position is the average; the median is somewhere to the left of the average). The reason for this probably lies in the electoral-system logic of Figure 2-12. Strikingly, both the Conservatives and the Liberals are seen to have located themselves at almost the exact mid-point between the two sub-electorates. Only the NDP are displaced towards the rest-of-Canada end, as a reflection perhaps of their historic infeasibility in Quebec. The mid-point solution suggests that, although the Quebec electorate is smaller demographically, it carries roughly the same electoral weight as the larger electorate outside the province.

If the national question was to be avoided, was commercial policy the issue to grasp? Recall that the electorate as a whole was almost as divided over commercial policy as over nationality. But also recall that, according to Figure 3-2, no party identification group was divided between French and English over commercial policy. The figure makes clear that a major source of division over commercial policy was party identification itself: Conservatives, taken all together, were almost as far from New Democrats, taken all together, as Québécois were from all others within each party.

The temptation for the Conservatives should be obvious in Figure 3-2: only the Conservative party lies near the pro-United States pole; its perceived position as a parliamentary and electoral organization is almost identical to the typical self-location of its decidedly numerous identifiers and this is true for both sub-electorates. The Conservative placement is a little closer to the median than is the placement of its polar opposite, the NDP, and so more votes may be gained than lost through forcing the issue. Although Liberal identifiers are closest of all to the whole-electorate median, this may be a dubious advantage should the Conservatives decide to force the issue – the very closeness of Liberal identifiers to the median may undermine their party's credibility as an opponent of the FTA. In any case, should the Liberals oppose closer ties with the United States, they have to compete with the NDP for control of the anti-American pole, whereas no such problem of competition besets the Conservatives.

Of course, the Conservatives *did* force the issue and this put both opposition parties in a tactical dilemma. Figure 3-2 indicates that the NDP owned the opposing side of the Canada–United States issue, so to speak. As the most credibly anti-American party they ought to have benefited from the Conservative initiative; indeed, the Conservatives may have intended this very thing. But credibility is not just a matter of taking a firm position. It also requires widespread belief in the party's feasibility as a government. Unfortunately for the NDP, its history has been one of electoral weakness, in contrast to the Liberals. Chapter 7 will reveal that voters somewhat discounted the NDP's favourable 1988 polls. But credibility in opposition has two parts. If the NDP failed the test of viability, the Liberals risked failing that of commitment: could a party located as it identifiers are in Figure 3-2 *really* claim to oppose closer US ties? Figure 3-2 bears witness to John Turner's success in demonstrating his commitment to such opposition.

That success came at a price. The Liberal party was viewed as markedly more anti-American than its own identifiers. Even outside Quebec, Liberal identifiers were markedly more favourable (0.085) towards close ties with the United States than was the party with which they identified (-0.23). In Quebec, Liberal identifiers were closer to the Conservatives than to their own party.

Given the high cost of demonstrating commitment, why did John Turner choose to be so close to the NDP? Spatial voting models suggest that the Liberals should have chosen a position at the median between the Conservatives and the NDP; the pull of the median could be heard in Mr Turner's insistence that he was not opposed to free trade as a philosophical position or on GATT terms. Yet Mr Turner chose a more extreme position. In part this may have been necessitated by the FTA itself. As a concrete product of negotiation it demanded a yes-no response. But, as we show in chapter 6, serious doubts persisted about John Turner's leadership capabilities. One way to resolve such doubts is to demonstrate commitment on an issue. By taking a clear position on the FTA he could mobilize Liberal identifiers and non-partisans in his favour and ensure that the NDP not undercut him. His own predilections ran against the FTA, to be sure. In this case conviction and self-interest were reinforcing.

Figure 3-3 shows the connection of class issues to commercial policy ones at the same time as it describes the NDP's enduring strategic dilemma. The first lesson of Figure 3-3 reinforces a message from Table 3-9: commercial policy and union policy attitudes were mutually reinforcing. Recall that in section B of Table 3-9 the strongest correlation between any factors, after the oblique rotation, involved class and commercial policy attitudes. Pictorially, this emerges in the clear northwest-southeast orientation of Figure 3-3. For party identification groups, pro-American orientations increase as support for the union movement decreases, and vice versa. The emphasis on commercial policy inevitably injected a sort of class consciousness into the election.

But which party's interests were served by this injection? Ironically, the party least well served was the party with the closest thing to a self-conscious class appeal, the NDP. Of all three parties the NDP was furthest away from the centre of mass opinion. Only New Democrats favoured more power for the union movement; all other groups wanted less. This was not just a byproduct of the fact that Liberal and Conservative identifiers count heavily in the non-NDP residual. Non-partisans (not shown on the figure), especially outside Quebec, were squarely in the negative side of the space. And if anything, Figure 3-3 understates the NDP's dilemma. The NDP's location on the class dimension is, as we mentioned, the average location of its identifiers. Had we asked a true party location item, as we did for ties with the United States and for French Canada, we may well have found that the NDP's perceived location was as far away from its own identifiers on the union dimension as the Liberal party's location was from its identifiers on commercial policy.

In light of this, the association between union-related attitudes and commercial policy attitudes could help the NDP only in that it might allow the party to push a class agenda in an economic nationalist disguise. But blocking this move was a Liberal party that could point to its own nationalist record since 1974, a record with little union movement baggage. Most recently there was John Turner and his Senate majority.

The NDP faces in exaggerated form a predicament common to parties of the left (Przeworski and Sprague, 1986). They start with a clearly defined organizational base. This is a considerable resource, even where the party-union links are as weak by democratic socialist standards as the NDP's are. But if the links provide a floor, they also inhibit brokerage and limit the party's growth potential. Compounding the NDP's problem is the fact that one potentially compatible part of the electorate on class questions, Quebec francophones, was difficult for the NDP to reach, through a combination of the party's own ethnically narrow legacy and the relatively pro-American orientation of Quebec voters. To the extent that the NDP articulates a classless agenda – and chapter 2 made the point that such an orientation has always been prominent on the Canadian left – it blurs its specific appeal to the union movement.

Figures 3-2 and 3-3 do suggest a way out for the NDP, but the route is perilous. Before 1984 both the Conservatives and the NDP were almost exclusively anglophone; after 1984 only one party fitted that description – the NDP. In 1988, almost in spite of itself, it probably had the most credibility as a party of the interests of English Canada, as against those of a bi-national definition of the polity. To move wholeheartedly in the English-Canadian direction might conceivably have netted the party some seats; it could well have made the FTA less decisive and the national question more decisive in the campaign. But it would have ruled the NDP out of contention to form a single-party government, much as was true of the Conservatives before 1984. As long as the possibility of a single-party government remains open, the NDP is forced into line with the other parties to remain credible.[27] The next chapter will indicate that the NDP adopted the one strategy left to it in 1988: to emphasize the virtues of its leader. This did not prove to be enough in the end, but it still seems to have been the best choice, particularly in light of evidence about that individual, Ed Broadbent, in chapter 6.

The predicament that Przeworski and Sprague articulated for parties of the left seems to us to apply to any party that considers or inherits a self-consciously narrow appeal. In Canada a variant of this logic has applied to the Conservative party for much of its history. The residue of that history appears in the astounding polarization over the national question (Figure 3-2) in its own support base. It is difficult to believe that the Conservatives can maintain the balancing act implicit in Figure 3-2 indefinitely. They are vulnerable to losing one or the other part – the francophones or the francophobes – of their coalition. The Reform Party is already looming on the English flank, and since 1988 the Bloc québécois has appeared on the other flank. Long-run survival may force the Conservatives to try and construct a coalition like the Liberal one. For now, though, the Liberal party itself commands the centre.

STRATEGIC CONSTRAINTS
AND TACTICAL POSSIBILITIES

Canadian parties are anchored to the country's social structure. Some two survey respondents in three say they identify with one party or another. These commitments seem resilient; certainly they were quite unaffected by the campaign roller-coaster. The third party system's religious, ethno-linguistic, class, and regional patterns persisted in 1988. Now, however, Conservative identifiers outnumbered Liberals. But the Conservative margin was small and the standoff that characterized the third system seemed fated to persist.

What does it mean to say that party identifications are ubiquitous? Do these bases require no reinforcement? Are they impervious to party positions on issues – that is, are they pure products of socialization? Alternatively, if issues matter, are the issues infinitely manipulable? We argue that issues do matter to party identification, that they constrain parties' movements. The constraints are not absolute; individual parties can move some distance and the positions they take relative to each other can be as important as the distance any one party moves relative to its base.

The issues of the previous century, as modified by the post-1960 evolution of society and the party system, burned through 1988's potential campaign agenda. The best-organized issues turned on Canada's enduring conundrums – the attraction/repulsion of the United States and the legacy of conquest and empire – supplemented by a union movement grown more powerful and represented by an increasingly plausible party.

These issues, in turn, helped organize party identification. Commercial policy did so in both English and French Canada. The national question sorted party identification within each language group as well, but did so in a way which was difficult to reconcile with the coalitional imperatives of Canada's single-member plurality electoral system. The national question was potentially explosive for each party, but especially for the Conservatives.

The stage as history set it dictated that parties would collude over the national question and divide over commercial policy. To do otherwise would risk rupturing their bases and compromising their hopes for broadly representative parliamentary delegations. A commercial policy emphasis allowed the Conservatives to unite their base. The same would be true for the NDP, but that party's own base was small and liable to a further squeeze if the electorate was polarized on one issue. For the Liberals the situation was even more complicated. The issue as forced by the Conservatives required the Liberals to choose. Making a choice was attractive in that it promoted a polarization from which the Liberals, as an historically major party, were well placed to benefit. But to choose was to abandon the median, where the Liberal party's own electoral base was located.

The parties, at least the big ones, had a powerful incentive to emphasize the FTA. How did they get that emphasis out to the electorate? Did the mass media cooperate? Could the parties and leaders, John Turner especially, get to voters directly?

4 The Campaign in the Media: Illusion as Reality?

If history sets the terms for the electoral game, the campaign creates a setting for the final contingencies to play themselves out. Increasingly, the campaign has become a media event. The images in the media, especially on the small screen, are as close as most citizens get to the "real" campaign. Indeed, such reality as the campaign possesses is largely manufactured for media consumption and re-transmission. The campaign has been described as "the contest waged by the parties and their leaders to determine the issues around which the national (ie, media) campaign will revolve. The object of the contest ... is to manage events so that the news coverage will come out as close to their preferred version of events as possible." (Fletcher, 1981, pp. 125–6)[1]

But some parts of the media are more manageable than others and each part has its own rhythm. Do these rhythms permit an accumulation of impact that could turn a campaign around? And do any of the messages actually get through to the electorate?

Four elements in the media campaign are worth distinguishing:

- *Television news* coverage of issues and of parties' campaigns is a critical source of information for voters and is, commensurately, the primary target of the heart of the campaign, the leaders' tours. News coverage tends to be episodic: it responds to specific events and does so quickly. It may also respond to an internal ethic of objectivity.[2] Together, these considerations make the news very hard for any party to control. They also militate against structural biases, or at least against biases for or against parties which the media see as clearly in the electoral game. General campaign news coverage thus may not be structured to produce a cumulative effect, of the sort that could swing a campaign one way or the other.

– *Opinion polls* are a part of the news that no agent, in either the parties or the media, really controls. To the extent that polls give clear horse-race indications, they may in turn make news which takes on a cumulative pattern. Polls thus have the potential to swing a campaign, provided the audience is paying attention.

– *Advertising* is something which individual parties can control, although they cannot advertise every day of the campaign and they face ceilings on the total amount of advertising they can buy. Non-party advertisers faced legal constraints on content but, given enough money, no constraints on time or volume. There is no guarantee, however, that a party's advertising strategy will prove successful. The marginal impact of any single play of an advertisement is likely to be smaller than the impact of a news item of comparable duration: viewers seek the item out; a viewer who sees an advertisement has had it forced on his or her attention. But if it does happen to succeed, it can be repeated *ad nauseam*; it faces no newsroom constraints. The other side of this coin is that an unsuccessful, or no longer appropriate, advertising commitment, once made, takes several days to undo.

– *Leaders' debates* are a media event in one sense: they cannot happen but for the existence of national broadcast media. Debates might seem to be the ultimate episodic event: they happen and then they are gone. Although debates are also news and so get reported at length after the fact, as a news item they suffer from the rapid turnover that afflicts all campaign news. But the audience for them is huge. They provide a chance, if a temporally delimited one, for parties to reach the electorate directly. Even as a debate recedes as a news event, it lives in the minds of its viewers. In that sense, it can swing a campaign more effectively than any other medium. Then again, the major players strive to anticipate and neutralize such a threatening event. And voters may be able to neutralize it for themselves.

This chapter is our first chance to confront the interaction of the mass media with their audience. Most empirical work has been sceptical of the role of the media, especially over periods as short as a Canadian campaign. Citizens who attend to the media directly may also turn to opinion leaders for interpretations of the event.

Voters who are relatively inattentive, if they are to be influenced at all, must depend even more on personal influence networks to mediate the impact of potentially disturbing campaign stimuli. This is the image of the two-step flow of communication, an image that has been around for at least four decades. The classic radio-era studies (Lazarsfeld et al., 1944; Berelson et al., 1954; Katz and Lazarsfeld, 1955) emphasized that social communication, for all the advances in broadcast media, retained an important personal element. A message originating in an impersonal medium would not necessarily reach much of its intended audience immediately. The first round would see a direct incorporation of the message by opinion leaders. Opinion leaders would, in turn, pass the message on to their family, friends, and co-workers. But as they did so, they subtly transformed the message, bringing its persuasive content into line with their predispositions. They thus minimized the message's effect even as they transmitted it (Klapper, 1960).

But more recent work, notably by Iyengar and Kinder (1987) and Popkin (1991), is less dismissive of the mass media. And chapter 1 indicated that Canadian media campaigns seem to have gained in importance and that the 1988 campaign, in particular, shaped the outcome. The presentation of the campaign in the media must, then, be given its due.

THE NEWS

This section concentrates on television news, the English CBC network in particular. We are not staking a claim that television is necessarily the most important medium for news. Although respondents' self-reports commonly give television as the primary source of news, other analyses yield a picture much more favourable to print.[3] Nor are we insisting that among television news programs only the English CBC is worth analysing. The problem, at bottom, is one of time. The coding of the news, both print and television, is very labour-intensive. We had to focus on particular outlets and particular places.

Our logic followed that of the parties. If a party's objective is to direct – or redirect – a national campaign, then it has little choice but to work through television. Of the mass media, only television is sufficiently centralized to have a unidirectional effect on the whole electorate. Where news in print is scattered across several outlets,[4] news on television is confined to a few channels. Canadians overwhelmingly choose *one* channel for national news, the CBC. Overall, about one-half our respondents who watched any national news watched the CBC exclusively. Another 20 percent watched CBC in combination with other sources. Less than one-third watched no CBC. The bias toward the CBC is greater in French than in English: in French only about one news watcher in five saw no Radio-Canada news. If we are to analyse only one outlet in each official language, that outlet must be CBC/Radio-Canada.

We recognize that this makes our analysis a partial one. Evidence suggests, however, that tracking the CBC gives a fair approximation of coverage on both other networks and in print. Writing about 1988, for instance, Frizzell and Westell (1989) remarked: "As in 1984, what is striking is the similarity in the coverage provided by the three networks and by the seven papers in [the Carleton Journalism Study]." From our perspective, then, the pack-like qualities of campaign journalism simplify the analysis.[5]

The emphasis on English news requires some further justification. Again the primary constraint is time, supplemented by space. There was a sense, though, that the forces driving the campaign originated in English Canada. To the extent that this was true, the CBC news program most central to the campaign, even in some respects in Quebec, was the English one, "The National." Once we get into the daily numbers, then, we typically focus on the English side.[6]

Issues

Policy questions dominated CBC campaign coverage.[7] On the English network issues took up nearly 54 percent of campaign news time. On the French network, the figure was slightly over 50 percent. Issue coverage, according to Figure 4-1, was dominated by the free trade agreement. In English the FTA took up fully half the issue time and thus about one-quarter of all campaign coverage. In French the FTA's dominance was nearly as great. Moreover, the second most important category in both languages – economic issues, including employment, fiscal policies, regional development, the deficit, and the like – overlapped the FTA conceptually. In English so did the third category, social policy (including women's issues). Two of the three issues which commanded more attention in French than in English reflected traditional preoccupations: cultural policy, and the constitution. More novel was the importance attached by Radio-Canada to the environment, presumably in the wake of the events at Saint-Basile-le-Grand.

The balance of FTA coverage shifted back and forth. "Balance" here means the net treatment of the issue, in seconds. For any news unit in which the FTA was mentioned in a positive light, the length

Figure 4-1
Policy Coverage on Television News: Radio-Canada (French) and CBC (English)

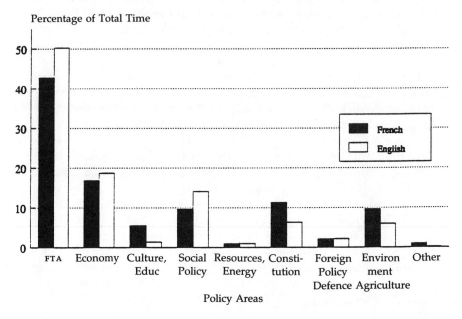

Percentage of Total Time

of that unit was added to the day's positive total. A corresponding rule governed units in which the FTA was cast in a negative light. The negative sum was subtracted from the positive sum to reach the daily balance. Similar counting rules were adopted for other media variables. Figure 4-2 gives the FTA's daily tracking for "The National."[8] It also gives a special seven-day moving average: in contrast with the moving averages in other chapters, these are *not* centred on the day of interest; rather they pool that day with the six preceding days. The intent here is to capture the cumulative impact, if any, of the media quantity. This anticipates discussions, below, of media impact.

In the first two weeks, coverage hardly moved off centre. Week three brought a shift against the agreement. The debates moved the coverage even further in the negative direction. Most striking of all was the evening of 25 October, which was dominated by report on the debate, most notably by repetition of Mr Turner's exchange with the prime minister.

But the balance quickly shifted back. Coverage in the week following 30 October was roughly even, although with two striking outliers. One came on Wednesday, 2 November, with coverage of business leaders' opinions and of strong statements by Brian Mul-

Figure 4-2
The Balance of FTA Reportage: CBC National News

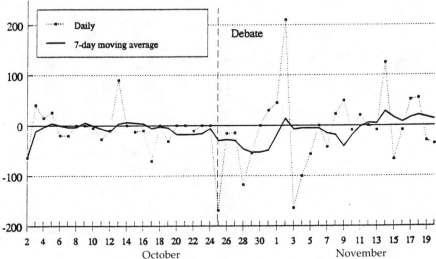

Net Treatment, in Seconds

roney and John Crosbie. This was by far the most one-sided day, positive or negative. But the second most negative reading of the campaign came the very next day, which was dominated by rebuttals of Emmett Hall's press conference. Thereafter, FTA coverage turned slightly positive.

The content of the coverage also shifted dramatically, according to Figure 4-3. The figure gives a crude categorization of the coverage, week by week, together with the pro/anti direction of that content.[9] Overlaid on the weekly breakdown of arguments is the weekly net balance across all arguments; this corresponds roughly to the seven-day moving average in Figure 4-2. In the first three weeks no issue tilted the coverage much. The moderately negative reading in week three was a compound of all issues. But the dramatic crash after the debates was almost entirely the product of sovereignty concerns. Coverage reflected – indeed repeated – Mr Turner's accusation that the prime minister had "sold us out." In week five the focus shifted more specifically to social programs. Emmett Hall notwithstanding, the social programs arguments which dominated that week's coverage were negative, opposed to the FTA; much of this was in specific rebuttal to Hall.

But the tide was clearly turning. By week six social programs, to the extent that they were covered at all, were back on centre. Neg-

Figure 4-3
Argument over the FTA: English Only

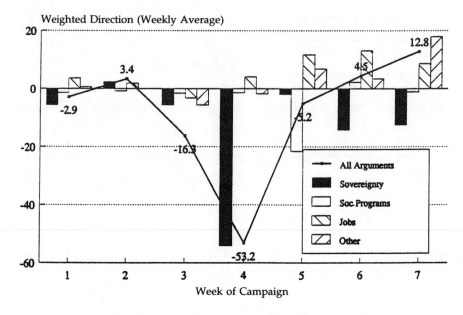

ative coverage continued to be dominated by sovereignty concerns. On the positive side, references to jobs emerged. The miscellany of concerns collectively labelled "other" also became generally positive. Notable among these by this time were references to American protectionism.

Taking the campaign as a whole, the CBC's coverage of the FTA is striking for its balance, at least in its representation of events and arguments. A sharply negative moment came at mid-campaign, mainly as the English debate was transformed from an event in its own right into an object of secondary coverage. But the news coverage quickly bounced back to a kind of balance.

Leaders

Most days, when coverage moved off issues it shifted to leaders.[10] In English, 60 percent of all references to political actors were to leaders. In French, the percentage was close to 50 percent. Parties as such received relatively slight coverage in both languages.

Coverage of the leader, like the FTA, did not appear systematically biased over the full campaign, according to Figures 4-4 to 4-6.[11] In the early going, both Mr Mulroney and Mr Turner tended to get

Figure 4-4
Treatment of Brian Mulroney: CBC National News

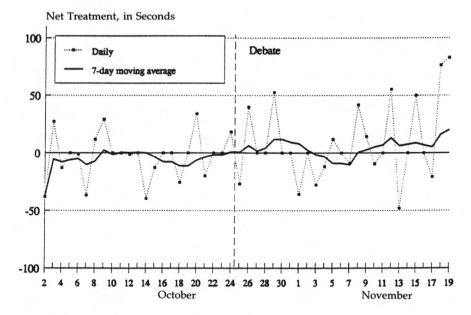

Net Treatment, in Seconds

negative coverage. Mr Broadbent got consistently positive coverage for almost the entire campaign. The real story of the early campaign was John Turner. On 5 and 6 October, for instance, came the child care and Dery fiascos.[12] In coverage terms, these two readings for John Turner were worse than any day in the entire campaign for Brian Mulroney. Yet they were only rehearsals for 17 October and the days immediately thereafter, perhaps as agonizing a period as any Canadian party's campaign has ever undergone. On the 17th, Mr Turner reaped a whirlwind for his improvisation on abortion policy. This set the stage for the report of the failed coup on the 20th.

Then came the debates, both of which generated positive coverage for John Turner. The English debate, of course, was the principal triumph: Mr Turner's coverage here was the largest outlier, positive or negative, for any leader before the last week. Indeed, three of the four days from 25 to 28 October were strikingly positive. Thereafter Mr Turner's coverage fell back towards balance. Never again, though, did he get as bad coverage as in weeks one and three.

Coverage of Ed Broadbent and Brian Mulroney did not ride the roller-coaster in the way that coverage of John Turner did. Especially notable is how they fared after the debates. Neither was treated in

Figure 4-5
Treatment of John Turner: CBC National News

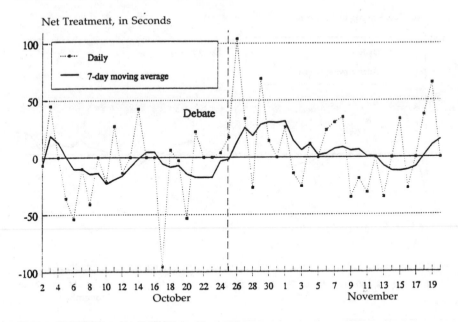

Figure 4-6
Treatment of Ed Broadbent: CBC National News

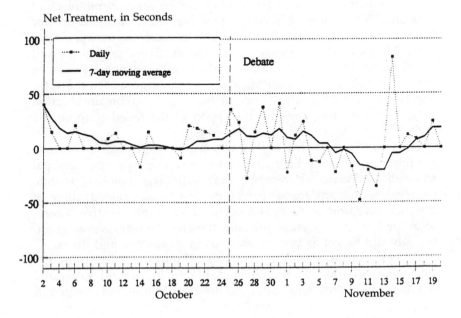

Table 4-1
Published Polls

Publication Date	House-Outlet	Party Share		
		Conservative	Liberal	NDP
October				
3	Gallup-*Star*	43	33	22
5	Reid-*Southam*	45	26	27
11	Environics-*Globe*	42	25	29
14	Insight-*CTV*	47	27	26
16	CanFacts-*CBC*	42	25	29
17	Gallup-*Star*	40	28	29
21	Insight-*CTV*	43	25	30
24	Gallup-*Star*	40	28	29
29	Reid-*Southam*	35	35	28
29	Insight-*CTV*	35	39	23
31	Gallup-*Star*	38	32	27
November				
1	Environics-*Globe*	31	37	26
4	Insight-*CTV*	40	37	20
7	Gallup-*Star*	31	43	22
9	Environics-*Globe*	35	37	24
10	Reid-*Southam*	39	35	24
10	CanFacts-*CBC*	38	38	21
11	Insight-*CTV*	39	39	20
14	Gallup-*Star*	35	35	26
19	Reid-*Southam*	41	33	23
19	Gallup-*Star*	40	35	22
19	Insight-*CTV*	43	32	20

Adapted from Frizzell et al. (1989), p. 95. Typos in their 10 and 29 October readings have been corrected. Two polls in the Frizzell compilation are not repeated here: the Gallup-*Star* poll of 10 October was not a national poll; the Goldfarb poll of 2 November received spotty coverage.

a particularly negative way; the CBC hesitated to comment on the *relative* performance of the leaders and thus the Turner positives did not automatically generate Mulroney-Broadbent negatives. Mr Broadbent's only real moment of agony came on 13 November, with a grilling over language policy. At the end, coverage of all leaders turned positive. The biggest beneficiary of this final turn was Mr Mulroney.

Polls

In the 1988 campaign, the media reported twenty-two national polls (Table 4-1), twice as many as in 1984 but many fewer than the

Figure 4-7
Parties' Shares in the Last Poll(s)

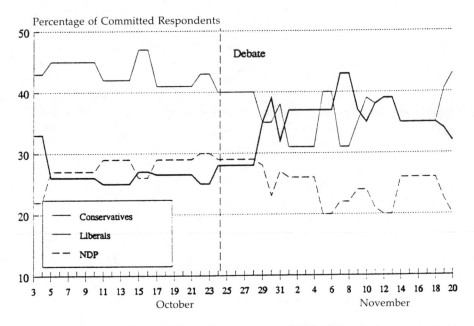

seventy-three polls in the 1987 British election (as reported by Butler and Kavanagh, 1987, p.125). In sheer volume, Toronto *Star*-Gallup and *CTV*-Insight Canada dominated with eight and six polls, respectively. Otherwise, polling tended to be driven by the cycles of the "real" campaign. Before the debates, only Gallup and CTV reported results more than once. Right after the debates, each of the four high-volume firms went into the field, with the result that a new poll appeared each day but one from 29 October to 2 November. Polling then subsided again, although all five outlets published a poll in the week which began with Gallup's so-called rogue poll (7 November). Then, after Gallup published its regular Monday poll on 14 November, an eerie silence prevailed, broken only at the end with three polls on the 19th.

Figure 4-7 shows for each day what a voter ought to have gathered from the most recently published poll about the three major parties' relative standing.[13] Before the debates the poll message about the likely winner was cumulative and consistent. Although Conservative support declined slightly, each poll showed the party with a comfortable lead. By 24 October the Conservatives had led nine consecutive campaign polls, not to mention pre-campaign polls in

September. The Liberals and NDP, in contrast, were stuck in a distant second-place tie.[14] On the eve of the debates an impartial observer of these polls would have concluded that a Conservative victory was overwhelmingly probable.

The debates ushered in uncertainty about the front-runners. Note, though, that poll confirmation of the debates' impact did not come until the 29th, four days after the English debate. It then became clear that the Conservatives had dropped and that the Liberals, not the NDP, had surged. But whether the Liberals or the Conservatives were more likely to win remained unclear until 19 November. From 29 October to 19 November the Liberals came out ahead five times, the Conservatives three times, and the two parties were tied four times. The NDP's situation, in contrast, became increasingly clear. Each post-debates poll confirmed that the NDP would finish third; by election day this had happened fourteen consecutive times. The NDP's actual share, though, did not clearly begin to drop until the second round of post-debates polls, starting with the *Insight*-CTV poll on 4 November.

If voters had trouble sorting this out for themselves, television news was ready to help. Figure 4-8 gives the balance of "horse-race" reporting for each party, by day, on "The National." This is probably as good a reading as can be obtained for universally available poll commentary. This is so, in part, for the reasons we gave above for focusing on the CBC. But it is probably even more true for poll coverage than for any other campaign news quantity. Print coverage of polls was actually quite spotty. Each major chain and each of two Toronto dailies, the *Globe and Mail* and the *Star*, had their own polling affiliate, as Table 4-1 indicates. On the day that the affiliated firm reported, only that firm would get front-page coverage. Other days, other polls might make the front page, but never with the detail that the affiliated poll received. In this respect, CTV, with its Insight Canada connection, was like a print outlet. The CBC, in contrast, conducted only two polls itself and was committed to comprehensive poll coverage.

Although frequent, horse-race coverage was not a daily event. Nineteen readings were discernible over the fifty-day span, most of them coinciding with poll appearances.[15] This episodic coverage makes the daily tracking hard to follow. For visual clarity only the seven-day moving appears in Figure 4-8.

The figure is set up to emphasize the most telling horse-race story, the Liberals' reversal of fortune. Up to 25 October, every mention of the Liberals was negative. The most negative of all, ironically, came on the day of the English debate. This was an updating of

Figure 4-8
The Reporting of the Horse Race

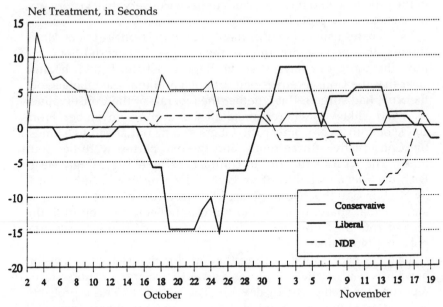

7-day moving average

cumulatively bad poll news. Over the same period, most mentions of the NDP were positive; what counted was not how far behind the NDP were, but how they were abreast, if not ahead, of the Liberals. That is, Liberal and NDP coverage was being driven by performance *relative to expectations.*[16]

The polls on the last weekend of October changed all that. From then to 19 November, all post-debates horse-race readings for the Liberals were positive, more positive even than for the Conservatives. Again, the critical factor seems not to have been how the Liberals were doing absolutely or even relative to the Conservatives. What counted was how well they were doing relative to expectations generated by their October nightmare. Most negative readings referred to the NDP; coverage reinforced the message of marginalization that the polls themselves implied. For the Conservatives, only one reading was actually negative: the day of the Gallup poll of 7 November.

At the end the frontrunners' situation sorted itself out: three separate polls showed the Conservatives with a comfortable lead. The Liberals had clearly fallen back but were in no danger of ceasing to be the official opposition. In the coverage, both the Liberals and the

NDP were treated negatively, the only time in the campaign that this happened.

ADVERTISING

With only four weeks to go, parties gain the right to place their own advertisements. In 1988 the advertising period began on Sunday, 23 October, and ended on Saturday, 19 November. Three facets of party advertising are obvious candidates for scrutiny: overall volumes for each party; treatment of the central issue, the FTA; and treatment of leaders, their own and each other's. Advertising by so-called third-parties (organizations or individuals not formally identified with a party or candidate) faced no time restrictions; in 1988 such advertising merits discussion only in relation to the FTA.

Overall Televison Allocations

Anecdotes of the campaign led us to expect a flood of Conservative advertising at the end. No such pattern leaps from Figure 4-9, which gives each party's daily overall prime-time (6 p.m. to midnight) advertising buy on Radio-Canada Montreal and CBC and CTV Toronto, in seconds.[17] If any party appeared to hold back for a last-week push, it was the NDP. For the three major parties combined, the pattern was one of week-by-week intensification. By the last week parties were spending one-and-one-half times as much on prime time as they had in the opening week, 23–29 October. Cumulatively, the Conservatives bought 39 percent of all the major-party advertising time on these channels, the Liberals 29 percent, and the NDP 32 percent.

The Conservatives were certainly the biggest buyers at the end, although not strikingly more so than at other points in the campaign. Their 13 November advertising placement was the biggest single one by any party on our three Toronto-Montreal channels. But the NDP was also highly active at the end. In the last week the NDP outbought the Liberals by quite a margin. And the NDP was the only party to tilt its outlay towards the end of that last week; it even bought more time than the Conservatives. The Liberals stood in contrast to both the other parties. Liberal advertising reached its single-day peak on 30 October and subsequently dropped before embarking on the final path of growth. But the Liberals never matched the Conservatives, nor did they join the NDP in concentrating on a final, big push.

All three parties aimed their advertising at areas of greatest strategic opportunity, locations where they were weak but plausible: where Conservatives invested in English Canada, Liberals and the

Figure 4-9
Party Advertising Volumes, by Day

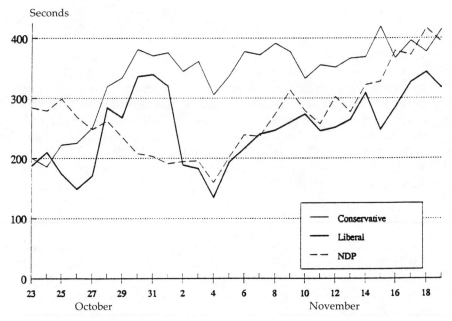

5-day moving average

NDP put money disproportionately into Quebec. Conservatives placed just 24 percent of the advertising on Radio-Canada, but they placed 46 percent of the total on the two Toronto television channels. This helps explain why the Conservatives' campaign seemed so overwhelming to English Canadians. The Liberals bought a meagre 24 percent of the English advertising, but on Radio-Canada Montreal they bought 41 percent. The NDP fell between these extremes.

For advertising allocation, then, the prime time story was not one of a Conservative juggernaut. Although the Conservative party spent more money than each of the others, the two anti-FTA parties combined outspent the Conservatives handily. Although the NDP was able to match the Conservative late-campaign advertising surge, the Liberals were not.

All parties were constrained by the medium. Television stations are obligated not just to parties but to other advertisers as well. Once a party books its "gross ratings point" maximum in a period, it is difficult for it to exceed that maximum at short notice. If the party suddenly decides to increase its exposure it is likely to have to do it outside of prime time. This is allegedly what the Conservatives did in the late going.[18]

Figure 4-10
Party Advertising on the FTA

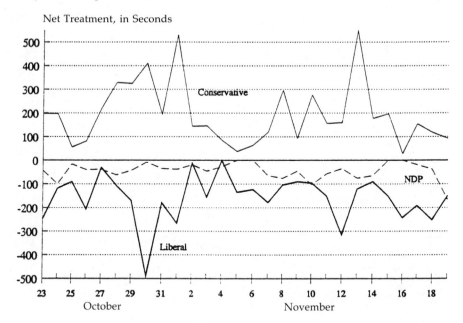

Advertising about the FTA

The party battle over the FTA was closely fought. Altogether, advertising against the agreement outweighed that in favour in seventeen days out of twenty-eight. Some of the other eleven days were very one-sided, although four of the five decidedly pro-FTA days came early in the party advertising period. When the four weeks of party advertisements ended, the Conservatives had mentioned the FTA positively for 5,440 seconds and the Liberals and NDP had attacked it for 5,718 seconds, roughly an hour and a half on each side. For all that, anti-FTA mentions cumulatively outweighed pro-FTA ones by only 278 seconds, or just over four minutes.

The margin was small because the NDP left the fight to the Liberals. According to Figure 4-10, NDP mentions of the FTA outweighed those by Liberals on only four days, and only on the last advertising day did the NDP make a decisive contribution. On most days the Liberals carried the ball alone. Cumulatively, the Liberals devoted some 63 percent of their total CBC and CTV advertising commitment to attacking the FTA. They contributed 4,458 seconds, 78 percent of the anti-FTA total. Although the Liberals often matched the Conservatives on individual days, cumulatively they could not. Like the Lib-

Figure 4-11
Third-Party Pro-FTA Advertising: Post-Debates

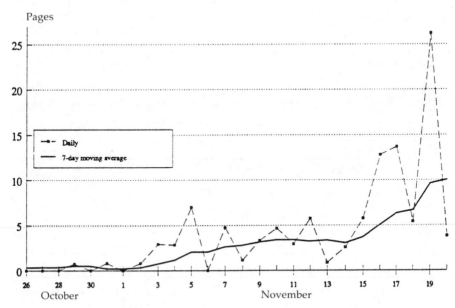

erals, the Conservatives targeted their advertising on the FTA;
57 percent of their total advertising time mentioned the agreement.
The NDP mentioned the FTA in only 1,260 seconds, 16 percent of
their total time. Had the NDP matched the Liberal commitment, party
advertising against the FTA would have outweighted that in favour
by about an hour, as opposed to four minutes.

The NDP's strategic choice may have been doubly significant in
light of the sound from off stage. The 1988 campaign saw the most
striking intrusion of third-party advertising in a national election in
over forty years.[19] Earlier elections had not as a rule provided much
of a field for such advertising and the Canada Elections Act, as
amended in 1983, prohibited it. But the pertinent provisions of the
act were struck down for Alberta in 1984[20] as inconsistent with
freedom of expression guarantees in the Canadian Charter of Rights
and Freedoms. The Alberta decision was not appealed and the chief
electoral officer advised his officials not to apply the law.

The result appears in Figure 4-11. The figure tracks the daily balance of third-party advertising for or against the FTA, culled from
fourteen-newspapers; to the best of our knowledge, third parties
did not place television commercials. The daily reading can be taken
as the total area, in pages, of pro-FTA advertisements.[21] The third-

party campaign responded to polls. Before 1 November, while the Conservative share still seemed robust, virtually no advertisements were placed. The next few days, when it was clear the Conservatives were in trouble, saw an order-of-magnitude shift: the average daily placement equalled about two full pages. The following week saw this grow by about a half: for 7–13 November the average daily placement was three full pages. The last week brought another order-of-magnitude shift: for 14–20 November third-party advertisements averaged ten pages, *per day*. A big fraction of this came on the last day of full circulation, Saturday, 19 November: roughly twenty-seven pages, close to two pages in each of our fourteen newspapers on that one day. About 65 percent of the total third-party advertising space was bought in the campaign's final week; the last Saturday alone took up 25 percent.

The Leaders in Party Advertising

The party which most consistently presented its own leader as a major asset was the NDP. Virtually all mentions of Ed Broadbent were positive, which is to say that almost all were made by his own party. The "negative" line in Figure 4-14 is the sum of Conservative and Liberal mentions of Mr Broadbent. Hardly any such mentions were made and these came well after the NDP had fallen back in the polls. Figure 4-14 is also striking in comparison with Figure 4-11. The NDP went out of their way to emphasize their leader and did so at the expense of the campaign's central policy question; cumulatively, Ed Broadbent was mentioned about 2.7 times as often as the FTA.

The old parties actually downplayed their leaders. They did not ignore them entirely, of course, but the own-party weights (the positive lines) in Figures 4-12 and 4-13 are markedly smaller than the NDP weights for Ed Broadbent in Figure 4-14. Altogether, the NDP mentioned Mr Broadbent almost twice as often as the Liberals mentioned John Turner and over 1.25 times as often as the Conservatives mentioned Brian Mulroney.

All three parties spent most of their leader time on the attack. From the outset, the primary target was Brian Mulroney. Although Mr Mulroney received fairly regular mention in Conservative advertisements, his own party was regularly drowned out by the other two parties (added together as "negative") and especially by the Liberal party. Much of this advertising was also – implicitly if not always explicitly – about the FTA. For instance, a Liberal advertisement about the demerits of the FTA explicitly linked the agreement

Figure 4-12
Brian Mulroney in Party Advertisements: English Only

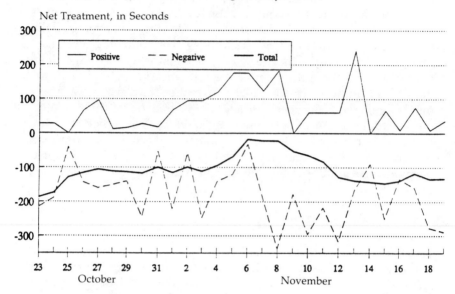

"Total" line is 7-day moving average

Figure 4-13
John Turner in Party Advertisements: English Only

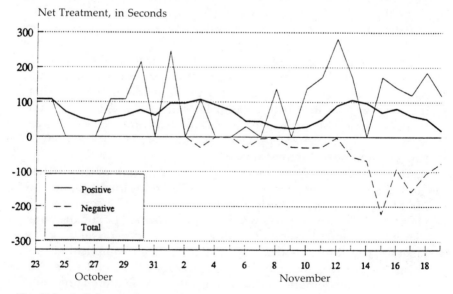

"Total" line is 7-day moving average

Figure 4-14
Ed Broadbent in Party Advertisements: English Only

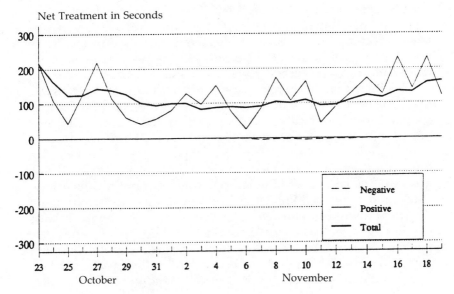

"Total" line is 7-day moving average

to the trustworthiness of its negotiator: "say one thing, mean another" went the trope.

The other main target was John Turner. Early on Mr Turner escaped: attacking him may have seemed unnecessary, as he was
already down. About a week after the debates, however, the Conservatives had awakened to the possibility that John Turner was the
source of the strategic predicament that now beset them. Thence
began attacks on Mr Turner, the "bombing the bridges" campaign
(Fraser, 1989, p. 322). The Conservative inventory changed from a
large number of individual positive advertisements, each getting a
small amount of play, to the opposite configuration: a small number
of negative advertisements, each getting a high frequency of play.
One advertisement made Mr Turner appear vampire-like and accused him of "misleading the Canadian people." Another distilled
the Conservatives' theme into one brilliant line: "He's out to save
his job, not mine." After 3 November the net treatment of John
Turner moved back and forth close to the zero line. Effort on both
sides intensified in the last week: the Conservatives ran one hundred
to two hundred seconds a day and the Liberals countered with a
like amount.

THE LEADERS' DEBATES

Chapter 1 indicated that, superficially at least, the 1988 debates were critical to the campaign. After them the Conservative share of vote intentions collapsed immediately; after a few days the NDP share also fell; the Liberals surged; the Conservative recovery was not automatic; and the NDP recovery was nil. Earlier parts of this chapter also testify to the pivotal role of the debates, as Conservative attacks on John Turner and third-party advertising on the FTA both responded to the tactical challenge posed by the debates. But their importance still comes as something of a surprise.

So far, evidence about debates in campaigns has accumulated in three countries. In the United States the bulk of the evidence suggests that debates have little impact. American presidential candidates tend to be well known before they are called to debate and the event should thus reveal little that is new. The event itself is highly staged, not least by the candidates. They typically anticipate possible dangers. After the fact, "spin doctors" work to neutralize any damage which might have occurred. For their part, members of the audience bring strong predispositions to the event. Besides, American presidential elections are commonly one-sided.[22] In Germany, however, the pattern is altogether different: debates come near the end of campaigns and can play a very significant role.[23]

The Canadian record is mixed. Where leaders are already well known, predispositions are likely to be confirmed and the impact small. This was the case in 1979. Although Joe Clark and Ed Broadbent were each leading their party in an election for the first time, each had been an MP for years and had led his party for, respectively, three and four years; Pierre Trudeau, of course, did not need a debate to be introduced to the electorate. In contrast, debates did seem critical in 1984. Figure 1–3 indicated that virtually all the massive surge to the Conservatives occurred sometime after the first two debates. That year saw both old parties led by new faces (or one new face and one new-old face). The French debate may have been critical in indicating that Mr Mulroney was the real francophone.[24] The first English debate featured an exchange over patronage appointments which seemed to galvanize resentment at Liberal governments' longevity and arrogance, and which also revealed Mr Turner's rustiness. Lanoue confirms that perceptions of his performance did play a role in his party's crash.[25]

By 1988 every leader was well known and well practised. The anticipatory preparation was also considerable. The media, for their part, seemed so dismayed by the alleged American record of spin-doctoring and manipulation that they appeared to struggle against being manipulated themselves. The *Globe and Mail*, for instance, anticipated events with articles about the debates' irrelevance.[26] Although the American pattern seemed to be one of offsetting rather than of one-sided manipulation, the Canadian media seemed to fear being lured into calling a winner. One observer claims that reporters exposed themselves to the Canadian parties' spin doctors only to interview them about the very phenomenon they represented.[27] A tracking of headlines in sixteen newspapers[28] also revealed a reluctance to call a winner: three newspapers had no electoral headline on the debate right after the event and nine had studiedly vague ones. Only four gave any indication that John Turner might have won. None of the four focused on the FTA exchange; two emphasized, of all things, patronage.

The three English television networks resolutely declined to give a summary judgment on performance.[29] In this they mirrored the diffidence of print. But the television news was not just in the business of calling winners and losers, it was also retailing images. Figure 4-5 indicated that the television news presentation of Mr Turner on the day after the English debate was overwhelmingly positive. It was also positive for Ed Broadbent, but mildly negative for Brian Mulroney. For Broadbent and Mulroney, though, 26 October hardly stands out; for John Turner, in contrast, that day brought by far his highest reading, indeed the highest one for *any* leader until the campaign's last week.

Voters themselves came to a pretty one-sided conclusion about the debates, according to Figure 4-15. In the days and weeks which followed the events, about 55 percent of our respondents claimed that John Turner had performed best. Brian Mulroney was given the nod by under 15 percent and Ed Broadbent by under 10 percent. Over twice as many people thought Turner had won as thought that anybody else had. As for who had performed worst, the only thing that respondents were clear on was that John Turner was *not* that person. Ed Broadbent was mentioned most often, but virtually as many respondents were unable to name anyone as named the NDP leader and the "don't know" percentage was higher for the loser than for the winner.

The event cut across through prior commitments: all party identification groups agreed that John Turner won, according to Figure 4-16. Only among Conservatives did less than a majority say so, and even in that group the percentage was close to 50. New Democrats were about twice as likely to name Mr Turner as to name their own leader. This said, party identification did have an impact in its

Figure 4-15
Who Won? Who Lost?

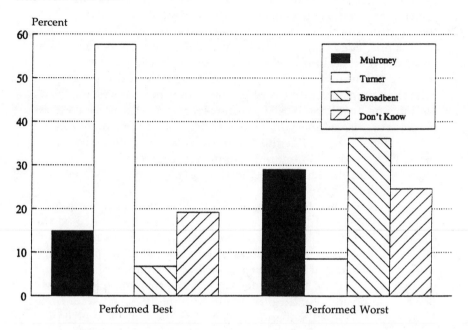

Respondents with vote intentions only

own right. Figure 4-16 indicates that each leader was named the winner in disproportionate numbers by his own party's long-term supporters. The difference was around twenty points for Brian Mulroney and Ed Broadbent and closer to thirty points for John Turner. But if the leader's own partisans were biased in his favour, no further bias was imparted by identification with any other specific party.

Of respondents who thought of themselves as "strong" or "fairly strong" partisans, over 60 percent watched a debate. The percentage for "not very strong" partisans and non-partisans was just under 50. Put another way, respondents in the the two most intense categories of partisanship constituted 54 percent of the debates' audience but only 41 percent of the non-viewer group. The strong partisan coloration of evaluations suggests one reason that debates' impact has traditionally been limited: *the audience consists disproportionately of intense partisans.*

But in 1988 partisan bias was less impressive than the openness many viewers displayed to the debates' manifest content. Few of the 55 percent of respondents[30] who actually saw a debate needed

Figure 4-16
Who Won? by Party

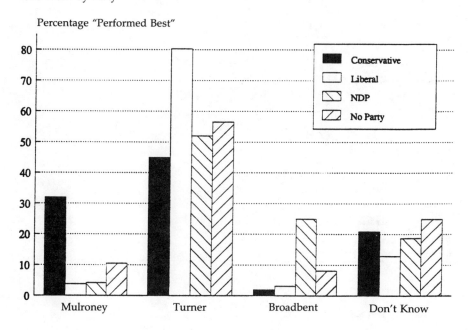

Percentage "Performed Best"

Respondents with vote intentions only

to be told who won. According to Figure 4-17, respondents who saw a debate claimed one-sidedly that John Turner won and made this claim right from the start.[31] In contrast, non-viewers took about a week to rally to the Turner-as-victor consensus. At the outset non-viewers were some twenty points less likely than viewers to name Mr Turner as the winner.[32] By early November the viewer/non-viewer difference had evaporated: around 60 percent of each group named John Turner as the winner; indead, for a few days, non-viewers were *more* likely than viewers to name John Turner.

Then the two groups diverged. Among viewers, Mr Turner's debate perception sagged some ten points. But the decay was gradual; most viewers, evidently, managed to treat this question as a factual one. Among non-viewers, however, the frequency of those claiming that Mr Turner had won dropped sharply after about 9 November. This slide bottomed out towards the beginning of the campaign's last week. The last five days brought non-viewers back in line with the viewers.

Figure 4-17
Perceptions of Turner's Performance, by Debate Viewership

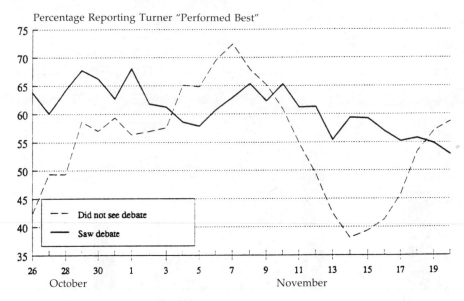

Percentage Reporting Turner "Performed Best"

5-day moving average

The non-viewers' pattern looks suspiciously like one of following cues. But what cues? The obvious place to look is to television, both news and advertisements. The debates generated several days of positive readings for Mr Turner, some readings which recounted the English debate itself, others which reported large, successful rallies and the like. Coverage cooled off rapidly, though, and even turned negative. Then at the end, Mr Turner shared in the positive reporting that all leaders received. The debates also ignited the advertising war over Mr Turner.

Table 4-2 ties this movement in news coverage and advertisements to perceptions of the debate. The basic strategy here and in later chapters is, for a given media quantity, to enter values lagged from one to six days before the day of interview into the respondent's data file, and then to use regression analysis[33] to estimate the links, if any, between the media stimulus on one hand, and the behavioural, perceptual, or attitudinal response on the other. The reason for using lagged values should be obvious: earlier sections of this chapter show how advertising and media coverage *follow* events. If we just lined the stimulus and response data up simultaneously we would ignore the complexities of causal direction. By lagging the media variables, we reduce the likelihood that they are merely track-

Table 4-2
The Impact of News and Advertising on Debate Perception

	(Generalized least squares estimation)			
	Did not see debate		Saw debate	
News				
1	0.020	(0.020)	0.032	(0.013)
2	0.013	(0.019)	−0.020	(0.014)
3	−0.011	(0.022)	−0.020	(0.017)
4	0.035	(0.019)	0.024	(0.015)
5	0.000	(0.020)	0.037	(0.017)
6	0.024	(0.019)	0.039	(0.015)
Total	0.081	(0.049)	0.092	(0.037)
Advertisements				
1	0.001	(0.007)	−0.018	(0.005)
2	−0.014	(0.007)	0.005	(0.006)
3	−0.015	(0.007)	−0.017	(0.006)
4	−0.002	(0.007)	−0.003	(0.005)
5	0.015	(0.007)	0.008	(0.005)
6	0.015	(0.006)	−0.001	(0.006)
Total	0.000	(0.017)	−0.026	(0.130)
Covariates				
Cons. Ident	−0.048	(0.047)	−0.164	(0.043)
Lib. Ident	0.123	(0.045)	0.263	(0.039)
NDP Ident	−0.086	(0.058)	−0.003	(0.061)
Quebec	−0.116	(0.044)	−0.027	(0.029)
Education	0.054	(0.008)	0.011	(0.006)
Intercept	0.240	(0.062)	0.505	(0.049)
R^2	0.18		0.27	
N	694		938	

Standard errors in parentheses

ing the thing they are supposed to explain. The particular lag structure we have chosen – all lags from one to six days – is agnostic: in other words, it allows for nearly immediate effects and also gives a media variable up to one week to have an effect, and it allows each day to have an impact.[34] In this chapter the independent variables are derived from Turner advertising and news balance (Figures 4-13 and 4-5) readings; units have been transformed into thirty-second "bites." The dependent variable is whether or not the respondent perceived Mr Turner as the winner.

Table 4-2 does not speak clearly. On one hand the overall impact from media variables was greater for debate viewers than for non-viewers, mainly because of viewers' greater responsiveness to news.

On the other hand non-viewers may be more open to advertising. For debate viewers only two advertising coefficients seem significant and both have the wrong sign, as does the "total" coefficient: if advertising is having an effect it is certainly not the intended one. Two significant coefficients also have the wrong sign for non-viewers, but here two coefficients also have the right sign. Advertising *could* have its intended effect in this group, but the timing had better be right: the greater part of a week would be required for an advertising message to sink in. The cumulative advertising effect for non-viewers is nil, however, and there seems to be little point in pursuing the matter further in this chapter. The most consistent effects here were from the news.

The debates thus yielded a story of both direct and indirect effects. Respondents who saw the debates were quick to make up their minds and then were relatively resistant to changing them. For the most alert citizens, the broadcast media were the necessary tool for making the event possible, but mainly as a passive conduit. Even for debate watchers, though, some scope remained for adjustment of perceptions and Table 4-2 indicates that some of that adjustment followed the news.

The dynamics of debate perceptions were consistent with some of the traditional two-step flow story but not with all of it. The fact that it was only after a week or so that non-viewers rallied to the consensus established among viewers is most readily explained by mediation through personal influence, although we have no direct evidence that this secondary social influence was exerted mainly through individual face-to-face discussion, as the Katz and Lazarsfeld thesis argues. But if this is consistent with the two-step pattern documented so long ago, the rest of what we have found is not so readily squared with it. First, the debates' immediate effect was great. A large fraction of the electorate viewed the debates and they re-evaluated Mr Turner swiftly. Secondly, it is hard to describe the effect as muted. For all that the debate audience consisted disproportionately of Liberal and Conservative identifiers and that these identifiers bent their perceptions to fit their predispositions, evidence for such immunizing tendencies was much less impressive than evidence for the sheer persuasive power of the event.

DISCUSSION

In the news, three elements stood out as potentially critical stimuli. The balance of FTA coverage moved roughly as the Conservative share did; it took a sharply negative turn at mid-campaign and then gradually moved to the positive side. The treatment of *John Turner* took roughly the opposite path: mainly negative in the early campaign, a dramatic turn for the positive after the debates, and then a slide back into the negative range. Turner coverage bounced back towards balance more quickly after the debates than did coverage of the FTA. At the end all leaders received positive treatment. Finally, published *polls* mirrored the same reality that our daily tracking, as reported in chapter 1, picked up.

Two patterns leaped from advertising. First, the party which emphasized its own leader the most was the NDP. This may have made sense in the early going, but even then the NDP was hardly feasible as a government. The NDP's emphasis on Ed Broadbent contrasted sharply with its lack of emphasis on the FTA. Secondly, major-party advertising was reactive, sometimes to polls, sometimes to the other side's advertising. As the Conservatives' share dropped, their advertising focused on Turner; by the second last week they had driven the balance of Turner advertising down roughly to the zero point. As Conservatives' preoccupation with Mr Turner increased, so did the Liberals' concern to defend him also increase. Even so, the weight of Conservative advertising was such that the last week began badly for Mr Turner. And the Liberals could not counter the sheer weight of third-party advertising on the FTA. As with Conservative advertising on John Turner, the third-party campaign did not get mobilized until well after the debates. Thereafter it simply grew and grew.

The lag in advertising reaction seems to have been roughly one week. Turning an advertising campaign around takes time and effort: that a problem exists must first be established; its source must be identified; advertisements designed to neutralize the source must be devised and tested; and the tapes with accompanying play instructions must be gotten out to the stations in the field. In the Conservative case, it must have been clear that the party was in trouble by at least the weekend after the debates. Their reaction to the predicament, a narrowing of the number and focus of their advertisements and a shift to a negative tone, did not become visible until 3 November. The Liberal response to the Conservatives' offensive took another week to get mobilized, although some of this delay may have reflected legal difficulties in getting access to debate footage. Third-party advertising in newspapers followed a different rhythm from party advertising on television, not surprisingly, but a week-long lag in getting the campaign going was visible here too.

The media campaign, including the debates, was about the FTA and about leaders. The balance of coverage and of advertising went up and down over the campaign. Did the media affect FTA opinion?

Did they affect perceptions of leaders, beyond the effect documented here for perceptions of debate performance? Did the polls affect voters expectations for parties' chances of success?

5 Free Trade and the Control of the Agenda

Just as free trade dominated the media discussion of issues, so did it dominate the consciousness of the voters. In dissolving Parliament on the issue the government took a major electoral risk. For many voters, free trade was an open question and by mid-campaign it looked as though the majority in favour of the FTA had been reversed. By the end of the campaign much of the status quo ante had been restored: although the FTA did not enjoy a majority in its favour, neither was there a majority against it.

This chapter describes how, politically, the FTA gamble seemed to be worth taking and how it ultimately paid off. It also describes how the gamble almost failed once again, how 1988 almost recapitulated 1891 and 1911. In the campaign the battle was over what considerations Canadians should invoke in making up their minds about the FTA. Early in the campaign, the opposition succeeded in implanting two kinds of argument unfavourable to the agreement. One kind emphasized the untrustworthiness of its main negotiator, Brian Mulroney; the other addressed the substance of the issue. Early on, substantive arguments against the agreement outweighed those for it. But some of these arguments were speculative. As such they could expand to envelop the FTA; for the same reason, they could deflate rapidly. Ultimately the government found arguments of its own to defend the agreement. As these arguments took hold in the electorate, they helped align voters' opinions on the FTA with their prior party commitments. Short-term issue dynamics helped serve a long-term goal: rebuilding each party's coalition.

Figure 5-1
The Importance of Free Trade

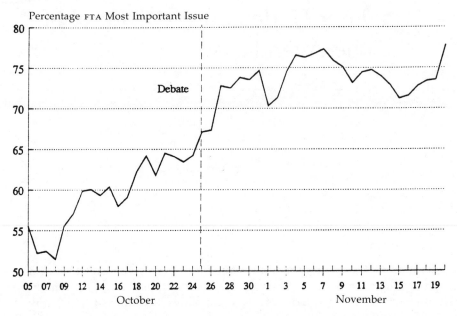

Percentage FTA Most Important Issue

5-day moving average. The base for the percentage calculation includes respondents who do not know which issue is most important for them.

THE DOMINANCE OF THE FTA

Right from the beginning, free trade was the overarching question. At the start, according to Figure 5-1, just over half the sample named it as the most important issue. This percentage increased steadily over the next two weeks and on the eve of the debates about two respondents in three named free trade as most important. The debates added about another eight points. Most of the shift was immediate, that is, *overnight*. After the debates, the share for free trade stabilized around 75 percent.

Although the debates had a discernible impact, the daily tracking does not support the assertion that the they "elevated free trade into the campaign issue."[1] Free trade was the issue well before the debates and was becoming steadily more so as each week passed. The pre-debates trend suggests that, even had there been no debates, the issue would have been about as dominant as it in fact was. The debates just accelerated matters.

Figure 5-2
Opinion on Free Trade: Environics

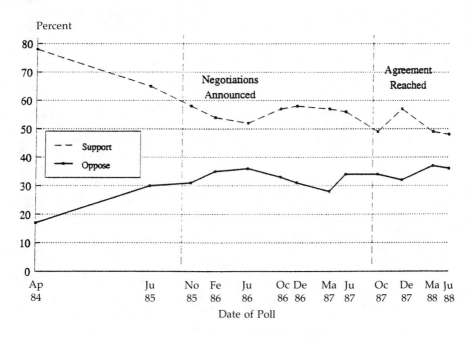

THE BALANCE OF OPINION

Before the Campaign

How risky was the 1988 free trade gamble? Survey evidence was ambiguous. Questions with an abstract wording and which sought only agreement-disagreement tended to elicit one-sided support for free trade. Environics and Gallup readings are cases in point. On the eve of negotiations (June 1985), according to Figure 5-2, Environics indicated that two-thirds of Canadians supported free trade.[2] Support weakened in subsequent months but the apparent pro-free trade majority was never reversed, not even as late as June 1988. Gallup told much the same story. About 50 percent of Gallup respondents agreed that elimination of tariffs would make Canada better off; only 30 percent believed the opposite (Figure 5-3).[3] In the fall of 1985, then, free trade appeared to be not that risky an enterprise.

Not all the evidence confirmed this rosy picture. When protection was named as an alternative to free trade, support for the latter

Figure 5-3
Opinion on Free Trade: Gallup

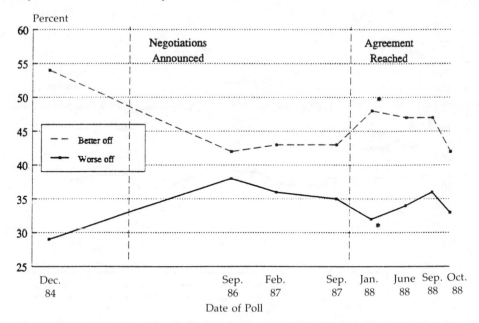

*Wording of question changed (see Chapter 5, note 5)

dropped dramatically. A Decima question along these lines produced clear majorities for protection in 1982 and 1983.[4]

Just as mentioning an alternative lowered support for free trade,
so did making the issue concrete. The mere announcement of negotiations was a case in point. Figures 5-2 and 5-3 each hint that
support for free trade dropped between the last poll before and the
first poll after the government's September 1985 declaration of intent. Opinion then seemed to stabilize until the two countries came
to a tentative agreement in October 1987. Environics indicated that
the announcement of an agreement brought a further five-point
decline in support (June-October 1987) for free trade as an abstract
proposition.[5] As for the agreement itself, support was lower still
than for free trade in the abstract: from December 1987 to October
1988 Environics had support and opposition in a virtual tie, according to Figure 5-4; compare this with Figure 5-2.[6]

On its substance, the draft agreement struck in late 1987 was
fraught with political risk. Under it, most tariff barriers between the
two countries would be gone within ten years. A continental energy

Figure 5-4
Opinion on the FTA: Environics

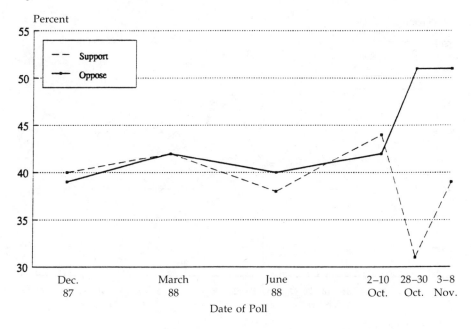

market would be created, as Canada foreswore export taxes on Canadian production and agreed that any rationing would fall proportionally across all North American contracts. Canada dropped
barriers to American provision of services, including financial services, and greatly increased the asset threshold above which foreign
investment became subject to review. Concessions on the American
side were much less dramatic. American tariffs on Canadian goods
would also disappear within ten years, but American barriers were
smaller than Canadian ones to begin with. Americans placed virtually no restrictions on Canadian capital movements before and so
had few to remove. America agreed to establish a joint review process for trade disputes. But the trade law to be jointly adjudicated
remained that of the country in which the dispute originated.

The agreement was vulnerable to being characterized as a sellout:
the United States gave up little while Canada bartered away its
sovereignty. This was an argument familiar from earlier trade initiatives. But the Conservatives might still reasonably have calculated
that electorally the FTA would save them, not sink them. However
low it might seem, support for free trade was at least as strong as
support for the Conservatives, probably stronger. The most

Figure 5-5
Support and Opposition to the FTA among Partisans

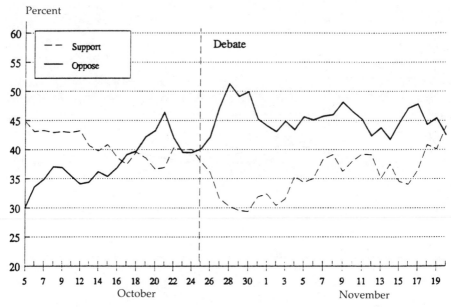

5-day moving average

pessimistic readings, the Decima "free trade versus protection" jux-taposition and the Environics question about the FTA itself (Figure 5-4) gave the free trade side about 40 percent of the electorate. This was a substantially larger share than the Conservative party received in published polls from late 1985 to the spring of 1988 (Figure 2-14). The challenge for Conservatives was to energize the issue just enough to bring more of the 40 percent pro-FTA camp into its partisan fold and yet keep opinion on the other side split between the two opposition parties. Of course, the Conservatives also had to hope that the decline in support for the FTA that pre-election polls had revealed would proceed no further.

THE BALANCE OF OPINION IN THE CAMPAIGN

Conservatives were disappointed in these hopes, as Figure 5-5 reveals. The figure tracks each side of FTA opinion among respondents who can give a party preference. The campaign revealed that the agreement was still strategically vulnerable: support slid and op-

Table 5-1
The Pre-Post Election Stability of FTA Opinion

Week	Pre-Post Correlation	N
4–9 October	0.68	253
10–16 October	0.66	439
17–23 October	0.66	421
24–30 October	0.65	431
31 October–6 November	0.71	481
7–13 November	0.66	437
14–20 November	0.75	449

Correlations are Pearson r's.

position gained right from the beginning. Just before the debates the two sides appeared to be at a standoff: by our measure, about 40 percent of the sample were on each side.[7] For supporters the worst was yet to come: after the English debate, support for the FTA plummeted and opposition surged. In four or five days, the 40:40 standoff became a 30:50 rout.

But the recovery began immediately. Opposition to the FTA subsided from its peak fairly quickly, although it never returned to its pre-debates levels. By the end of the campaign about 45 percent of voters opposed the agreement. The support side recovered more slowly but the recovery was more complete: by the end, support reached at least the pre-debates level and perhaps even the 5 October level.

The magnitude of the recovery raises questions about the reality – indeed about the general characteristics – of the debate-induced decline. Did the debates do no more than momentarily disturb opinion? Or did they produce a new alignment that could only be pushed back to its original form by some active intervention? Consider Table 5-1, which presents weekly correlations between response to the pre-election question and to its post-election counterpart. If the debates did nothing more than temporarily destabilize opinion, one indicator would be a drop in the pre-post correlation in the debate week and, perhaps, in the following week. This would indicate that FTA opinion measured in those weeks did an especially poor job of predicting respondents' final positions on the issue, in contrast with opinion measured before and after the debate hiatus. No such drop is visible. What the debates did do was take a roughly stable rank order of (unmeasured) underlying pro-/anti-FTA dispositions and move the whole distribution away from FTA support. The later campaign took the same distribution and pushed it back towards its starting point.

This takes us back to the campaign tracking of Figure 5-5. Did the distribution bounce back by itself – suggesting that the debates were sound and fury, but of no lasting significance – or did the distribution have to be *pushed* back? The figure suggests that both things happened. All of the subsidence on the "oppose" side took place within a week of the initial surge. This suggests that some of the debate impulse decayed by itself, without external intervention. The "support" side tells the opposite story. The recovery in support did not begin until the surge on the opposition side had been accomplished. The recovery was fitful and the final push did not come until the campaign's last week. Supporters of the FTA could assume, then, that some impact from the debate was transient. But the elimination of this impact – a shift from the 50–30 distribution to a 45–30 one – still left the agreement in deep trouble. The rest of the recovery, apparently, could not be taken for granted; it had to be won. Certainly the government seemed to think so, in light of the resources it and its allies poured into the fight.

For the rest of this chapter, the FTA position will be represented graphically by a single summary variable, scored +1 if the respondent favoured the agreement, −1 if he or she opposed it, and 0 if the respondent was ambivalent or indifferent. All apparent differences between the support-side and opposition-side dynamics can be reconciled with a model which posits that underlying dispositions on the FTA are roughly normally distributed.

Even though the decisive debate seems to have been the English one, its greatest impact was among Quebec francophones, according to Figure 5-6. Outside francophone Quebec, support was drifting downwards well in advance of the debates. This slide continued after the debates but was not obviously accelerated by them. Among Quebec francophones support may also have been slipping before the debates, but on this Figure 5-6 is inconclusive. What is clear is that FTA support in francophone Quebec dropped abruptly around the time of the debates. Figure 5-6 makes the drop appear to *predate* the debates, but this is an artifact of pooling; the raw daily tracking (not reported in the figure) makes it clear that the first day of the crash was 26 October, the morrow of the English debate.

If Quebec francophones differed from other Canadians in their response to the debates, they did so also later in the campaign. The recovery outside francophone Quebec was under way within a week of the debates and was accomplished by 10 or 11 November. In francophone Quebec, opinion seemed to sway back and forth and the final recovery came suddenly and only in the last week.

Figure 5-6
FTA Opinion in French and English Canada

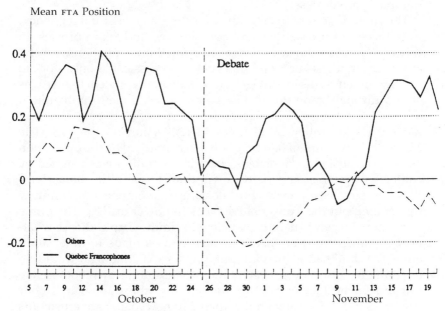

Mean FTA Position

7-day moving average

WHAT PRODUCED THE MOVEMENT IN FTA OPINION?

The campaign tapped into uncertainties about the negotiator and about the agreement itself, which were latent before the campaign. This helps to explain the shift against the FTA. The fall in FTA support was not across the board, however. The mid-campaign shift brought FTA support in line with long-standing party identification. So did the recovery, for that matter. And what fuelled the recovery? In part it reflected a rhetorical breaking of the link between the FTA and some of the arguments against it; this reduced the sense of uncertainty about life with the FTA. At the same time FTA protagonists sought to increase voters' sense of unease about life *without* the agreement.

Uncertainty over the Agent

John Turner's sellout metaphor – "I happen to believe that you have sold us out" – personalized concerns for sovereignty by joining them to fears about the agent. By confronting Mr Mulroney directly with his responsibility for the free trade agreement, Mr Turner echoed weeks of preparatory rhetoric by the two opposition parties and by non-party advocates.

The rhetoric sought to take advantage of voters' natural tendency, in the face of uncertainties and complexities, to look to proxies, in this case to ask who was responsible for the negotiations. Liberal and NDP strategists believed that such a process could only work to the agreement's disadvantage: they repeatedly styled the FTA as "the Mulroney trade deal." The Liberal party's platform-highlight document, for instance, placed this expression in bold face and named Mr Mulroney three times in its section on the FTA. The Mulroney government had regularly been attacked by the opposition as mendacious and unreliable. The administration was plagued by conflicts of interest and petty corruption. Harmful in themselves, these problems sat poorly with the campaign emphasis on honesty that helped put the Conservative party in power in 1984. The prime minister was seen as habitually telling his immediate audience whatever it wanted to hear, heedless of promises made to other audiences. And he had gained a reputation as someone who would do anything to close a deal, even at the expense of his own bottom line – if indeed he had one. Over the summer the Canadian Labour Congress had elaborated on this theme in newspaper advertisments with the following exchange in headlines: "Mulroney says the trade deal will work for us ... He also said he wouldn't sell Air Canada." The text in the ad asked: "Can we believe anything Brian Mulroney says?"[8] If the strategic premise in these advertisements was right, the FTA was vulnerable to the reputed untrustworthiness of the agent principally responsible for it.

The government itself seemed to concede the point. In its early advertisements it adopted what might be called a third-party approach to the FTA: rather than emphasize its own responsibility for the agreement, it recited FTA endorsements by independent groups. At least six different FTA-oriented advertisements appeared in which the name of the Conservative party was revealed only at the end. Two were compilations of newspaper editorial excerpts; three featured an employer in his plant describing the virtues of the FTA; and a fourth had a fruit grower in front of her property doing the same. No early advertisement featured Mr Mulroney speaking directly on the agreement.

To assess the agreement's vulnerability to doubts about its negotiator, we administered not one FTA support/oppose item to our respondents but two, with random assignment of respondents to one or the other version. For half the sample "Canada" negotiated the agreement. This places a mild burden of proof on rejecting the agreement. To the extent that it does, this version mirrors Conservative late-campaign rhetoric which asked: what would be the effect of rejecting the FTA on Canada's image abroad as a good-faith negotiator?[9] For the other half the negotiator was "the Mulroney government." This treatment goes straight to the prime minister's reputation.

The greatest impact of our experiment in question wording should have come in early campaign. Indeed, much of the impact may have been absorbed by the time our fieldwork began, so intense over the summer had been the opposition's attempts to link the FTA to the prime minister. To the extent that opinion remained unengaged in October, however, the "Mulroney" treatment should have had an adverse impact on support for the FTA. As the campaign wore on this impact should have weakened. Early in the campaign the consideration may not be ordinarily accessible to the respondent's consciousness. At this point if the consideration is introduced into consciousness it should move survey response. By late campaign the consideration may come to be factored into the latent response disposition. At this point, invoking it serves only to reinforce opinion on one side and is likely to be discounted by the other side.[10] By then the consideration's impact should be not so much *internal* to the experiment as *external*, in the ebb and flow of FTA support itself.

Figure 5-7 suggests that the opposition's pre- and early-campaign strategy was well conceived. In the weeks before the debates, respondents in the "Canada" treatment were palpably closer to the supportive end of the FTA scale than respondents in the "Mulroney" treatment. In percentage terms, the typical pre-debates difference in Figure 5-7 translates into about a ten-point larger share of FTA support in the "Canada" group. The difference cannot be accounted for by chance. The experiment's impact evaporated within a week of the English debate. Support for the FTA fell in both groups, but fell further in the "Canada" than in the "Mulroney" group. Thereafter differences between the groups were largely sampling error.

The existence of an impact from the experiment before the debates indicated the potential for discrediting the FTA by linking it to Brian Mulroney. The disappearance of this effect after the debates indicated that the potential was realized in the campaign – distrust of Brian Mulroney was now biting in the electorate at large. We had implanted uncertainty about the agent in the "Mulroney" treatment group. After the debates this treatment had little further impact: all respondents – even those assigned to the "Canada" treatment – now came to us with Mulroney-related doubts about the FTA already in

Figure 5-7
Identity of the Negotiator and FTA Opinion

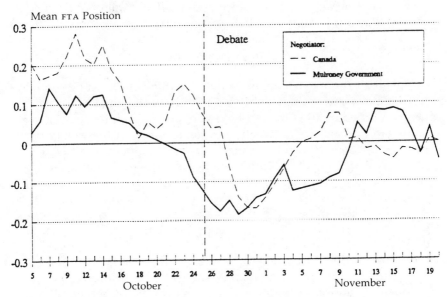

7-day moving average

place. We no longer needed to remind them of the linkage between the prime minister and the FTA; John Turner's accusation that Brian Mulroney had sold us out did the job for us. Consequently, both treatments yielded about the same level of support for the FTA, and the experimental impact faded. It faded as FTA support in the "Canada" treatment fell precipitously after the debates; "Canada" respondents got from the debates the message that "Mulroney" respondents had been getting all along.

Before the debates, both treatment groups drifted against the FTA at roughly the same rate. All convergence between treatments occurred after the debates. Clearly, something was working against FTA support even before the debates. But whatever it was, it must have been unrelated to uncertainty about the negotiator. Had the negotiator been the issue before 25 October, the difference would have narrowed. What else was at issue?

Uncertainty over the Agreement's Impact

One plausible interpretation of the earlier decline in FTA support is the debate over its substance. Three lines of attack seemed especially

Figure 5-8
The Dynamics of the Challenges

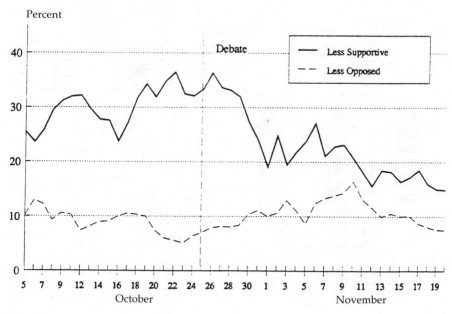

5-day moving average

promising as the campaign began: the apparent abrogation of *sovereignty* over key elements of the economy; threats to Canada's *social programs*; and fear of *job displacement*. Arguments available to supporters of the FTA seemed politically weaker. Two arguments, nonetheless, had emerged by the eve of the campaign: a standard comparative-advantage claim in terms of *lower prices*; and an historically specific argument in terms of insurance against *American protectionism.*[11]

Each of these arguments was mirrored in the 1988 study by a challenge contingent on initial FTA opinion. Supporters were given, at random, one of the three opposition arguments and asked if this made them less supportive. Opponents were given one of the two supportive arguments and asked if this made them less opposed. Respondents were not asked if they changed their minds, just if they felt less of whatever it was they initially claimed to be.[12] Again, we should expect the impact of challenges to follow the logic in Zaller (1984) and diminish as the campaign wore on.

Figure 5-8 suggests that opponents did indeed have the rhetorical advantage. The figure combines response to each side's set of challenges. Before 1 November arguments against the FTA moved two

Figure 5-9
Impact of Arguments by Stage of Campaign

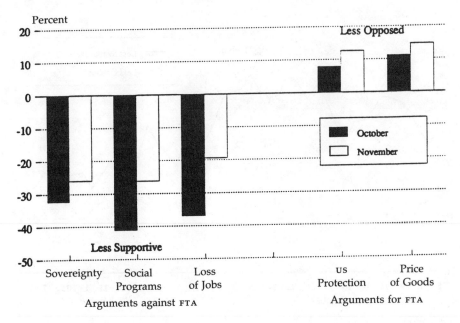

to three times as many FTA supporters as arguments for the FTA moved opponents. In the last week of the campaign, however, the corresponding ratio was only about 1.5 to 1. All decay in impact was on the opposing-argument side. The campaign had done its work, evidently, by helping FTA supporters cope with opposition arguments and by moving erstwhile supporters who were truly vulnerable to opposition considerations to the place where they belonged: the opposition camp.[13]

This interpretation still requires substantiation. It sits rather awkwardly with the exact time path of decay in challenges' effectiveness: anti-FTA challenges' impact *increased* before the debates and did not begin to drop until three days *after* the debates. A full estimation of the process must take account of a powerful selection bias that reflected the very force of the campaign's arguments: just as arguments reached their peak of intensity or effectiveness, the group to which they are directed was being depleted of its most marginal members. The interaction of endogenous resistance and exogenous force requires much more unpacking than we can provide here.

Figure 5-9 gives a crude account of impact from specific challenges. The "social programs" challenge proved the most powerful. In the early going it was nearly four times as powerful as either

Figure 5-10
The Evolution of FTA Opinion within Party Groups

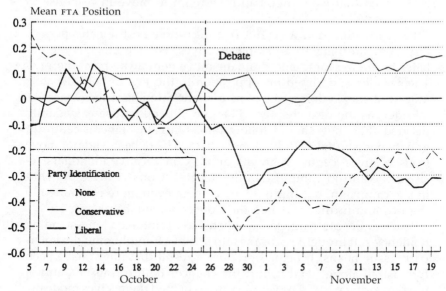

7-day moving average

challenge on the other side; indeed, it moved two FTA supporters in five to reconsider.[14] On the pro-FTA side there is a hint that the "US protectionism" challenge gained some bite. But challenges to FTA opponents underlined just how hard pro-FTA arguments were to make. Typically, they failed to move all but one in ten of the agreement's opponents. In rhetoric, at least, supporters of the FTA occupied a strategically vulnerable position.

Party Identification

The debates seemed to turn the Conservatives' strategic logic on its head. Where the Tories may have hoped to ratchet their vote up by appealling to FTA supporters, the debates instead brought FTA support down by catalysing long-standing party commitments.

This is the lesson of Figure 5-10. In it, the daily FTA reading is centred on the 5–25 October mean value for the identification group in question. This suppresses differences between party identification groups before 25 October, but those differences were marked.[15] Instead, visual emphasis falls on differences in group dynamics, in response to the English debate; late-campaign shifts can also be compared readily to mid-campaign ones. Because of small daily sample sizes, NDP identifiers do not appear in the figure. Suffice it to say that New Democrats began the campaign onesidedly anti-FTA and stayed that way; they had little room to move in response to the debates.

Party identification was critical to the whole post-debates period. First compare Liberals and Conservatives. For the Liberals the debates brought a rapid and dramatic movement away from the FTA. Their leader underlined his opposition to the FTA in both debates; indeed, it was in doing so that he demonstrated his effectiveness as a leader, as the next chapter will argue. Liberal partisans evidently decided that they should follow him. Once the Liberal centre of gravity had shifted, it did not move back. The debates did not move Conservatives' centre of gravity at all; Conservative identifiers resisted the anti-FTA impulse in the debates. Conservatives did shift in late campaign, but this only made them even more committed to the FTA and further widened the Conservative-Liberal gap.

Thus far the campaign looks only to have reinforced long-standing tendencies. It brought partisans into line by strengthening the voter-party-issue nexus. It helped produce a result that might have been forecast all along. And it hurt the chances both of the FTA and of its sponsoring party. The Conservatives helped themselves modestly by the late-campaign squeezing of more FTA support out their own partisan camp.

Now consider the non-partisans. Early on, non-partisans resembled Liberals in their net movement away from FTA support. But the similarity was superficial. For non-partisans it is not even clear that the debates were critical: their movement was not obviously faster after the debates than before. And where Liberals stuck with their opposition to the FTA, non-partisans drifted back towards support. Winning them back was a vital part of the Conservatives' success.

Movement in FTA opinion, then, seems clearly to reflect the prior history of the party system. The shifts only reinforced the ongoing alignment of voters and parties. The respondents most obviously susceptible to the critical events in the campaign were those identified with parties. Once partisans shifted they did not shift back. Non-partisans did respond to the campaign; they were the only one's who moved first in one direction and then in the other on the FTA.

The Recovery

How did the Conservatives turn the screws on their own supporters as well as win non-partisans back for the FTA? To get some purchase

Table 5-2
The Structure of FTA Considerations, Post-Election

	Control Key Sectors	Social Programs	Loss of Jobs	US Protection	Market Size
			$(N=2,922)$		
A. Post-Election Mean Rating					
	−0.08	−0.24	+0.14	−0.04	+0.45
B. Correlations among the Considerations					
Social Progs	0.61				
Loss of Jobs	0.44	0.49			
US Protect	−0.12	−0.13	−0.13		
Market Size	−0.31	−0.36	−0.23	0.33	

Correlations are Pearson r's.
Correlations on same side of argument in bold.

on the place of substantive arguments in the recovery, we must resort to the post-election wave. There, four of the five challenges were recast as items asked of all respondents.[16] The challenge about the price of goods was replaced by one about access to a large market – an argument that gained increasing prominence as the campaign progressed. The usual form of the argument went thus: but for the FTA, Canada would be the only industrialized country without guaranteed access to a market of one hundred million or more. In substance, this argument overlaps the "American protectionism" item. But the emphasis in the large-market argument was structural, on an abiding characteristic of the market for Canadian products. Rhetorical emphasis on the American protectionism seemed more in terms of active harassment, under countervail proceedings, which could go on irrespective of the tariff level.[17]

The pre- and post-election contrast is startling. Table 5-2 gives the mean post-election ratings for the five items. The results are a surprise in light of the record of campaign-wave challenges. On the anti-FTA side the rank order of ratings was the reverse of the rank order of challenges' impact: respondents were *less* likely to agree with the "social programs" item than with any other. The balance of opinion was also slightly in disagreement with the "key sectors" claim but also with the "US protectionism" claim. The two consid-

Table 5-3
The Impact of FTA Arguments, Post-Election

	(Ordinary least squares estimation; N = 2,359)	
Consideration	Coefficient	Standard Error
Control Key Ind	− 0.31	0.04
Social Programs	− 0.57	0.05
Jobs Losses	− 0.54	0.04
US Protection	0.26	0.04
Large Market	1.19	0.04
Intercept	− 0.30	0.05
R^2	0.60	

erations on which the balance of opinion was positive were the "job loss" (anti-FTA) and the "market size" (pro-FTA) ones.

It seems unlikely that balance of agreement with the social programs consideration was so negative for the entire campaign. The power of the campaign-wave challenge, discussed above, corresponded to the repeated invocation of that argument in the campaign and with the free fall of support for the FTA in mid-campaign. The Conservatives themselves paid attention to the issue, once they had awakened to the danger. In addition to stepping up advertising concentration on the consideration, they marshalled seemingly independent witnesses. One key event was the press conference by Emmett Hall. His claim that the health care system and other social programs were not at risk under the FTA received voluminous coverage, as chapter 4 indicated. Liberals and New Democrats were put on the defensive: were they prepared to call the father of medicare a liar? The integrity of social programs was also a major theme in third-party advertising. The post-election evidence indicates that these arguments worked.

Table 5-3 sheds further light on the relative power of the arguments. It gives the contribution of each argument to summary FTA opinion, as measured in the post-election wave. After the election we elicited FTA opinion on a nine-point scale (as opposed to the crude acceptance-rejection item of the campaign wave). A coefficient in the figure indicates how many units on the nine-point scale a respondent was moved, other things equal, by a unit jump in the degree of agreement with a pro- or anti-FTA argument. Just as Table 5-2 indicated that agreement was greatest with the "large market" and "job loss" considerations, so does Table 5-3 reveal that agreement or disagreement with these two items was most consequential for overall evaluation of the FTA. *The greatest leverage by far was exerted by the market size argument.* On the anti-FTA side, the social programs consideration was a close rival to fears for jobs. But this is only to say that the remaining few who still accepted the social programs argument were, not surprisingly, powerfully moved by it.

So far this has been an account of *persuasion*. Did the Conservatives also *distract* the electorate from arguments which otherwise told against the FTA? Distraction is the other side of priming. At issue is the shifting of the weights attached to various considerations, which can take place quite apart from any movement in the background distribution of opinion. Answering the question takes two steps. First, did the structure of response to the pro-/anti-FTA arguments admit this sort of agenda manipulation? If pro-FTA arguments were one tight bundle of opinions, if anti-FTA arguments another tight bundle, and if the two bundles were negatively correlated with each other, little prospect for manipulation would exist; the situation would be just too polarized. In fact, opinion was *not* very polarized, according to Part B of Table 5-2, and such polarization as occurred told against the anti-FTA forces. Most closely linked were the anti-FTA "key sectors" and "social programs" considerations. Throwing both arguments into play would evoke agreement from much the same group of people; few coalitional gains would be made by adding one argument to the other. Arguments on the pro-FTA side possessed more strategic potential: the two pro-FTA arguments were much more loosely related to each other than were any two arguments on the opposition side. This was strategically advantageous: invoking both might have expanded the anti-FTA forces. This coalition might have been shakier than the other side's, more vulnerable to being split, but it only had to hold together for one day's polling.

No less critical, however, was the looseness of the connection *between* the pro- and anti-FTA considerations. Correlations across the boundary were negative, to be sure. But they were much lower than the correlations within the anti-FTA group. Most critically, the most powerful anti-FTA consideration ultimately, fear of job loss, was less negatively correlated with the pro-FTA arguments than either of the other anti-FTA arguments. Each side thus had an argument with the potential to split the other side's coalition. Put another way, only 11 percent of the sample agreed with both of the two pro-FTA arguments and disagreed with all of the three anti-FTA arguments, and only 8 percent did the opposite. Most respondents agreed with at least one argument on each side of the question.

Distraction, then, was possible. The second step in determining its role involves estimating the relative impact of pro- and anti-FTA considerations at various stages in the campaign. Did the Conservatives succeed in making pro-FTA arguments weigh more heavily than anti-FTA ones towards the end of the campaign? Ideally we would employ questions put to respondents in the campaign itself to answer this question, but by framing the arguments as challenges we rendered that impossible. We can, however, use the post-election questions to examine the dynamics during the campaign. Even if the overall distribution of the five FTA items shifted from before the election to after, the rank ordering of individuals on any given question ought not to have shifted, apart from random error. We should thus be able to enter post-election self-placements into estimates, with the campaign-wave FTA opinion as the dependent variable. If people initially considered a particular argument in forming their FTA opinion and then were distracted from considering it, we would expect their views about the argument to become less important as an explanation of their FTA response. For priming we would expect the reverse.

To check for changes in the importance of the five arguments over time, we did separate weekly regressions of FTA support on summary pro- and anti-FTA scales. Table 5-4 reports how the coefficients of these regressions changed over time. The pattern is not consistent with agenda shifts through distraction or priming. Over the campaign, we might have expected to see coefficients on the anti-FTA scale shrink (at least in late campaign) and coefficients on the pro-FTA scale grow. Neither occurred. The pro-FTA coefficient remained roughly stable and the anti-FTA coefficient may even have grown. The real action in the week-by-week comparison was in the intercepts: these fell and rose roughly as the pro-FTA share did. This suggests that Canadians were not distracted; rather they were persuaded, first by the anti-FTA arguments and then by arguments on the other side.

The particular fate of the social programs consideration may be an object lesson in political vulnerability, which was the flip side of its power. The argument touched Canadians' deepest fear – that American pressure would somehow undermine one of Canada's distinctive features, its highly developed social services. But arguments about the impact of the FTA on the welfare state were highly speculative. As such, they could expand to make the FTA appear one step short of the apocalypse. For the same reason, they were vulnerable to rapid compression. By the late campaign, the social programs arguments still available to FTA opponents were highly convoluted, strained in the telling.

Table 5-4
Arguments for and against the FTA: Impact by Week

Week	Intercept	(Ordinary least squares estimation) Anti-FTA	Pro-FTA	R^2	N
4–9 Oct.	−0.06 (0.06)	−0.89 (0.14)	0.34 (0.16)	0.32	196
10–16 Oct.	−0.01 (0.04)	−0.77 (0.09)	0.48 (0.09)	0.35	331
17–23 Oct.	−0.10 (0.04)	−0.74 (0.10)	0.78 (0.11)	0.36	333
24–30 Oct.	−0.20 (0.04)	−0.78 (0.09)	0.80 (0.09)	0.48	363
31 Oct.–6 Nov.	−0.14 (0.04)	−0.78 (0.09)	0.54 (0.10)	0.35	399
7–13 Nov.	−0.26 (0.04)	−0.90 (0.09)	0.75 (0.09)	0.45	356
14–20 Nov.	−0.12 (0.04)	−0.97 (0.08)	0.61 (0.09)	0.44	369

Scales standardized to −1,1 interval.
Standard errors in parentheses.

In contrast, arguments that the FTA entailed labour market displacement and a de facto loss of sovereignty were less controvertible. The FTA, like any international agreement, constrained Canada's freedom of movement. The fact that it would set the terms for long-term capital investment meant that the costs of changing it, once it was in place, would be very high. And proponents of the FTA could not deny that the agreement inevitably entailed dislocation.

THE MEDIA AND THE BALANCE OF FTA OPINION

What was the external mover of opinion on the FTA? We have already established that the debates played a major role, although the balance was already shifting well in advance of them. The debates were not decisive at the end. By 20 November opinion had returned to a standoff rather like the one on the eve of the debates. But the restoration of that balance of opinion did not appear to have been automatic or foreordained; it had to be earned. The visible evidence of the effort lies in the media series of the last chapter.

Table 5-5 presents estimations for four plausible avenues of media impact: news treatment of John Turner, news treatment of the FTA, the treatment of John Turner in party advertising, and third-party advertising on the FTA. News and third-party advertising on the

Table 5-5
The Impact of News and Advertising on FTA Opinion

| | (Ordinary least squares estimation; N = 2,760) | | | |
	Turner		FTA	
News				
1	−0.006	(0.018)	0.116	(0.091)
2	−0.025	(0.018)	0.033	(0.078)
3	−0.033	(0.018)	−0.091	(0.093)
4	−0.016	(0.018)	−0.144	(0.089)
5	0.000	(0.017)	0.169	(0.096)
6	0.017	(0.017)	0.036	(0.079)
Total	−0.063	(0.043)	0.119	(0.215)
Advertisements				
1	0.013	(0.008)	0.016	(0.008)
2	−0.017	(0.010)	−0.001	(0.010)
3	−0.023	(0.009)	−0.004	(0.012)
4	−0.008	(0.013)	−0.014	(0.011)
5	−0.001	(0.013)	0.034	(0.012)
6	−0.025	(0.014)	−0.039	(0.015)
Total	−0.061	(0.027)	−0.008	(0.028)
Covariates				
PC Ident	0.659	(0.039)		
Lib Ident	−0.339	(0.041)		
NDP Ident	−0.489	(0.051)		
Quebec	0.251	(0.035)		
Education	0.023	(0.007)		
Intercept	−0.243	(0.068)		
R^2	0.266			

Standard errors in parentheses.

FTA need little further justification; news treatment of the FTA (Figure 4-2) roughly paralleled the movement of FTA opinion itself. Third-party advertising (Figure 4-11) responded to the crash in FTA support and reached its own peak just as the recovery in FTA support occurred.

Why not advertising by the parties, in total or on the FTA? Neither the overall outlays by all three parties nor party treatment of the FTA looked a plausible candidate for moving FTA opinion. The sheer volume of advertising moved up steadily over the last four weeks, but not in a manner that suggested a systematic advantage for one party over the two others. Party advertising on the FTA was a stalemate, in the sense that neither opponents nor supporters established a clear dominance over the other for any length of time.

Where systematic patterns did occur was in the news and advertising treatment of John Turner. In advertisements, only the Liberals bothered to mention him early on. The Conservatives did turn their attention to him in the last two and a half weeks. They did so in a way that impugned both his leadership ability and, critical to this chapter, his credibility as an interpreter of the FTA. By reminding voters of his leadership problems, they supplied an alternative interpretation of why he opposed the FTA: he did so not because he really believed the words he was saying but because only by saying them could he save his own job. News treatment of Mr Turner was also often implicitly about the FTA. This was especially so in the period right after the debates when Mr Turner's attacks on the agreement finally broke through to dominate coverage of the campaign.

Why should we expect *any* of this material to seep through? Advertising effects tend to be greeted with even more scepticism than claims for effects from the news. The handful of studies that start from the premise that media effects in campaigns are worth exploring all emphasize the news.[18] But the folk wisdom about 1988 and other recent campaigns makes much of the media, especially of advertising.[19] And the campaign's surface features, as revealed in chapter 1 and earlier in this chapter, tell us that 1988 exhibited dynamics in spades. But so, according to chapter 1, have other campaigns in the post-1960 period. It seems unreasonable, then, to dismiss the possibility that these dynamics responded, at least in part, to the event's most manipulable components, media images.

The basic strategy here is that outlined in chapter 4's account of debate perceptions: opinion on one day is related to each media quantity for each of the six preceding days. We begin with the coefficients and then turn to daily tracking.

Three of the four media groups had effects consistent with expectations, but only two sets met or even approached the minimum criterion for statistical significance. About the FTA news lag structure not much can be said: the sum of the coefficients is large and positive, as we might expect, but little should be made of this, as the estimated standard error for the total coefficient is roughly twice the size of the coefficient itself. Third-party advertising coefficients defy substantive interpretation: some are large and significant but the pattern is offsetting and the total coefficient effectively zero. Both sets of FTA terms may be stumbling over a statistical difficulty, multicollinearity: for both news and advertising variables, each lag term is highly correlated with the other terms in its set as well as with other terms in the overall media package. This inflates the standard errors for these terms; put another way, collinearity renders the

Figure 5-11
Impact of Turner Media Variables on FTA Position

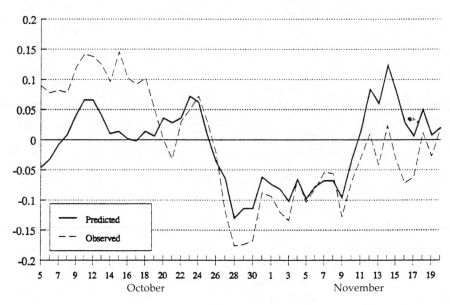

5-day moving average

coefficients unstable and mutually dependent. For neither set of Turner media variables was collinearity a problem and both sets performed consistently with expectations. News and advertisements had subtly different patterns. News effects – at least the negative ones we expect – tend to have short lags. Advertising effects tend have long lags.

Figure 5-11 carries this through to the bottom line, to the daily tracking of FTA opinion. To create daily predictions the twelve FTA media terms were dropped.[20] All impact from the Turner media variables came after the debates. For advertising this is no surprise as the first party advertisements were placed only on 23 October, just one day before the French debate. The early-campaign downward drift in FTA support was being fuelled by something other than reports of John Turner's campaign. Of course, the reports in this early period were hardly favourable to Mr Turner (Figure 4-5). But media variables really started to kick in the days after the debates. Indeed, the closeness of the post-debate fit between predicted and observed would be almost worrisome, were it not for the lack of pre-debate fit.

Figure 5-12
Separate Impact of Turner Advertising and News

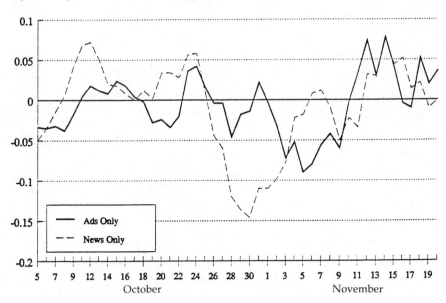

5-day moving average

Was it news or was it advertising? The fact that the media started to bite into FTA opinion only after the debates might make one suspect that the operative factor is really advertising, the factor that started up only on the eve of the debates. Figure 5-12 sorts out news and advertising by simulation. The simulation indicates that news and advertising each had an effect but at different times.

Right after the debates, opinion was driven by the news. The advertising line implies only a gradual decline in FTA support, less dramatic a drop even than the gradual one already occurring before the debates. The news line, in contrast, drops like a stone and drops just as far as the total prediction in Figure 5-11. The power of the news is corroborated by another fact about the post-debates plunge in FTA support: the English debate was clearly critical to the balance of opinion (Figure 5-5), but actually seeing a debate was not. This last point is made by Figure 5-13. In this figure the report of debate viewership is from the post-election wave. This allows us to distinguish the specific fact of viewing the debate from the general predisposition to attend to the media; pre-debate differences between debate viewership groups allow us to identify how much of what

Figure 5-13
Debate Viewership and FTA Opinion

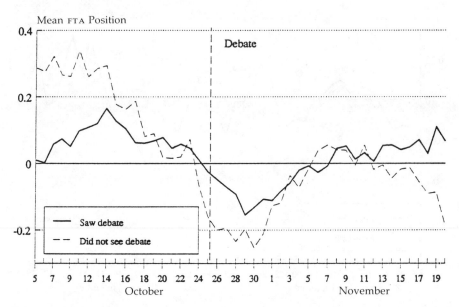

7-day moving average
Debate viewership from post-election

appears to be a debate effect is really attributable to general media attentiveness. Both viewers and non-viewers responded to the debates. Both lines appear to turn down before the debates, but this is an artifact of the seven-day pooling. Note, though, that the drop in FTA support was greater for non-viewers than for viewers (in contrast with the pattern in chapter 4 for the re-evaluation of John Turner). Figure 5-13 thus reinforces Figure 5-12, in emphasizing how critical the post-debate news was in mediating the debate's impact on FTA opinion.

If news drove the immediate aftermath of the debates, advertising dominated the endgame. The predicted advertising boost in the FTA support (Figure 5-12) is over half the total predicted media boost (Figure 5-11). News coverage did also play a role, though. The news line jumps at roughly the same time as the advertising line, just not as far. At the end, both factors worked to the FTA's advantage.

Are we *really* picking up influence from outside voters' own political psyches? Or are we simply picking up autonomously generated movement in the campaign's endgame, which would occur anyway and which happened to coincide with a furious media campaign? Keep in mind that we always employ media terms from days before the day of interview. We have also noted periods in which all or some factors have no effect. The weakness of effects in some periods increases our confidence in the reality of the effects we do find; otherwise, we might be engaged in little more than a curve-fitting exercise. The evidence is still circumstantial, however. But at this point, there is little reason to pursue the alternative interpretation. It is best to take it up when we come, in chapter 8, to media estimations for the politicians' bottom line – vote shares.

DISCUSSION

If history set the stage, the play did not unfold as the Conservatives wanted it to. All along the FTA harboured tactical weaknesses. One was the negotiator. Another was the string of substantive arguments that could be marshalled against it. Although the slide in FTA support predated both the debates and the drop in Conservative popularity, the leaders' debates helped unleash the anti-FTA arguments and produced a marked drop in support for the FTA. The recovery in FTA support was not automatic, any more than was the recovery in Conservative support. There was, to be sure, an initial decay in the impulse imparted by the debates. But once this had happened, opposition still led support by a comfortable margin. The last shifts in FTA support had to be won. Whatever the precise channels by which they were driven home, the most effective attacks in the early going were couched in terms of threats to Canada's social programs and in terms of Brian Mulroney's credibility as a negotiator. In the late campaign, John Turner was put on the defensive. And, most dramatically, the social programs argument seemed to be completely nullified.

The short-term dynamics of the campaign served the long-term interests of the system's dominant parties. As FTA opinions shifted, they tended to fall into line with the parties. The debates moved Liberals towards FTA opposition and the endgame moved Conservatives towards support.

6 Traits, Debates, and Leaders' Fates

When John Turner confronted Brian Mulroney with the sellout charge, he was trying to solve several problems at once. He was trying to engage what he believed were the electorate's long-standing doubts about Brian Mulroney's character. By doing so he hoped to discredit the Conservatives as a government. He was also trying in one stroke to discredit the FTA by association and make its rejection the central task for voters. But he was also trying to divert attention from questions about his own character and, perhaps even more damaging, about his competence.

All this presupposes that leadership rivals substantive policy as a factor in Canadian elections. An emphasis on leadership makes for a great story: vivid personalities; a dramatic moment on prime time television; and the questions of motivation and morality that enthrall the viewers of soap operas. But does such a story just substitute narrative for analysis? As it happens, leadership has long been an emphasis in analytic accounts of Canadian elections and is becoming more so in electoral studies elsewhere.[1] Canadian elections, in common with elections in other Westminster-style systems as well as with presidential elections in the United States, inevitably turn on the question of who – which individual – shall form the government. Elections may turn on other things as well, but the operation of other factors – even such overpowering ones as the FTA – will almost certainly be conditioned by judgments on persons.

Some of these judgments will be about party leaders as potential executives. *Competence* for the job is an obvious place to start. The narrative in chapter 1 hinted that John Turner had a serious competence problem; many of his doubters were Liberals. Also important is *character*. Here it is easy to become lurid, but the fact remains that the offices to be filled are ones of trust. Voters ought to care about whether or not their agents are persons of integrity and empathy.

But whether or not an agent can be trusted to serve one's interests is not just a matter of personal character. It is entirely reasonable to ask how much like oneself the potential agent is. The more an agent resembles oneself the more he or she might be expected reflexively to understand and act on one's own interests. This point requires some care: we do not necessarily want our agents to be *exactly* like us; think of how we choose physicians, for example. But we might reasonably prefer leaders who embody our own basic demographic characteristics. In Canada the traditionally critical characteristics have been ethno-religious and regional. Chapter 2 emphasized the pivotal contributions of Laurier, Diefenbaker, and Mulroney. Each was, in Hollywood terms, cast against type; his accession signalled that his party was now prepared to take a hitherto neglected region or group as seriously as it possibly could. Each leader recast the entire party system. But each also illustrates the pitfalls of ethno-religious and regional appeals that risk being *too* focused.

Finally, 1988 put leadership on the table in a wholly new way. The most popular leader of all seemed to be Ed Broadbent, leader of the system's weakest party, the NDP. It is tempting to conclude that Mr Broadbent's popularity was a sideshow, a function of his party's very infeasibility. But the NDP seemed far more credible in October 1988 than it had ever been before at a comparable stage in the electoral cycle. And an NDP leader had never before been the most highly regarded one; hitherto what had rubbed off on its leaders was the party's *lack* of credibility. Certainly, NDP strategists believed that Mr Broadbent was an asset.

The surface features of the campaign emphasized considerations such as these. Did the electorate respond accordingly? Were leader perceptions regionally and linguistically biased? Could voters form realistic and differentiated appraisals of each leader? Were these appraisals modifed by the campaign? If so, by what means? Were some voters especially likely to modify their views?

THE LEADERS: ORIGINS, IDENTITIES, AND EVALUATION

Brian Mulroney might have been invented specifically to solve the Conservatives' tactical dilemma. In making his case to the party in 1983, he put the logic of Table 2-12 in his own pithy terms: "There are 102 ridings in the country with a Francophone population over 10 per cent. In the last election the Liberals won 100 of them, we won two. You give Pierre Trudeau a head start of 100 seats and he's going to beat you 10 times out of 10."[2] In Quebec the Conservatives had taken only one seat in 1980 and no more than eight seats in any of the seven elections since 1963. In 1984, with Brian Mulroney as leader of their party, the Conservatives won fifty-eight of seventy-five seats in Quebec.

Brian Mulroney was born in Baie-Comeau on Quebec's northern shore. His father, an electrician, had moved to Baie-Comeau to work at a new paper plant. Although he grew up as an anglophone Irish Catholic, francophone Canada was never far away in his experience. At Laval law school he learned to speak French fluently and he made francophone political friends to go with the anglophone ones he had made earlier at St Francis Xavier University in Antigonish, Nova Scotia. All of this might have made Brian Mulroney a Liberal, but he became a Tory, "the only smart Tory anyone knew in Quebec: a regular sounding board for journalists and political operators anxious to have Quebec's mysteries translated to them" (Fraser, 1989, p. 24).

If Brian Mulroney was from somewhere, John Turner seemed to be from everywhere. He was born in England, raised mainly in Ontario, went to university in British Columbia and England, first represented St Lawrence–St George, a Montreal seat, then represented Ottawa Carleton, moved to Toronto after his first retirement from politics in 1975, and returned to British Columbia to represent Vancouver Quadra. He thus claimed ties to three provinces, but two of the three associations were fleeting and dated. Although John Turner is younger than Pierre Trudeau, he represents an older version of the Liberal party, perhaps even an older one than Lester Pearson's. In any case, when he returned to politics in 1984, he seemed unfamiliar with the new order of things:

... he – and the nation – seemed genuinely confused as to whether he was a lawyer, a board director, or a politician; and because he had trouble psyching himself into his political persona after more than eight years away from it, everyone noticed how rusty his speeches and his manner had become ... He wasn't even up on the buzz words, the changing lexicon that allows a politician to deflect or obfuscate potentially dangerous issues. During the campaign, for example, he persisted in referring to reporters as "the gentlemen of the press," "the boys," or "guys," even though there were women on the bus. (Graham, 1986, p. 188)

Of the three leaders, Ed Broadbent seemed the most comfortable in the role. But then he had had the most practice: by the time Brian

Mulroney seized control of the Conservative party, Ed Broadbent had already been leader of his party for eight years. In 1988 he could claim thirteen years on the job. Under his leadership the NDP had moved up to 20 percent of the total vote; in 1980 and 1984 the party's election-day share was higher than most observers predicted from pre-election polls, which redounded to Mr Broadbent's credit. Ed Broadbent's pedigree as a New Democrat was impeccable; he did not present his party with a conundrum in quite the way that Brian Mulroney or John Turner did theirs. But he was from Ontario, the second leader in a row from central Canada, an awkward fact for a party whose roots and greatest appeal were in the west. Moreover, the NDP's elevated place in the polls encouraged Mr Broadbent and his advisors to think like a government in waiting – or at least like an opposition in waiting. In Canada, as chapter 2 reminded us, this means making the Quebec campaign pivotal. But the NDP had no history of success in the province and its organizational rank and file was typically uneasy with the kinds of appeals that go down in Quebec. The party's policy history was centralist and not focused on cultural questions. To the extent that the NDP had come around on cultural policy, it was to the Trudeau position: bilingualism and multiculturalism, not the Quebec-focused nationalism that seemed to control the high ground in 1988. Ed Broadbent had to steer an uneasy path between his own party's sense of itself and what he believed the party needed to form a government.

Figure 6-1 presents the average "feeling thermometer"[3] evaluations of leaders by region during the early weeks of the campaign. Three things stand out. First, Ed Broadbent had the highest evaluations in all regions except Quebec, where Brian Mulroney rated slightly higher. Secondly, John Turner's ratings were much lower than either of the other two leaders, and were lowest in Quebec. Finally, Brian Mulroney's ratings were much higher than John Turner's and were especially high in Quebec. The other side of Mr Mulroney's Quebec strength was the regional differentiation of his appeal: he was weakest in the west, his party's heartland.

Underpinning differences in Figure 6-1 are attitudes to the place of French Canada in the larger whole. Figure 6-2 takes respondents' self-placement on the item on "promoting French" (chapter 3) and subtracts their placement of each leader. Response is compared between between Quebec francophones and all others.[4] A positive value means that, on average, members of the group rate themselves as more favourable than the leader towards promoting French. A negative value means that, on average, members of the group rate themselves as less favourable than the leader. Typically, Quebec francophones thought that Brian Mulroney was only slightly less

Figure 6-1
Leader Evaluations before Debate by Region

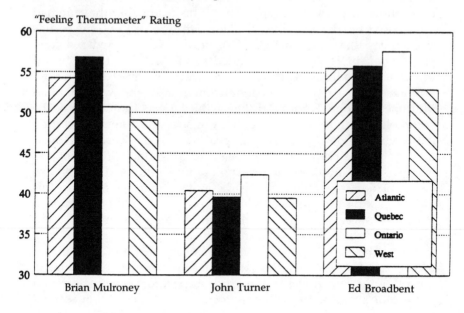

Figure 6-2
Leader Distances on Promoting Interests of French Canada

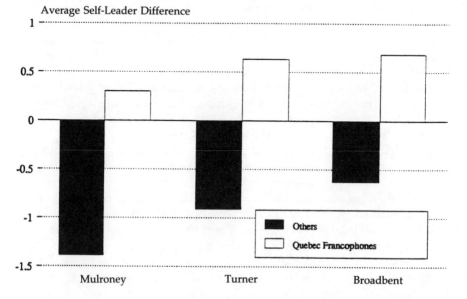

Figure 6-3
Leader Ratings by Day

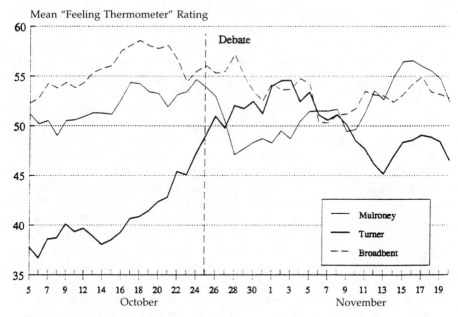

5-day moving average

favourable towards promoting French than they were. Compare this with John Turner, who was seen as hardly more favourable to French Canada than Ed Broadbent.

Differences between voters and leaders and among leaders themselves were sharper on the English side. The difference for Brian Mulroney was stunning: the typical English Canadian saw Mr Mulroney as fully one-third the maximum possible distance away on the measure. Ed Broadbent was seen as closest to anglophones on the issue, but even he seemed as far away from anglophones as from Quebec francophones.

THE COURSE OF LEADER EVALUATIONS

Region and language differences in leader evaluation set the stage for the campaign. Figure 6-3 indicates that the campaign had plenty to work with. The figure plots the ups and downs of "feeling thermometer" ratings, smoothed by the five-day moving average. Most striking is the surge in John Turner's ratings. He was on the way up even before the debates, notwithstanding his frequently bad press. The debates appear to have accelerated the rise. The post-debate surge required about a week and moved the ratings up some ten points. The total gain, pre- and post-debate, was about fifteen points. Brian Mulroney's ratings, in contrast, dropped about five points in the three days right after the debates. But then they began to climb and they ultimately returned to the pre-debate level. Immediately John Turner's ratings peaked, they began to drop; the decline was especially severe over the second-last weekend. At the end, his ratings were scarcely higher than they had been on the eve of the debates. Ed Broadbent's ratings fell slightly after the debates.

Another aspect of Figure 6-3 deserves mention: the strength of Brian Mulroney. For the first half of the campaign the most highly regarded leader was Ed Broadbent. Even so, his margin over Mr Mulroney was small compared with both their margins over John Turner. As his ratings surged, John Turner passed Mr Mulroney and even caught up with Ed Broadbent. But he did so as Mr Broadbent's own rating was sliding. At the end, *Ed Broadbent was no more highly regarded than Brian Mulroney.* The level and resilience of Mr Mulroney's rating is striking in light of his government's and his own apparent earlier unpopularity and in light of the success of the opposition strategy to discredit the FTA by association with its negotiator. What accounted for Brian Mulroney's ratings?

THE SOURCES OF EVALUATION: COMPETENCE AND CHARACTER

In an 8 June 1988 interview with Graham Fraser Brian Mulroney talked about competence: "We've had a rough time ... We know we're doing well in leadership. We know that. I've never run worse than second behind Mr Perfection [NDP Leader Ed Broadbent]. Turner always runs third." Later in the interview, Mr Mulroney quoted a *La Presse* poll from memory: "Who is most able to govern Canada? Mulroney first, Broadbent a poor second, and then Turner who is so far behind you can't see him" (Fraser, 1989, p. 41–42).

John Turner agreed that leaders were important: a few months before the campaign, he told the Liberal mayor of Moncton, New Brunswick, "Never talk about the Free Trade Agreement. Call it the Reagan-Mulroney Trade Deal" (Fraser, 1989, p. 71). John Turner was not talking about competence, though. His emphasis was on Brian Mulroney's character.

Character was also to be an NDP theme, at least when they went on the attack against the FTA. George Nakitsas, Broadbent's chief of staff, made three strategy recommendations in a January 1988 paper:

First, the less we use the words free trade the better. We should instead focus our attack on the Mulroney deal or on the Mulroney/Reagan deal ...

Second, we should at every occasion relate the Mulroney deal to our key message and deal with it as the last straw in a long list of examples where Mulroney has not been open, honest or fair with average Canadians ...

The third recommendation is to deal with the Mulroney deal as the last straw. Specifically, this would mean referring, whenever possible, to other issues where Mulroney has not been fair, open or honest when discussing the Mulroney deal or aspects of it. By doing this, we can keep the focus on the last three years and use the trade issue to reinforce our strengths and Mulroney's weaknesses. (Fraser, 1989, pp. 129–30)

If Brian Mulroney was vulnerable for his character and John Turner for his competence, what of Ed Broadbent? For all that the NDP saw Mr Broadbent as a major asset, their presentation of him was rather formless. A 1 June strategy paper suggested that the campaign theme should be that "Decent Ed has been there, working hard, fighting for ordinary folks" (Fraser, 1989, p. 133). The emphasis seems to be empathy. In hindsight Mr Broadbent's popularity still seems to need explaining. Fraser speculated that it stemmed from "his old-shoe familiarity. He had been leader of his party two and a half times as long as Brian Mulroney and three times as long as John Turner." In addition, unlike Turner and Mulroney who had had to live with failure, scandals, and the grubby exercise of power, Ed Broadbent had no such record. For all this, his popularity seemed to have dropped since 1984 (Frizzell et al., 1989, p. 120). Indeed, longevity seems to undermine all leaders' popularity (LeDuc and Price, 1990).

In their preparation for the campaign, then, all three leaders and their staffs talked about the importance of manipulating *trait* impressions. Their strategies rested on three basic assumptions: that traits differ perceptibly across leaders; that perceptions of traits change with time and campaigns could manipulate voters' assessments of traits or at least voters' attention to certain traits; and that changes in traits have an impact on vote intentions.

Measuring Traits

"Trait" psychology presumes that traits can be measured and that they explain behaviour across a wide set of circumstances. This theory is a matter of controversy. There is some agreement that abilities such as intelligence and knowledge can be measured, substantially less agreement about the possibility of measuring capacities for leadership or visionary thinking, and virtually no agreement about the theoretical utility and measurability of trustworthiness, morality, compassion, and capacity to care. These controversies need not detain us. For us it is not important whether or not individuals' own traits explain behaviour. What matters is that individuals employ the language of traits to assess others, specifically, party leaders.

Our 1988 election study put eight questions, adapted from an American battery, about each leader. Respondents were asked how much each of the following words or phrases described each leader: *intelligent, knowledgeable, provides strong leadership, man of vision, moral, trustworthy, compassionate,* and *really cares about people like me.*[5] These words and phrases form the pairs and tetrads in Figure 6-4. The grouping follows both from a commonsense reading of each item and from empirical work on how these trait attributions cohere (see Kinder, 1983; Aldrich et al., 1988). In this chapter, traits are analysed either separately or combined into two scales, for competence and character. Competence is measured as the average of responses for intelligent, knowledgeable, provides strong leadership, and man of vision. The character scale averages response for moral, trustworthy, compassionate, and really cares about people like me.[6]

What Do Traits Measure?

To make a trait judgment, people must act as naive psychologists, and attribution theory suggests that people base their assessments of others upon how those others act in salient and important situations. Voters may base their assessments of leaders upon the ongoing political drama reported by the press – precisely the events described above for each leader. Moreover, these assessments probably vary according to one's evaluation of what constitutes competence or character. One person may think that competence consists of championing a certain idea, whereas another may believe that favouring the idea suggests utter incompetence. At the same time, some people may believe that taking a bold stand – even an incorrect one – is better than taking no stand at all. This may be especially true of political partisans who would rather have a bold and decisive leader who takes incorrect stands than one who seems to waffle and take no stands at all. Finally, trait evaluations may be

Figure 6-4
Trait Items and Dimensions

Trait Item	Trait Dimension

Intelligent

Knowledgeable
} Intellectual Abilities

Provides Strong Leadership

Man of Vision
} Leadership Abilities

} Competence

Moral

Trustworthy
} Integrity

Compassionate

Really Cares about People
} Empathy

} Character

coloured by independently formed likes or dislikes for the leader.
In sum, trait evaluations should be affected by:

– sources of information and news;
– political partisanship;
– programs and ideas proposed by leaders; and
– basic likes and dislikes for the leader.

Attention in this chapter will be focused on the first two factors.
On sources, the deepest divide should be between francophones in
Quebec and all others. Within a language group, media outlets compete to tell the *same* story. Within each language group, the most
abiding source of differentiation is the voter's prior partisanship.

Figure 6-5
Trait Ratings by Leader

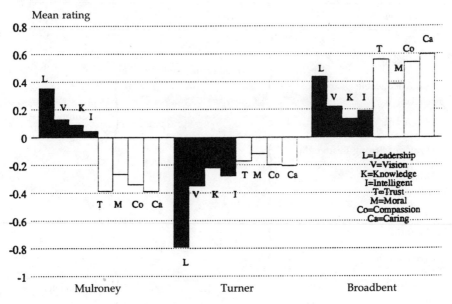

Ratings centred at average across all
three leaders for trait in question

The linguistic and partisan distinctions have two great virtues: each is unequivocally prior to trait ratings; and our measure of each is stable over the campaign – the language measure for obvious reasons, and the party measure as described in chapter 3.

The same cannot be said for issue positions and for likes and dislikes for each leader. It is entirely reasonable to expect each to be an independent factor in trait perceptions. But we shall show that trait ratings also had a life of their own.

Overall Ratings

The first assumption made by the leaders and their strategists is that something is at stake in trying to manipulate the images of leaders, that trait ratings can and do vary across leaders. Figure 6-5 validates the assumption and confirms journalists' stereotypes.

If Ed Broadbent was not absolutely "Mr Perfection" on the five-point trait scales, his ratings nonetheless hovered just below the ceiling. Mr Broadbent was especially strong on character traits: one-

Figure 6-6
The Relative Appeal of Mulroney and Turner

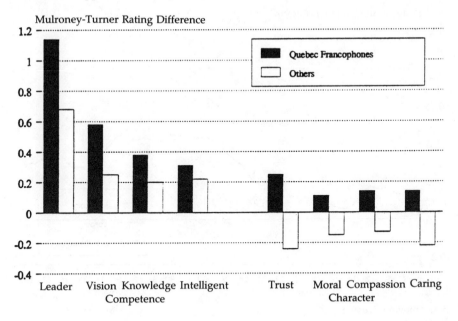

half to three-quarters of a point higher on all four such traits than the second place leader, John Turner. He was also the highest on all four competence traits, although here he barely edged out Mr Mulroney. Brian Mulroney was thought to be nearly as competent as Mr Broadbent and much more so than John Turner. His character, however, was as much in doubt as Mr Turner's competence. Mr Mulroney's problems paled before the troubles visited on John Turner. Mr Turner was seen as of only marginally better character than Brian Mulroney. And he trailed both other leaders badly on perceived competence. Especially weak was his rating on leadership.

Region-Language Differences

The summary ratings mask sharp regional-linguistic differences, especially between ratings of Brian Mulroney and John Turner. Figure 6-6 breaks down the Mulroney-Turner difference between francophone Quebecois and all others, trait by trait. Among Quebec francophones, Brian Mulroney was more highly rated across the board, but especially on competence: his leadership advantage was nearly one point greater in Quebec than elsewhere. Even on char-

Figure 6-7
Competence Ratings by Day

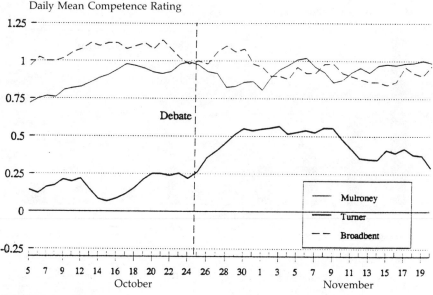

Daily Mean Competence Rating

5-day moving average
Ratings centred at zero

acter, Mr Mulroney had the advantage in francophone Quebec. The character-competence tradeoff between Turner and Mulroney was a perceptual conundrum only outside Quebec.

THE DYNAMICS OF TRAITS

Overall Pattern

Trait ratings have an air of reality about them, or at least of the version of reality the media had repeated for four years or more. Campaign strategists are right in thinking that there is something at stake in trying to project an image of leadership ability, intellectual mastery, integrity, and empathy. Could it be, though, that these images are so deeply rooted in the social structure (as suggested by the previous section) or in the electorate's cumulative experience with the leaders that nothing in the short span of a campaign could change them? Figures 6-7 and 6-8 give the basic patterns which address this question. Henceforth, we combine trait items into two indices, competence and character.

Figure 6-8
Character Ratings by Day

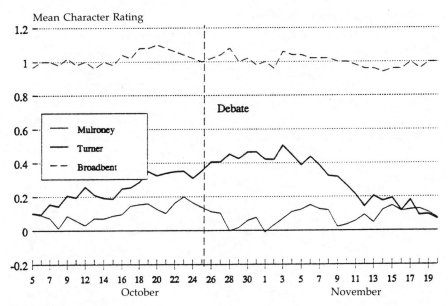

5-day moving average
Ratings centred at zero

The primary story of the campaign was about John Turner's competence. Once again, the key moment was the English debate. Before the debate, not a single reading lay *above* 0.25. After the debate not a single observation was *below* this value.[7] At the end, Mr Turner's ratings fell off, also a pattern familiar for other variables. But his ratings did not revert all the way to the pre-debate level.

Otherwise trait ratings remained fairly stable. Brian Mulroney's competence ratings were essentially undisturbed, while Ed Broadbent's ratings went down slightly, but not in response to any obvious single event. For character perceptions, all leaders' ratings fluctuated very little. Such systematic movement as appeared was all for John Turner, but the range of movement was small compared with the range for his competence ratings. In a sense the contest was really between Brian Mulroney and John Turner: Mr Turner was slightly ahead of Mr Mulroney on character; Mr Mulroney was initially markedly ahead on competence, but this lead was dramatically cut. And as we know from chapter 1, the debates dealt Mr Broadbent's party out of the race to form the government. To simplify the exposition in what follows, then, we focus on the Turner-Mulroney difference.

Figure 6-9
Turner-Mulroney Trait Differences among Conservative Identifiers

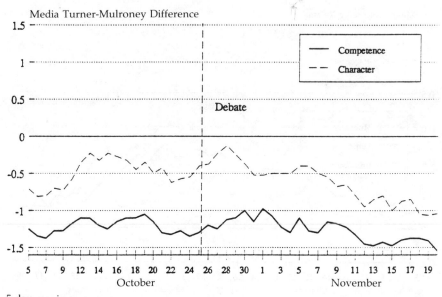

5-day moving average

Trait Ratings and Partisan Identity

Why *should* a voter alter his or her perception of a leader? We have,
after all, shown how perceptions can be socially rooted. The profile
of individual traits and leaders also reflected a cumulative story. Yet
we see critical shifts for at least some leaders and some traits. Who
has a stake in re-evaluation, in effecting such a perceptual shift?

The answer is: Liberal identifiers. Chapter 3 indicated that there
were plenty of Liberals left in the electorate, almost as many Liberals
as Conservatives and more Liberals than Conservatives, strikingly,
in Quebec. But their party had saddled itself with a leader about
whom many had doubts. The doubts were especially pointed about
his competence, about whether he was up to the job of leading his
party. Liberals, above all, had a stake in resolving such doubts. This
is the lesson of Figures 6-9 to 6-11 taken together. In each figure
the daily moving averages are given for the *difference* between Turner
and Mulroney ratings for competence and for character. The higher
the value the greater is John Turner's rating advantage over Brian
Mulroney, and vice versa.

Not surprisingly, Conservatives rate Brian Mulroney more highly
than John Turner for both competence and character: both lines are

Figure 6-10
Turner-Mulroney Trait Differences among Liberal Identifiers

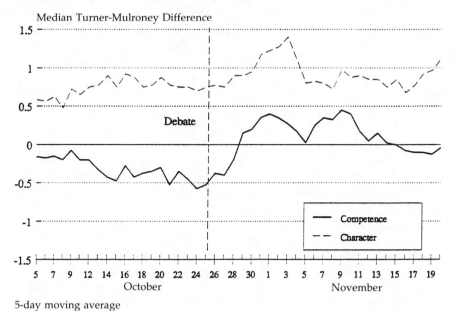

5-day moving average

Figure 6-11
Turner-Mulroney Trait Differences among Non-partisans

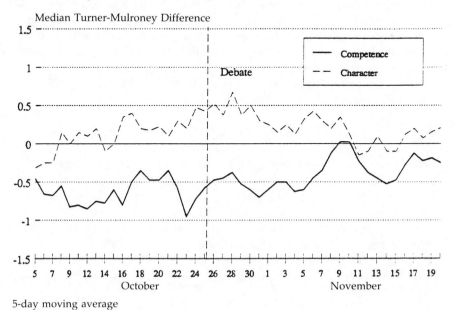

5-day moving average

below zero. The margin is much smaller for character than for competence and there is a hint that, briefly, John Turner was virtually tied with Mr Mulroney in character ratings among Tories. The real story, however, is that the campaign had virtually no net impact on Tories' relative rankings of the old parties' leaders, apart from a mild reinforcement of the long-standing disposition (indicated by the fact that both lines drift downwards over the last fortnight).

The non-partisan story is much the same, according to Figure 6-11. Character ratings changed very little until a modest slide over the last fortnight. The competence difference also changed little. In the last two weeks it crept upwards for a few days, then downwards, and finally stabilized above where it began. Non-partisans were no more affected by the debate than were Conservatives.[8]

Now consider Liberal identifiers, in Figure 6-10. The debates had a strong and significant impact on John Turner's competence ratings relative to those for Mr Mulroney: Mr Turner's relative standing improved by about three-quarters of a point. His character rating also improved relatively speaking, but with no enduring effect. Although Liberals did revise their relative perceptions of Mr Turner's competence in the last ten days of the campaign, the net positive impact of the debate was still about half a point on our scale.

To recapitulate, the campaign *did* have an effect on the electorate's perceptions of the leaders' traits. But its impact was highly selective. Two of the three leaders escaped largely unaffected; perceptions of character, whatever the leader, were fairly stable; and most groups were immune to perceptual shifts. The affected individual was John Turner, the leader with the most to gain. The pivotal trait was his competence, the one on which he needed to gain the most, and the perceptual gains were greatest in the group for which such gains resolved cognitive tension – Liberal identifiers. In being focused, the shifts were tactically potent at least in the short run.

TRAITS AND THE MEDIA CAMPAIGN

The key shifts in trait ratings, especially for John Turner, correspond to patterns that have emerged in the previous two chapters. The debates marked a critical turning point. Later, some or all of the debates' impact was nullified. The second-last weekend seemed critical for John Turner's overall standing, and for perceptions of his competence in particular. Did actually seeing a debate make a difference to his perceptions and evaluations? Did the nullification of the debates' impact correspond to any media quantities and, if so, to which ones?

Figure 6-12
Debate Viewership and Perceptions of Turner's Competence

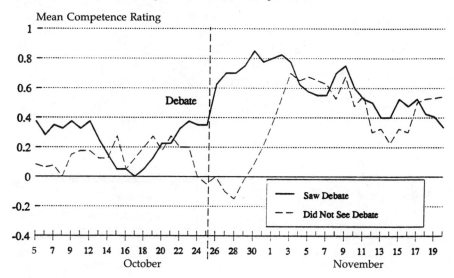

5-day moving average
Report of viewership from post-election wave

Traits and Debates

Our expectations for debate viewership cannot be hard and fast. On one hand, chapter 4 indicated that seeing a debate accelerated the formation of a consensus that John Turner performed best. On the other hand, the same chapter revealed that Liberals were disproportionately likely to watch a debate (but then so were Conservatives). The debate audience might already have rated Mr Turner relatively highly and might thus have been less responsive than non-viewers to its persuasive impact. It is one thing to admit that John Turner won; it may be quite another to alter a settled judgment on his competence. And chapter 5 indicated that the impact of the debates on FTA opinion was entirely a mediated one: non-viewers may even have been more responsive to the debates than viewers.

Figure 6-12 makes clear that seeing a debate mattered for perceptions of John Turner's competence. This figure and Figure 6-13 use the post-election debate viewership question to help distinguish true debate effects from party-motivated self-selection bias. In these figures and in the rest of the chapter we focus on the leader most affected by the campaign, John Turner. Turner's pre-debate com-

Figure 6-13
Debate Viewership and Perceptions of Turner's Character

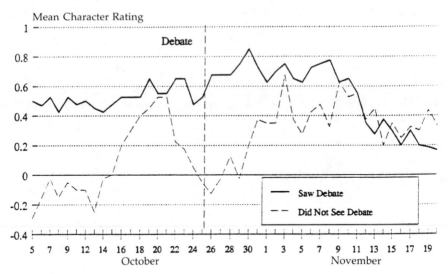

5-day moving average
Report of viewership from post-election wave

petence ratings did not differ between viewers and non-viewers; if Liberals in the audience imparted any bias, it must have been offset by Conservatives. In the debate audience, Turner competence ratings surged. The immediate surge occurred *only* in that audience: if anything, ratings dropped among those who did not see one of the debates. Within a few days, however, non-viewers' ratings began to rise and by 4 November, ten days after the English debate, the groups were indistinguishable.

For character ratings, the picture presented in Figure 6-13 is more obscure. Debate viewers began with a bias, relative to non-viewers, in John Turner's favour. They also did seem to respond positively and immediately to the English debate. But the response was much less impressive than for competence ratings. Meanwhile, non-viewers were slow, apparently, to revise their character judgments. The issue is clouded by an unaccountable pre-debates surge in non-viewers' character ratings. Also clouding the issue was the late decay in viewers' rating; their late, negative re-evaluation of Mr Turner's character was sharper than their concomitant drop in viewers' competence ratings.

Notwithstanding the awkward patches in the character series, the debates do seem to have mattered. They produced a sharp upward revision in John Turner's most manipulable perceptions, of his competence. Their effect was partly direct, in the immediate revision of the audience's perceptions, and partly indirect, in the later rallying of respondents not in the audience. The pattern here recapitulates that in chapter 4, for judgments on the winner. The contrast is with with FTA opinion, to which direct debate exposure was not critical. The key factor may be the object of assessment. Opinion on the FTA may require too much ancillary reasoning and reinforcement to respond overnight to a television spectacle. As well, the elements that go into opinion change may be as available, at much the same time and on the same terms, to respondents who did not actually see a debate as to those who did. But for judgment on the debates' actual participants, direct exposure may be critical.

Ratings, News, and Advertising

The impact of the debates did not endure. For both competence and character ratings, the late campaign brought downturns. Was the downturn induced by the furious advertising attack on John Turner? Or was it the result of bad press? Alternatively, did the bubble burst on its own, independently of the media fury? For that matter, how much of John Turner's initial post-debates' surge can be laid at the door of the media? We saw that the debate audience was quick to re-evaluate Mr Turner, but even in that group not all of the effect was immediate. To address these questions we turn to media estimations. As before, we begin with the estimation of coefficients in an equation and then move to that equation's fit to the daily tracking. The only media quantities that make sense here are the two Turner ones: the daily balance of positives and negatives in all parties' advertising and the same daily balance for national news broadcasts. The Turner rating variable is the summary one, the "feeling thermometer."

From Table 6-1 a familiar pattern emerges. Where advertising and news are each measured in thirty-second bites, the impact of one such bite is greater for news than for advertising. The cumulative effect of a sustained thirty-second news advantage is estimated as over three points on the thermometer scale. The corresponding impact from an advertising advantage is 0.8 points. Both effects are cumulatively significant; indeed, the advertising coefficients have a more straightforward interpretation here than in, say, chapter 4. Also familiar is the relative speed of advertising and news. The news has a more immediate impact: we estimate it to peak within two days, although its effect continues for six days. Advertising does not really kick in until day four.

Table 6-1
The Impact of News and Advertising on Ratings of John Turner

(Ordinary least squares estimation; N = 2,750)		
News		
1	0.316	(0.319)
2	1.173	(0.324)
3	0.437	(0.348)
4	0.219	(0.327)
5	0.391	(0.325)
6	0.717	(0.321)
Total	3.253	(0.802)
Advertisements		
1	−0.160	(0.149)
2	0.127	(0.150)
3	−0.055	(0.152)
4	0.334	(0.158)
5	0.235	(0.156)
6	0.317	(0.148)
Total	0.798	(0.373)
Covariates		
PC Ident	−4.916	(0.853)
Lib Ident	8.522	(0.898)
NDP Ident	−1.537	(1.128)
Quebec	−0.538	(0.767)
Education	−0.586	(0.158)
Intercept	50.358	(1.178)
R^2	0.11	

Standard errors in parentheses

The summary impact of news and advertising appears in Figure 6-14. Before the debates, media quantities were just not relevant. In the case of advertising, this should be no surprise: there were no advertisements before 23 October. News there most assuredly was, however, much of it very bad for Mr Turner. The bad news did not affect his ratings, which gradually drifted up before the debates. After 25 October the media clearly became a factor in John Turner's fortunes, for both good and ill.

News and advertising impact, Figure 6–15 reveals, followed markedly different trajectories. Cumulatively, though, each made about the same contribution, notwithstanding the disparity in their coefficients. The news impact was more immediate: it helped promote John Turner's early post-debates surge. Thereafter the news contributed to a gradual slide in his ratings. Advertising was still not

Figure 6-14
The Predictive Power of Media Factors for John Turner's Ratings

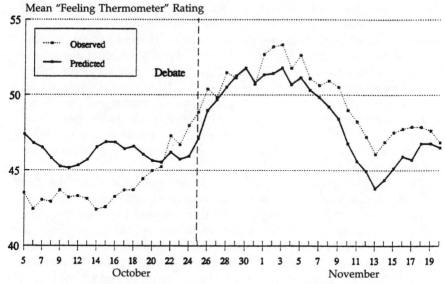

5-day moving average

Figure 6-15
Separate Impact of Advertisements and News on Turner Ratings

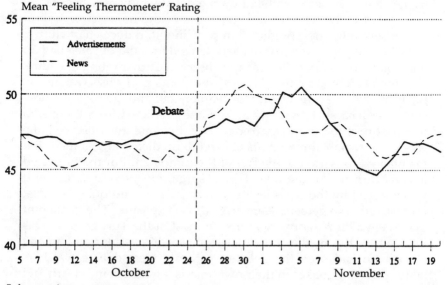

5-day moving average

really a factor as late as 30 October, one week after the French debate. Undoubtedly this reflects the long lags on advertising effects (Table 6-1). But when advertising kicked in, it evidently helped sustain the surge: note that the estimated advertising peak came just under a week later than its news equivalent. Roughly speaking, the news induced about two-thirds of the total media effect at this stage; where the estimated news-induced gain was five or six points, that for advertising was two or three degrees. The total gain was about ten points. After John Turner's ratings peak, advertising seems to have been the more potent factor. It induced a drop of more than five points and was the factor primarily responsible for the late-campaign turns in the series, reflecting Conservative salvoes and Liberal return fire.

Figures 6-14 and 6-15 raise an awkward question about the debates. We argued above that Turner ratings, unlike FTA opinion, were affected by direct viewing of the debates. Here we provide evidence of early dramatic impact from the post-debates news, a pattern which indicates that media did what their name says they should do, namely, *mediate* the debates' impact, tell the audience what it should think. Can these interpretations be reconciled?

The attempt at reconciliation is Figure 6-16. Here we present predicted media effects for both watchers and non-watchers. The story that emerges is complex. The first point is familiar from the earlier account: the really striking dynamics, at least before the very end of the campaign, are exhibited by the debate audience. Because of the lack of early post-debates dynamics in the non-viewer group, we present only their predicted impact line, to reduce chart clutter. Now look at the two debate-viewer lines. First, the debates had an immediate, unmediated effect: the observed Turner rating line turns up immediately after the debates (the pooling of observations actually makes it seem to turn up earlier, but this just shows how swift the debates' impact was). The line predicted from the media does not turn for another two days. By this time, the observed line was some two or three points above the predicted line, a margin it maintained for virtually the rest of the campaign. But the predicted line *did* turn up; of the total Turner surge, most (70 to 80 percent) was induced by the post-debates media barrage and only a modest fraction (20 to 30 percent) came from direct exposure. The final point may seem a bit paradoxical at first: if most of the Turner surge was induced by the media, nonetheless it was almost entirely among those who had seen the debate. Not only were debate watchers better placed to make up their own minds – which some clearly did – but they were also in a better position to be responsive to the news

Figure 6-16
The Debate or the News?

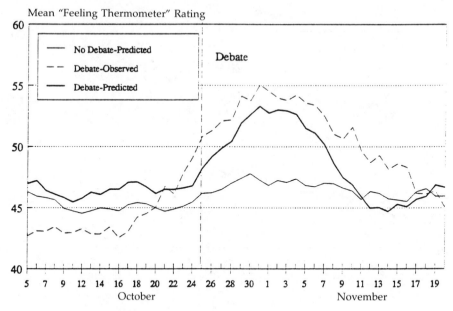

Mean "Feeling Thermometer" Rating

7-day moving average

and to opinion leaders on the broadcast media. This point is reinforced, ironically, by the pattern for modest media impact visible for non-viewers: their ratings were predicted to rise over early November, then fall, then rise again, as they felt the impact from advertising. Attentive voters were affected dramatically by both news and advertising; inattentive voters were affected modestly by advertising alone.

REASSEMBLING THE LIBERAL COALITION

We have preliminary indications that Liberals were disproportionately responsive to the mid-campaign events; they had the most at stake in John Turner's rehabilitation. But not all Liberals are equal in this respect. Liberals who were already in the voting fold before the debates may already have made their peace with John Turner; indeed, they ought to have been naturally more favourably disposed to him. But many Liberals had strayed. The Liberal vote in 1984 was scarcely larger than the party's share of identifiers, as reported in chapter 3. Many of these supporters must have defected in that year

Figure 6-17
Turner Ratings by Party Identification and 1984 Vote

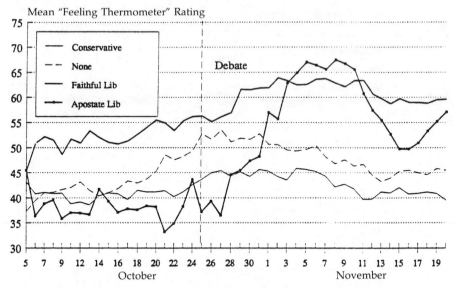

7-day moving average

and may well have still remained out of the Liberal voting coalition early in the 1988 campaign. If they were looking for a reason to return, the debate supplied it.

Figure 6-17 indicates that the 1984 apostate Liberals were indeed the pivotal group at mid-campaign. Before the debates, apostates rated Mr Turner as poorly as did the Tories. Pre-debates gains in his ratings came entirely from non-partisans or from Liberals already on side. After the debates, apostates came all the way back home: by early November, they rated John Turner as highly as did their more constant brethren. The vicissitudes of the last week may have caused them temporarily to stray (then, again, this may have been just sampling error) but on election eve apostates and faithful were scarcely distinguishable. The leadership battle helped reconstitute the underpinnings of the third-party system. It did not create decisional tension; it resolved it.

THE TRAIT FOUNDATIONS OF OVERALL EVALUATION

All that remains is to close the circle, to connect movements in trait perceptions to the dynamics of overall leader evaluation. Certain

Table 6-2
The Impact of Trait Perceptions on Overall Evaluation

	Traits	(Ordinary least squares estimation) Leader		
		Mulroney	Turner	Broadbent
Cross-section	Character	16.35 (0.71)	7.94 (0.80)	9.30 (0.81)
	Competence	8.82 (0.80)	12.61 (0.80)	11.70 (0.93)
Time-series	Character	20.78 (5.27)	−7.02 (3.79)	5.60 (4.84)
	Competence	17.44 (5.71)	39.05 (3.48)	14.26 (4.04)

Standard errors in parentheses.

parallels were especially suggestive; the most visibly manipulable judgments were on competence and were so especially for John Turner. But competence judgments were also powerfully rooted in the party system and the social structure. And if movement in competence perceptions seemed to parallel flux in John Turner's overall standing, the parallels were less clear for the other leaders.

To tell a story about campaign effects we need to concentrate on the dynamic elements in our data. If we want to make a case that one key to Mr Turner's overall recovery was a dramatic upgrading in his perceived competence, we have to separate impact attributable to that upgrading from potential confounding information. If we just regressed respondents' summary thermometer ratings for him on their competence ratings, we would confound the longitudinal variation produced by the campaign with all the abiding cross-sectional variance which is not of primary interest here.

Table 6-2 reports the results from time-series cross-sectional estimations. Dependent variables are the 100-point thermometer scales. Independent variables are character and competence ratings split into their "time-series" and "cross-section" parts. The time-series part is the average competence rating for the day the respondent was interviewed. All respondents interviewed on a given day get the same rating; the values are exactly the ones which appear in Figure 6-8. The cross-section part is each respondent's own score with the day's average score subtracted from it. Alternatively put, individual respondents' scores are deviations from the mean score for the day; this variation comes from differences in party identification, region, free trade opinion, and the like.

The first two lines in Table 6-2 show that for all three leaders there is a strong cross-sectional impact on overall evaluation from both character and competence. Interestingly, each evaluation of Brian Mulroney and John Turner was most powerfully affected by the traits on which he was weakest: Mulroney by character judgments and Turner by competence ones. Judgments on Ed Broadbent were more balanced.

The next two lines are the really critical ones. Taking all three leaders together, the driving force of evaluative dynamics is perceived competence. Depending upon the leader, a one-point change in competence ratings produces a fifteen- to forty-point change in leader evaluations. For John Turner this was the whole story. From just before the debates to about one week after, his competence perceptions surged just over one-quarter of a point on our arbitrary scale (Figure 6-7). The predicted impact of such a surge is roughly ten thermometer points and just such a surge was the full extent of the thermometer rating gain in Figure 6-3.

Only for Brian Mulroney was time-series variation in character perceptions a major factor. Figure 6-3 did record a serious drop in Mr Mulroney's overall rating. The coefficients in Table 6-2 and visual examination of Figures 6-6 and 6-7 indicate that his drop was a compound of heightened doubts – ultimately passing ones – about both his competence and his character.

DISCUSSION

When voters evaluate leaders, two things appear critical: where voters themselves sit in the social and political structure relative to each leader, and how each leader has performed over the previous months and years. Whatever each leader's objective merits, each also is a stylized embodiment of a set of policy preferences. For instance, Brian Mulroney enjoyed better ratings in Quebec than elsewhere, across the board and for individual traits. But the reality of a leader's own performance also intrudes. For instance, even in English Canada, Mr Mulroney was seen as more competent than John Turner. Through the biases imposed by background, voters can produce a picture that is differentiated both within and between individual leaders and done in a way which corresponds well with received images of each person.

But considerable evaluative slack remained at the beginning of the campaign. The campaign moved overall ratings as it did judgments on individual traits. In 1988 the biggest movement was for John Turner, especially for perceptions of his competence. Not all trait perceptions or all leader images are equally manipulable all the time. "Manipulation" may not even be the appropriate word. Its associations imply an inability of voters to think or to search out information for themselves. Perceptual shifts were rare among uninvolved voters. In 1988, *seeing* a debate made all the difference. Some of a debate's effect was from the event itself, from the dramatic exchanges taking place before viewers' own eyes. Some reflected not so much the event as the viewer. A level of political involvement high enough to make a voter see a debate also makes him or her more open to media influence after the debate. Even in the debate audience not everyone shifted their perceptions. Shifts were greatest where the stakes were highest, for instance among Liberals wanting to know if it was all right to come back.

All this leaves open several major questions:

– What groups are most likely to re-evaluate a leader? The most dramatic shift in 1988 involved apostate Liberals. The debates and their aftermath allowed such Liberals to resolve cognitive tension. But is the resolution of tension always the dominant dynamic? A long-standing and persuasive literature in social psychology and political science suggests that it should be (Zaller, 1991), although rumination on other recent Canadian campaigns makes us hesitate to generalize. The first English debate in 1984, for instance, would seem to have had the opposite effect. Unlike 1988, the 1984 episode produced a displacement of preferences from the long-standing norm. But is this the same thing as increasing cognitive tension? Perhaps the 1984 debate just confirmed doubts about the Liberals, doubts that had been temporarily set aside. This is just speculation. As it applies to debates, this question points to the need to accumulate more cases. The question applies to news and advertising as well. And the concluding phase of the 1988 campaign saw a net increase in Liberals' cognitive tension: evaluations of John Turner went back down.

– Of whom are perceptions most malleable? The 1988 example suggests that the answer is leaders about whom there is some doubt. The operative word is doubt. Many voters had a low estimation of how trustworthy Brian Mulroney was; this was not something they doubted. The task for the opposition was not to implant doubts about Mr Mulroney's trustworthiness, but to activate concerns already in place. This activation showed in FTA opinion more than it did in evaluation of Mr Mulroney himself, although the character coefficient for Mulroney perceptions in Table 6-2 is not trivial. About John Turner, arguably, there truly were doubts. On one hand, he had not performed well in the years since 1984. On the other hand, he had survived and his earlier political record was one of considerable success. The record was sufficiently mixed that a bravura show of competence might bring to voters' cognitive foreground the successes rather than the failures in his record. The greatest doubts of all tend to be about newcomers. They have the most to gain from debates and commonly they press for them. But they may also have the most to lose.

- What trait perceptions are most susceptible to media manipulation? It is tempting to suggest that competence is the pivotal trait, that the 1988 pattern is the norm. Perhaps voters sense that public morality differs from private morality and that, while it would be nice to have someone of impeccable character in charge, it is of first importance to have someone who is truly up to the job. Here we are on speculative ground. The answer could just as well be that any trait about which there is doubt, in the sense conveyed in the preceding paragraph, is open to campaign manipulation. This question also points to the need for more cases.

Finally, does it all matter? Was the leader soap opera only a sideshow to the real issue, the free trade agreement, or was it just another path along which the standing alignment of parties worked itself out? This is a question for chapter 8.

7 Expectations: Self-Fulfilling Prophecies?

The single-member plurality electoral system that Canada shares with other Westminster-style democracies makes voters' expectations about the election's outcome potentially important to their own behaviour. No electoral system is truly neutral in the way it translates seats into votes; all systems compound the advantages of larger parties and the disadvantages of smaller ones. But under the plurality formula this compounding reaches its highest pitch. Figure 1-1 indicated, for instance, that the Conservative party could gain an outright seat majority with as little as 39 percent of the popular vote. The tone of the plurality formula is set by a feature which has also become a nickname for it, "winner take all": for each constituency a mere plurality – as small as one vote – gives a party all of the representation for that place. Another telling nickname is "first past the post." The image is of a horse-race and so it is not inappropriate that at least some media time, especially the sponsoring and coverage of polls, is spent on the campaign's horse-race features. Voters' interest in the horse-race is not just political voyeurism: some voters have reason to vote strategically, others might have good reason to jump on a bandwagon.

BEHAVIOURAL POSSIBILITIES

Strategic Voting

Expectations, whether derived from polls or from other sources, can inform *strategic voting*. In essence, to vote strategically is to vote for one's second choice the better to defeat one's last choice – in other words, a half-a-loaf calculus. A voter may prefer party A to party B and party B to party C. But the voter may also reckon that A does not have a serious chance of winning and may instead support B in hopes of defeating C.

An awkward fact about second-choice voting in mass electorates is that, however much it may resemble the process that we have come to see as the essence of rational choice, the maximization of expected utility, it is usually nothing of the sort. In expected-utility models[1] of behaviour the actor is deemed to take only those actions which truly serve his or her ends. In the world of voting, a choice, to be worth making, must have two characteristics. First, the voter must be able to discern a difference between the parties or candidates in question; one alternative must yield greater utility than the other. Secondly, the voter's own action must make a difference to the outcome. If it does not, then the outcome is a collective good, something the voter gets whether he or she "pays" for it or not. A voter who generally prefers the NDP to the Liberals might also prefer the Liberals to the Conservatives. But in the usual formulation, only if the voter has a realistic chance of helping the Liberals defeat the Conservatives should he or she vote Liberal; otherwise, the voter might as well go ahead and support the NDP. In reality, few voters have a realistic chance of making a difference to the outcome, even in their own riding, much less in the electorate as a whole. If we define "making a difference" as creating or breaking a tie, then even locally the probability of doing such a thing is on the order of one in several thousand. An actuary would characterize this as a moral certainty, in this case a moral certainty of ineffectiveness. It is sometimes claimed from this logic that voters should ignore strategic information and always support their first preference (Meehl, 1977).[2]

There is, however, another way for a voter – and for students of the process – to think about electoral choice. The question needn't be, How likely am I to create or break a tie? A more sensible question might be, What is the set of feasible alternatives? It seems reasonable to confine my own choice to such alternatives, unless, of course, I just cannot stomach any of them. The definition of feasibility is a matter of expectations, not of expectations for one's own efficacy but of *expectations for a party's chances of winning*.[3]

Bandwagons

In the folklore of elections, the role for polls and expectations is not in motivating strategic choice; it relies on a simpler notion, the creation of a bandwagon. By this is meant the relentless reinforcement of the frontrunner's initial advantage.[4] Voters are presumed to rally to the party in front, which in turn allows that party to increase its lead still further. This rallying is a form of contagion, much like fashion in dress or the tendency for baseball fans who emerge only in October to root for the team on the verge of winning the World Series (Bartels, 1988).

It is hard to square such a process with the 1988 pattern in the electorate as a whole. The Conservative party's high standing before the debates failed to arrest its reverse after the debates. The reverse itself was largely bereft of any self-replicating momentum and was entirely accomplished before the first post-debates polls were published.[5] Had it been a bandwagon, its momentum would have carried the Conservatives further and further down, to the party's irreducible base.

But the logic of a bandwagon may be important for an important section of the electorate: Quebec francophones. Chapter 2 revealed that Quebec plays a pivotal role in the formation of governments. Its seats tend to come en bloc, as befits a nation within a nation. The importance of cohesion was clear from the moment that francophones were joined politically to anglophones in 1840. Figure 2-12 indicates that whichever party holds the bloc is strategically privileged in the parliamentary game. Chapter 1 outlined two models for the bloc's formation. In one model, Quebeckers go with winners; they detect the way the wind is blowing elsewhere and trim accordingly. In the other model, Quebeckers *make* the winner; simply by bloc voting they overcome whatever natural majority exists in the rest of Canada.[6] Only the first model is really about a kind of bandwagon. Chapter 3 indicated that Quebec francophones were socially and sentimentally well placed to act as a moveable bloc, one available for a bandwagon; a smaller proportion than in the rest of the electorate identified with a party, and the social foundations of party choice were remarkably weak. Chapter 2 suggests, however, that historically the more adequate model is the second: Quebeckers have ensured that they are represented in government not by following an other-Canada lead but by concerting their efforts to ensure that their preferred party enjoys a strong parliamentary position come what may in the rest of Canada. Indeed, it was the movement in Quebec, well in advance of movements outside the province, that put the Liberals in power in 1896. Since that time, the Conservative party was rarely acceptable and thus could not generate much of a bandwagon. But after 1983 the Conservative party attained an acceptability in Quebec not seen since the early 1890s. Although Liberals and Conservatives championed subtly different conceptions of the place of French Canada in the country as a whole, in 1988 many Quebec voters could live with either party. If ever there was a year for a bandwagon among Quebec franco-phones, 1988 was it.[7]

The Level of Aggregation

The most readily available strategic information comes from media coverage of polls. Poll coverage tends to focus on the national stand-ings. In part this reflects time constraints in the newsroom. It also typically reflects a concern not to overinterpret results based on small region or province subsamples. But why should expectations for a party's chances *in the whole country* be a driving force for strategic voting?

In the expected-utility variant of the strategic voting model, if voters employ any strategic information at all, it should be local information – at a level where they might have at least a ghost of an effect – rather than national information – at a level where they can have no effect whatsoever. In the feasible-alternatives version of strategic voting it may not matter what the spatial scale of the information is; national expectations are as relevant as local ones. As it happens, the empirical record suggests that voters do incor-porate both national and provincial strategic information, as well as local information, into a strategic calculus.[8]

But national and local strategic information may conflict. It may be true that national information sets the boundaries of feasibility for forming a majority government. It may also be true that national poll information registers in voters' consciousness more clearly than does local information. But in 1988 forming a government was not the only definition of the game for Liberals and the NDP. The alter-native definition was stopping the Conservatives from forming one. And stopping the Conservatives ought to have been the primary objective of FTA opponents. To the extent that national information overrode local information, voters may have been induced to sup-port a party whose local chances, whatever its national standing, were still negligible.

For the bandwagon, national information is at least as valuable as local information. Indeed, for a potential bandwagon in Quebec it may be the *only* relevant information.

THE PATTERN OF EXPECTATIONS

Figure 7-1 gives the daily tracking of national expectations for each party.[9] Respondents could rate a party's chances from 0 to 100,

Figure 7-1
Expectations about the National Outcome

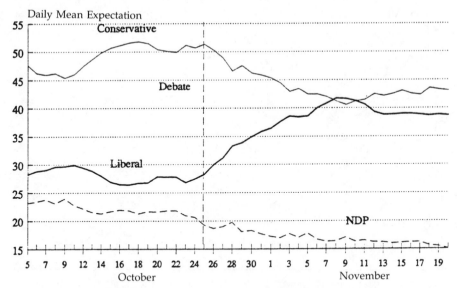

Daily Mean Expectation

5-day moving average

where higher means better. Conservatives entered the campaign
with average ratings in the high forties, the Liberals started in the
high twenties, and the NDP began in the low twenties. Down to the
debates, Conservative ratings strengthened while Liberal and NDP
ones weakened. Movement for each party was gradual, but the
Conservatives' expectations edge was palpably greater on 25 October
than it had been three weeks before.

The debates brought a dramatic reversal in trends for the old
parties: Liberal ratings surged and Conservative ratings dropped.
The movement was clearly well under way before the first post-
debates horse-race poll was released on 29 October. Although by
this time two polls[10] had confirmed the popular sense that Mr Turner
had won the debates, neither poll gave any hard information about
vote intention.

The Conservative decline and Liberal surge continued after the
first polls were published. By one reading the trends continued to
about 8 November. Then they reversed a second time. By election
day the Conservatives were perceived to be just ahead of the Liberals. Another reading of Figure 7-1 suggests that the Liberal surge
had already peaked by about 2 or 3 November and that the party
had settled in at, on our scale, an average expectations rating of
about thirty-eight. The Liberal boomlet in the middle of the second

Figure 7-2
NDP Expectations

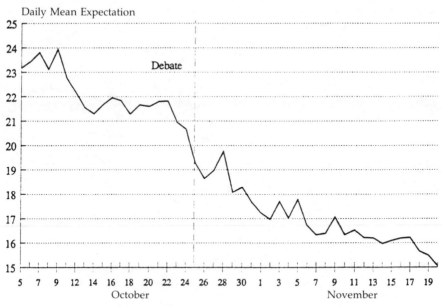

Daily Mean Expectation

Debate

5
7
9
12
14
16
18
20
22
24
26
28
30
1
3
5
7
9
11
13
15
17
19

October

November

5-day moving average

last week may not have been the culmination of a trend. It may instead have been a creature of the Gallup "rogue" poll published on 7 November (see Figure 4-7). This reading is corroborated by the speed with which the Liberal expectation retreated back to the high 30s almost immediately upon the publication of the next few polls.

NDP movements after the debates bear closer scrutiny. By the standards of Liberal and Conservative expectations, NDP movement was small and gradual. This was as it should be. The logic of the plurality electoral system dictates that gains in expectation induced by vote-share movements from the high twenties to the high thirties – the gains the Liberals enjoyed – should be much more dramatic than losses in expectation induced by vote-share losses from the high twenties to the high teens – the losses that befell the NDP. This was a lesson of Figure 1-2. The Liberals went from a very poor chance of forming the government to having a very good one. The NDP went from already having a very poor chance to having a poorer one still. The NDP had very little more to lose.[11] As a result of this compression, the scale of Figure 7-1 masks the pattern by which the party lost ground. Figure 7-2 brings the NDP into sharper

Figure 7-3
Expectations about the Local Outcome

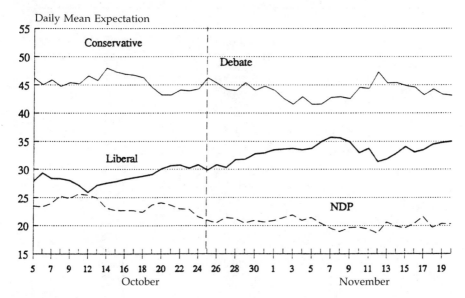

5-day moving average

relief. By the middle of the campaign's second week the party's expectations appeared to have stabilized in vicinity of twenty-one or twenty-two points. The debates immediately knocked about two points off the daily mean; this drop took only a couple of days. Then the NDP rating slide seemed to pause. The daily mean dropped again after 30 October and continued a gradual further slide right to the end. The second drop and subsequent slide followed the publication of the first post-debates polls.

The local expectations story begins in Figure 7-3. In a crude sense local expectations mimic the national ones, especially in Liberal growth and NDP decay. But differences are no less striking than similarities. Most important is that local expectations did not move remotely as much as national ones did. For Liberal and NDP expectations, the whole-campaign shift was only about half as great as for national expectations. For the Conservative party the local shifts were even smaller. This too is as it should be. Although a party's national seat total is just a summing up of local results, the upgrading of a party's chances of forming the government still leaves its probabilities of local success largely unchanged in most ridings. The seats that actually turn the result are not that numerous. Their number

Table 7-1
Sources of Liberal Expectations

	(Ordinary least squares estimation; N=2,792)	
	National	Local
Atlantic	2.08	4.93
	(0.99)	(1.37)
Quebec	−1.65	0.26
	(0.65)	(0.89)
West	−1.47	−10.29
	(0.64)	(0.87)
pc Id	−1.82	−3.38
	(0.65)	(0.89)
Liberal Id	4.93	7.76
	(0.69)	(0.94)
ndp Id	−1.72	−2.67
	(0.87)	(1.19)
26–28 Oct. Interview	2.67	2.80
	(0.99)	(1.36)
Liberal % last poll	0.89	0.48
	(0.05)	(0.06)
Constant	5.53	17.98
	(1.58)	(2.17)
R^2	0.160	0.148

Standard errors in parentheses.

is magnified by double counting: every one subtracted from one party is added to the other.

SOURCES OF EXPECTATIONS

Expectations emerge from voters' introspection as well as from their reading of external cues. The internal and external sources often interact and reinforce each other in producing a realistic appreciation of the situation. At other times they conflict. The less access a voter has to external information the more he or she resorts to introspection. External information is richer for national expectations than for local ones. Table 7-1 illustrates some of these propositions. It focuses on Liberal expectations, but the story is essentially the same for each other party. The figure is based on a multivariate OLS estimation; all variables in Table 7-1 were in the estimation simultaneously. Look first at the regional basis of expectation. The table gives an estimate of the difference made, other things equal, by living in a region other than Ontario. [12] For local expectations, regional coefficients are huge. They *should* be huge. Respondents were not all asked to evaluate the same strategic situation: perception of Liberal strength in the Atlantic provinces and of Liberal weakness in the west accorded with reality. Conversely, national expectations were only modestly differentiated by region. This is reassuring, for here all respondents were asked to evaluate the same situation. Even so, regional differences did appear for national expectations. For the west and the Atlantic regions, national-expectations differences were milder versions of local-expectations ones. The *prima facie* indication is that there is a modest projection from local experiences onto national expectations.

The other source of projection was party predisposition. Identifiers with each of the three parties are compared in Table 7-1 with non-partisans. Conservatives and New Democrats rated the Liberal party's chances lower and Liberals rated them higher than did non-partisans. But national expectations offered less scope for projection; poll standings were too well documented. Where for local expectations a Liberal tended to rate his party about eleven points higher than a Conservative did, the national-expectations difference was under seven points. The relative impact of party identification on local expectations must be interpreted with some care. Region of residence does not capture all of the geographic variation in parties' chances; much of the variation is within regions. To the extent that this is so and, further, to the extent that party identifiers tend to cluster in areas of their own party's strength, some impact from local strategic intelligence has undoubtedly leaked into party-identification coefficients. Still, we suspect that a big part of the local-national difference in degree of partisan bias reflects the poorer local information. Corroborative evidence appears below.

So far expectations look to be heavily prey to projective bias. But all is not bias and projection. The first evidence presented in this chapter was of campaign dynamics, which are hard to square with projection from fixed predispositions. Some of these dynamics undoubtedly involved respondents' noticing that their own ballot preferences had changed and then projecting this change, not unreasonably, onto others; the early surge of expectations after the debates looks something like this. But the general course of expectations had other dynamics, which suggested that outside information was also at work. Conservative expectations continued to decay long after that the party's vote share had stopped dropping. The mirror image was true for Liberal expectations and the Liberal share. And the 7 November Gallup poll had a discernible impact on Liberal and Conservative expectations, as did the neutralization of that Gallup by the next three polls.

Figure 7-4
Attention to Published Polls

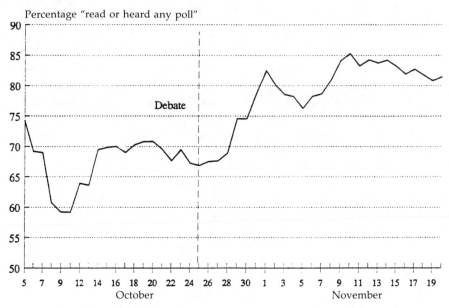

5-day moving average

Table 7-1 also testifies to the impact of polls. The poll variable is the Liberal share in the most recently published poll.[13] Because of arbitrary scaling factors the coefficient looks small. In fact it is huge: nearly one to one for national expectations. Specifically, a one-point increment in the Liberal share in the most recent poll translated into nearly nine-tenths of a point gain in expectation rating. The impact on the local rating was, appropriately, more muted: the coefficient was roughly half the size of the national one.

Figure 7-4 indicates that polls penetrated deeply into the electorate. In the pre-debates period around 70 percent of respondents with a vote intention claimed to have read or heard of a poll in the last seven days. After the debates the percentage surged to over 80 percent. The surge came just as the publication of polls reached its highest frequency, in the days after 28 October.[14]

Actually reading or hearing about a poll was vital to reacting to it. Table 7-2 is constructed along the same lines as Table 7-1. Here only national expectations are considered. The comparison is between those exposed and those not exposed to a poll. Reading or hearing about a poll more than doubled the rate at which the Lib-

Table 7-2
Poll Awareness and Liberal Expectations, National Only

| | (Ordinary least squares estimation) | |
	Read/Heard Poll	No Poll
Atlantic	1.00	1.89
	(0.05)	(1.83)
Quebec	−0.67	−5.20
	(0.71)	(1.41)
West	−0.40	−5.26
	(0.69)	(1.43)
PC Id	−1.38	−2.98
	(0.72)	(1.41)
Liberal Id	5.43	4.42
	(0.76)	(1.46)
NDP Id	0.49	−7.28
	(0.97)	(1.76)
26–28 Oct. Interview	1.56	4.44
	(1.18)	(1.81)
Liberal % last poll	1.05	0.47
	(0.05)	(0.10)
Constant	−1.33	22.92
	(1.77)	(3.40)
R^2	0.209	0.131
N	2,062	710

Standard errors in parentheses

erals' poll share was translated into expectational gain or loss. At the same time, poll exposure depressed the impact of irrelevant locational or dispositional factors. Among poll watchers no regional differences appeared, to all intents and purposes, in the national expectation. Among respondents not exposed to polls, regional differences were marked. Similarly, party identification sharply biased expectations among unexposed respondents. Among the exposed, in contrast, Conservatives and New Democrats gave the Liberal party essentially the same rating as non-partisans did; only Liberals seemed significantly biased. Awareness of polls thus dramatically tilted the balance towards information that was both current and in the public domain and away from information that was inside the voter's head. Figure 7-5, which juxtaposes the last-poll coefficients for each party from estimations like those in Table 7-2, confirms that this is true for all three parties.

The impact of poll awareness on the aggregate dynamics of expectations appears in Figure 7-6. Poll-aware respondents supplied the bulk of those dynamics at virtually every point in the campaign.

Figure 7-5
Poll Awareness and Impact of Last Poll, National Expectations Only

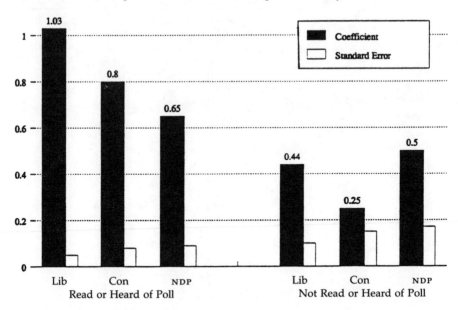

Before the debates the widening of the Conservative advantage occurred only among the poll-aware. Even at the beginning, the
Liberal-Conservative rating difference was around twice as great in
the aware group as in the unaware group. After the debates, the
closing of the gap proceeded much more rapidly in the aware group.
In part, this difference in speed is an artifact of the smaller gap that
the unaware group had to close. But after the gap had closed, the
sum of Liberal and Conservative ratings was still smaller in the
unexposed than in the exposed group: by implication, unexposed
respondents had still not ruled the NDP out as definitively as more
aware respondents had.

Two awkward patches must be traversed, however. First, exposed
respondents were more open than unexposed ones to non-poll information; the Liberal surge and Conservative decay among those
aware of polls began before the first post-debates poll. Among those
who reported not having seen or heard of a poll, the movement
began only after the first polls were published. The indication is that
the unexposed also tended to miss the debates[15] and thus were ill
placed to use the debates to revise their expectations. Whether the
unexposed then responded to the grapevine about the post-debates
polls or were only adventitiously exhibiting a lag from the debates

Figure 7-6
Poll Awareness and Aggregate Dynamics of Expectations

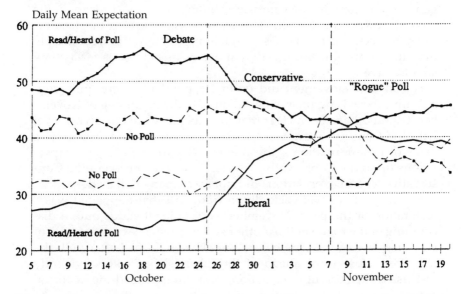

5-day moving average

remains an open question. Secondly, the unexposed were more responsive to one particular poll, the 7 November Gallup rogue poll. Not only did unexposed respondents alter the two parties' ratings more than did exposed respondents, but they did not revert to the socially dominant ranking: from 7 November to the end the unexposed persisted in ranking the Liberals higher than the Conservatives. They were sensitive to the drama that the poll initiated, but they did not grasp fully the import of the accumulation of contrary evidence which began shortly after.[16] Could it be that the real problem with polls is with citizens who are not routinely aware of them? Such citizens respond to the highest-profile polls but seem unable, in contrast to poll habitués, to place them in context.

DISCUSSION

Expectations mixed reality and bias. The more exposed the voter was to current information, the more realistic was his or her appreciation of the strategic situation. But the realism was not just a matter of response to poll information. High-exposure individuals also came relatively quickly to appreciate the Liberals' strengthened position after the debates; much of the revising antedated the polls. Poll exposure is not so much an indicator of polling as of individuals' general openness to the campaign. In any case, most respondents did claim awareness of polls. This was especially so after the debates. Thus expectations for parties' national performance moved sharply over the campaign. But did they move as quickly or as far as they should have?

For all that movement did occur, respondents were quite conservative in revising their expectations. By the beginning of November it should have been clear that the Liberals were effectively level with the Conservatives. Yet it took another week and, arguably, a piece of misinformation – the rogue poll – to push Liberal expectations up to the Conservatives' level. [17] The reassertion of the Conservative lead in expectations did not accompany poll evidence that the Conservatives were actually in front. All that happened was a restoration of the pre-7 November expectational status quo, a discounting of the rogue poll. Another striking instance of conservatism was the place of the NDP before the debates. In poll after poll, the NDP were close to or ahead of the Liberals. But voters evidently distrusted the current information, preferring instead the historical record, and thus they discounted the NDP's chances.

Perhaps the Canadian electorate was exhibiting the conservatism in the face of novel information which has become a staple observation in cognitive psychology:

An abundance of research has shown that human beings are conservative processors of fallible information. Such experiments compare human behavior with the outputs of Bayes' theorem, the formally optimal rule about how opinions (that is, probabilities) should be revised on the basis of new information. It turns out that opinion change is very orderly, and usually proportional to the numbers calculated from Bayes' theorem – but it is insufficient in amount. [18]

On the other hand, the respondents were about right in the end, even in advance of the last three polls; events vindicated them in rating the Conservatives' chances above those for the Liberals. They may have been right, then, to discount current poll information. The confidence intervals claimed by the major polling firms were large enough to make the difference between victory and defeat or between a minority and a majority result. And we cannot dismiss the possibility that some of the apparent sluggishness in expectations reflected error in our own measure. In light of all this, Canadians' adjustment of their expectations may have been about right –

grounded firmly in visible reflections of reality but muted in its dynamics.

In any case, by the standards set by local expectations, national ones were not sluggish at all. Local expectations were more infused with local content. The local boats that are raised or lowered to any significant degree by national tides are not that numerous. The fact that local expectations were both more differentiated geographically and less variable longitudinally than national expectations makes perfect sense. But what if local and national information conflict? Would voters abandon the locally indicated party for the nationally favoured one? For that matter, did voters employ any of this information, and if they did, was it to strategic ends or just to jump on a bandwagon?

8 Asking the Right Question: The Campaign Agenda, Priming, and the Vote

What undid the Conservatives' early advantage? Why were the Liberals, not the NDP, the beneficiaries of Conservative misfortune? How did the Conservatives restore their fortunes? Were the dynamics the same in English and French Canada? Did the campaign – as a site for strategy and counter-strategy, as opposed to a general heightening of the political sound level – even matter?

In principle two things can happen in a campaign. One is persuasion; the campaign can move opinion and perception and these in turn can move the vote. We have seen already that each of three potential factors – FTA opinion, perceptions of John Turner, and expectations for each party – moved dramatically. How much of this movement translated into shifts in vote intentions?

The other, more intriguing, possibility is that parties seek not so much to change voters' opinions as to change the very basis of the choice. This was one of the earliest themes in electoral research (Berelson et al., 1954). It was a central preoccupation of chapter 3, which indicated that different parties had different stakes in the potentially dominant free trade issue, that all parties had an incentive to avoid the national question, and that the NDP was in an especially tight-fitting box. Chapter 6 showed that one possible route out of the box was for the NDP to emphasize its one indisputable asset, Ed Broadbent. Such moves have come to be called priming, and are at the core of our notion of "letting the people decide."

Priming is the electoral manifestation of the elite struggle for control of the agenda. To substantrate an agenda-control argument it does not suffice to look only at what actually dominates the choice. Equally important is to ask what, among plausible policy questions, is *not* on the agenda. In 1988 one obvious alternative to the FTA as a central question was the Meech Lake Accord. The accord's long-run implications for the Canadian polity rivalled those stemming from the FTA. Only a month after the election, conflict over restrictions on commercial signs in Quebec exposed the divisions registered in Figure 3-2. Showing how the accord was kept off the agenda, then, is an important part of our story. This is central to demonstrating that the campaign mattered as more than just a place for generating sound.

If priming occurs, by what method is it accomplished? Answers to this question are readily to hand: the debates and the media campaign. Not only do these events and factors change opinion about key considerations, they can also increase or decrease the very importance attached to each consideration.

However they were affected, what was the relative importance of issues, leaders, and expectations as dynamical factors? Did their impact differ between French and English Canada? One possibility is that English Canada divided over the FTA and that French Canada followed the English Canadian lead. Another is that the two electorates differed in their attentiveness to leaders. Then again, distinctions between the two electorates may have been overdrawn, especially for 1988 and its overarching issue. After all, the party positioning in Figure 3-2 reflects the fact that in 1988 all three parties sought to cut right through the ancient cleavage, to force French and English to divide the same way.

Could it be, though, that the final result was fated all along by the underlying distribution of party identification? Vote shares at the end were uncannily close to the breakdown of identifications that prevailed, according to chapter 3, from the beginning. Although we look for and find evidence of a homing instinct in party identifiers, we also find that the campaign cut through parties' bases.

POSITION-TAKING AND PRIMING

The 1988 campaign could have been about one or both of two issues: the FTA or the Meech Lake Accord. Alternatively, it could have been about which person gets to form the government. Personality and issue considerations can overlap, as shown by the "Canada-Mulroney" free trade experiment in chapter 5. If an issue such as the FTA pitted the Conservative party against the other two parties, then the campaign was also bound to raise a strategic question:

Figure 8-1
Percentage Able to Place All Three Parties on Scale

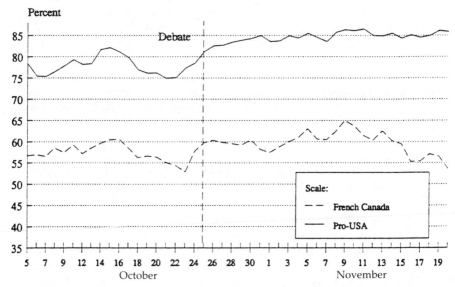

7-day moving average

Which anti-FTA party had a better chance to block the Conservatives?

How did the parties establish the campaign's issue agenda? Figures 8-1 and 8-2 tell the essence of the story: on free trade the parties worked hard at distancing themselves from each other and talked *ad nauseam* about their differences; on Meech Lake they converged and said as little as possible. Figure 8-1 makes a general comparison between the United States and French Canada as themes, with a daily tracking of respondents' ability to place all three parties on one or the other dimension (these are the party placement items that appeared earlier in Figure 3-2). Only respondents who could place themselves on the dimension in question figure in the calculation. Most striking is the distance between the lines: of those who could place themselves on the French Canada scale, only about 55 to 60 percent could also place all three parties; for the pro-United States scale, the corresponding figure was 75 to 85 percent.[2] The campaign further sharpened awareness of party positions on the pro-United States scale but not on the French Canada scale. The precise timing of the sharpening is not clear, as awareness of parties' positions wandered up and down before the debates (this was also true for the awareness of positions on the French Canada scale). What is clear is that by the end of October awareness of party po-

Figure 8-2
Placement on Pro-US Scale, by Party

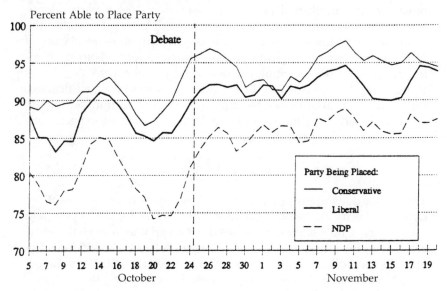

5-day moving average

sitions on the pro-United States scale reached its maximum value and stayed there for the rest of the campaign. Awareness of party positions on the French Canada dimension did not gain over the campaign. By election day, the gap between the two questions was about thirty points.

Figure 8-2 shows which parties talked most about the FTA: the Liberals and Conservatives. It may have helped that in their speech-making and advertising on the FTA, Conservatives and Liberals mentioned not just themselves but each other regularly, the Liberals from the beginning and the Conservatives once they realized they were in trouble.

The parties made voters aware of their positions on the major issue of free trade, even as they were remarkably successful at obscuring the field for the potential rival issue, French-English relations and the Meech Lake Accord. The next question is, did the parties get voters to use the strategically favoured issue in their own choices?

THE ESTIMATION OF CAMPAIGN EFFECTS

The estimation which addresses this question is necessarily complex and requires explication. First, it includes all potential factors: respondents' positions on the FTA (-1, through to $+1$); their positions on the Meech Lake Accord (also -1 to $+1$); their evaluations of each leader (feeling thermometer, o to 100); the Liberals' standing in the most recently published poll; and respondents' own party identification (three dummy variables, one for each party). Secondly, the estimation separates time-series effects – the true dynamical ones of primary interest here – from cross-sectional effects. Thirdly, it attempts to represent priming by or around the debates.

Including two issues and three leaders requires little justification. What need discussion are the time-series-cross-section setup, the representation of priming, and the representation of expectations by an external factor, poll results.

Separating Time-series and Cross-section

The estimations attempt to separate time-series from cross-section, dynamic from static. Two considerations argue for the separation: First, there is no *a priori* reason to expect a variable to have the same effect when it moves through time as when it sorts individuals relative to each other at any one time. If we do not split the variable, we risk conflating the two effects, possibly of masking them. A case in point is FTA opinion in relation to the NDP vote. At any given moment, FTA opponents should be more likely than supporters to vote NDP. Does it follow that increasing the anti-FTA share will also increase the NDP share? The discussion in chapter 1 suggested that NDP strategists did *not* expect this to happen and chapters 1 and 5, taken together, bear that expectation out: the post-debates surge of anti-FTA opinion accompanied a decline in the NDP share.

Secondly, the conflation is especially vexatious when the cross-sectional component of the variable carries unwanted baggage. In this estimation *all* variables of interest do just that. Chapter 5 indicated that FTA opinion reflected prior party identifications and that this became, if anything, even more true as the campaign progressed. Chapter 6 indicated the same for leader evaluations, especially for John Turner as his debate performance won 1984 apostates back. By including dummy variables for party identification itself we neutralize some of this projective impact. But measurement error remains; there will still be closet partisans. To the extent that the cross-sectional component of a variable carries such projective force, the coefficient on the variable would lead us to overestimate its true dynamic significance.

How then do we achieve this separation? The simplest way would be to take, for some variable, the between-day variation in daily means as the time-series component, and the within-day variation around the daily means as the cross-sectional component. This was exactly the strategy we used to estimate character and competence effects on the summary feeling thermometer rating for each leader. The major disadvantage of this approach is that a large part of what it labels as time-series variation is nothing more than sampling error. What is more, sampling error in one variable will covary with sampling error in the others; for instance, a daily replicate that comes up relatively Conservative will also come up pro-FTA, pro-Brian Mulroney, and so on. Out of this may come serious overestimation of the time-series component. In the case of the character-competence estimations, we had no choice but to adopt this strategy and this did not prejudice either factor relative to the other.

We do have a choice for the issue and leader measures. Instead of anchoring the analysis on the putative time-series indicator, the daily mean, we anchor it on the best available cross-sectional indicator – respondents' *post*-election position on the issue. Once the campaign ended, virtually all effort on persuasion and priming ceased. Parliament was summoned to pass the FTA and debate was vehement, but both opposition parties explicitly conceded the government's right to proceed. Accordingly, no temporal dynamics appeared in the post-election wave. Although the whole distribution quickly shifted in an apparently pro-FTA direction,[3] the post-election wave's cross-sectional positioning of respondents relative to each other was essentially correct. And Table 5-1 suggests that, apart from measurement error, as an indicator of cross-sectional locations within the campaign, respondents' relative location post-campaign is almost as good early as late. With the postelection FTA position in the equation as the cross-sectional indicator, the untransformed campaign-wave item becomes the best available time-series indicator.

The crux of this setup is the quality of the post-election item as an indicator of respondents' pre-election relative positions. There is no denying that precision about the initial location of an individual is lost in resorting to the post-election wave. In the end, though, we believe that any precision gained by using cross-sectional information from the campaign wave itself would be more than offset by using the sampling-error-ridden daily mean to anchor the time-series–cross-section split.[4]

The Representation of Priming

Priming appears as a shift in the time-series coefficient, that is, the coefficient on the campaign-wave item. We allow for possible shifts by creating interaction terms for each factor on which priming is plausible – the two issue factors, and each leader rating. For specific issues we have specific predictions: the impact of the FTA should increase over the campaign; such impact as we find for the Meech Lake Accord should decrease. The simplest interaction is between issue position and a pre-/post-debates temporal split: respondents interviewed after 26 Ocotber (the date of the English debate) score one, and respondents interviewed before then score zero on a dummy variable (called "debate" in the tables); this dummy variable is then multiplied by the respondent's campaign-wave issue position. The coefficient on the interaction term indicates the pre-post-debate shift. The main-effect coefficient becomes the time-series estimate for the pre-debate period; the post-debate coefficient is the sum of the main-effect coefficient and the interaction coefficient.

Polls for Expectations

For expectations, time-series effects cannot be separated from cross-sectional ones with the pre-post setup. As an inherently future-oriented factor, expectations could not be measured in the post-election wave. Direct estimation of the separate effects would have required anchoring on the campaign-wave daily mean, with all of the problems that that entails. For expectations, a comparison of particular interest is between French and English Canada. Given that the daily sample size for Quebec francophones is roughly one-third that for the rest of the electorate, sampling error in that sub-sample should be roughly twice as large as in the larger subsample; this would compromise the comparison irretrievably.

   In addition to these statistical considerations, there are good reasons to suspect that individual variation at a specific moment in the campaign is nothing more than projection and measurement error. Where we can expect real individual variation on issues and leader assessments, there is no obvious reason, except possibly ignorance about the campaign, why at any moment different people should have different expectations about parties' chances of forming the government. In fact the major source of expectations is poll results, and these vary, apart from sampling error, only over time.

   The best representation of expectations, then, and the route of least resistance, is to direct estimates of poll effects. The poll variable is the same as in chapters 4 and 7: party standings from the most recent poll. Using such a variable is *not* tantamount to having our poll track theirs, so to speak. Fieldwork for a published commercial poll takes place some days before publication and polls are not published every day. The "last-poll" reading for the typical interview date in our survey reflected commercial firms' fieldwork from about a week before. When we split the sample between French and English Canada, the data sets become even more independent, as the last-poll reading will be dominated by commercial-poll respondents outside francophone Quebec. The fact that commercial polls themselves are subject to sampling error is neither here nor there for our purposes; their samples are large and, in any case, the party shares they publish are political facts in their own right.

The connection between polls and expectations was a matter for chapter 7. Our sense is that as a proxy for expectations, polls embody roughly offsetting errors. On one hand they understate the electorate's adaptability: Liberal and Conservative expectations began to move right after the debates, before the first post-debates polls were published. On the other hand expectations respond to polls themselves somewhat sluggishly. One thing is clear, though – the last-poll variable is utterly devoid of any projective content; it is absolutely exogenous.

Last-poll standing of whom? As party shares add up to virtually 100 percent, all three parties cannot appear in a single estimation. Confining the analysis to two parties still raises problems of collinearity. The pivotal share was the Liberal one: FTA opponents ought to have compared Liberal and NDP chances; Quebec francophones may have compared Liberal and Conservative chances. The simplest way to proceed is to include only the Liberal standing.

THE ELECTORATE AS A WHOLE

The heart of this chapter is Table 8-1 and Figures 8-3 and 8-4. Table 8-1 presents three separate estimations, one for each party. In each case the dependent variable is scored one if the respondent said he or she intended to vote for the party and zero otherwise. The coefficients in the table can be read as the percentage point (typically, the fraction of a percentage point) increase in party support that comes from a unit change in the variable.[5] For most factors three lines appear in the table. Topmost is a line labelled "Pre": this is the reading on the variable from the campaign wave and stands as our estimate of the pre-debates time-series effect. Next is a line labelled "Pre x Debate": this is the coefficient for the interaction term and indicates the shift around the debates. The line labelled "Post" gives the post-election reading on this variable. This when added to "Pre" gives this cross-section estimate.

As expected, the campaign made the FTA more important and Meech Lake less important. Before the debates Meech Lake attitudes may well have had some impact, just under half the impact of shifts

Table 8-1
Time Series-Cross Section Estimation: Vote Intentions

	(Generalized least squares estimation; BON = 2,090)					
	Conservative		Liberal		NDP	
FTA Position						
Pre	0.115	(0.015)	−0.023	(0.012)	−0.021	(0.011)
Pre x Debate	0.074	(0.016)	−0.069	(0.014)	0.006	(0.012)
Post	0.042	(0.01)	−0.045	(0.011)	−0.031	(0.006)
Meech Lake Position						
Pre	*0.045*	*(0.010)*	*−0.014*	*(0.009)*	*−0.005*	*(0.008)*
Pre x Debate	*−0.047*	*(0.011)*	*0.023*	*(0.012)*	*0.015*	*(0.010)*
Post	*0.007*	*(0.006)*	*−0.001*	*(0.006)*	*−0.003*	*(0.006)*
Mulroney Rating						
Pre	0.232	(0.035)	−0.105	(0.038)	−0.106	(0.033)
Pre x Debate	−0.119	(0.036)	0.010	(0.039)	0.034	(0.035)
Post	0.041	(0.017)	−0.041	(0.020)	−0.013	(0.009)
Turner Rating						
Pre	−0.097	(0.035)	0.216	(0.039)	−0.143	(0.038)
Pre x Debate	0.000	(0.040)	0.043	(0.044)	0.040	(0.042)
Post	−0.064	(0.018)	0.022	(0.020)	−0.047	(0.020)
Broadbent Rating						
Pre	−0.108	(0.034)	−0.159	(0.036)	0.236	(0.033)
Pre x Debate	0.119	(0.036)	−0.040	(0.038)	−0.061	(0.035)
Post	−0.042	(0.020)	0.011	(0.022)	0.085	(0.021)
Liberal % Last Poll	−0.040	(0.110)	0.421	(0.122)	−0.210	(0.119)
Party Identification						
Conservative	0.314	(0.019)	−0.102	(0.014)	−0.107	(0.015)
Liberal	−0.110	(0.014)	0.429	(0.020)	−0.123	(0.015)
NDP	−0.109	(0.015)	−0.183	(0.016)	0.570	(0.022)
Constant	0.369	(0.42)	0.174	(0.046)	0.254	(0.044)
R^2	0.856		0.739		0.714	

Standard errors in parentheses

in the FTA position. This may be an overestimation for Meech, as its post-election coefficient is a nullity; perhaps cross-sectional impact is leaking into what we present as the time-series coefficient. This hardly matters, though, as the debates utterly cancelled all impact from Meech Lake attitudes; for each party the debate interaction is at least as large as the pre-debate main effect and of the opposite sign. The cancellation was especially precise in the Conservative case.

The contrast with the FTA could not be more sharp. For Conservative vote intentions, the debates increased the FTA's dynamic impact by more than half. Before the debates, moving from support to opposition reduced a voter's likelihood of choosing the Conservatives by just over 20 percent, other things being equal (the coefficient gives the effect of moving from neutrality to support or from opposition to neutrality; for the full jump from one side to the other the coefficient must be multiplied by two). After the debates, shifting from one side to the other was worth almost forty points.

For Liberal choice, the FTA's dynamic impact was between three and four times larger after than before the debates. Where early in the campaign, a shift from support to opposition added about five points to the likelihood of voting Liberal, other things being equal, after the debates the difference was between eighteen and nineteen points.

The Liberal shift was a compound of two effects. In part it was just the mirror image of the Conservative shift, reduced slightly by the fact that there were still two alternatives on the anti-FTA side. But the shift also reflected the fact that the Liberals were now winning the battle for control of that side. The NDP interaction coefficient, although small and statistically insignificant, is positive; the debates may have weakened the FTA-NDP nexus slightly.

The debates made Brian Mulroney and Ed Broadbent less relevant, at least for direct impact on party choice. Mr Mulroney's dynamic significance for Conservative choice was cut roughly in half. This was a good thing for his party, as his ratings were declining just as this happened. There is a hint that he became less important for each of the other parties as well. Ed Broadbent lost importance across the board. He was always most important for his own party and remained so to the end. But before the debates he had been as important as John Turner in Conservative choice. After the debates he ceased utterly to be a factor.

John Turner may have become more important in choice of his own party and less important for the NDP. Then again, his role may not have changed at all. Either way, the debates made John Turner stand out by default. Before the debates each leader was pivotal for his own party and was so to a remarkably equal degree. After the debates John Turner stood out: he was roughly twice as important, dynamically, for the Liberal vote as Ed Broadbent was for the NDP or Brian Mulroney for the Conservatives.

Liberal poll standings had an independent impact on the Liberal share itself and on the NDP's share, but they had no effect on the

Figure 8-3
Factors in the Conservative Fall and Rise

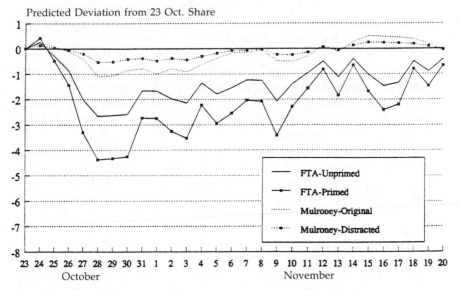

Predicted Deviation from 23 Oct. Share

5-day moving average

Conservative share. This a picture *of strategic voting*. The parties with the complementary relationship were the two opposed to the campaign's major agenda item, the FTA. The impact of polls was not small; net of all other factors in the estimation, a unit shift in the Liberals' poll standing induced roughly 0.4 point further shift. This is just the first-round impact. Unlike other factors, polls are reflexive; earlier shifts induce later ones, as their impact is registered in subsequent polls and further transmitted back into expectations and preferences.[6]

Figures 8-3 and 8-4 convert the big parts of the Table 8-1 story into pictures. In each figure, effects are presented as relative to the 23 October baseline. The date is two days before the English debate and is meant to represent the situation on the eve of the debates; the extra two days was necessitated by the five-day averaging. Wherever both the unprimed and primed lines appear for the same factor, the two lines will have same pattern – for example, both solid or both dashed. The unprimed line will have no symbol to mark the day but the primed line will have boxes as daily markers. For some factors only the primed line appears and it, too, will have boxes as markers to remind that reader that the line is primed. Only the two

Figure 8-4
Factors in the Liberal Rise and Fall

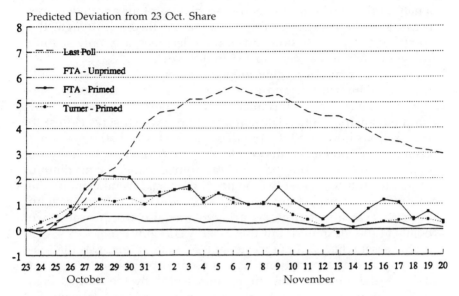

Predicted Deviation from 23 Oct. Share

5-day moving average

old parties are considered. The dynamic story for the NDP was mainly driven by expectations. As Table 8-1 indicated, other considerations – especially the one the NDP itself tried to emphasize, Ed Broadbent – were muted by the debates.

For Conservative voting, two factors merit close inspection: evaluations of Brian Mulroney, and positions on the FTA. Figure 8-3 presents each factor twice, once for what would have been its effect had the pre-debates coefficient in Table 8-1 remained in force, and once with the coefficient as it became after the debates (the sum of the main- and interaction-effect coefficients). For the FTA coefficient this is a difference between "unprimed" (solid line, no marker) and "primed" (solid line, marker); for Brian Mulroney it seems better to talk about "original" (dotted line, no marker) and "distracted" (dotted line, marker).

Had Mr Mulroney's ratings remained as important after the debates as before, their decline would have cost the Conservative party at the maximum about one point. The muting of his effect cut this already small impact in half. Either way, Mr Mulroney's popular standing was restored at the end. Much more telling was the FTA. Had the pre-debate coefficient remained in force, the shift of FTA opinion would have cost the party just under three points at the maximum. The priming of the issue increased this effect by about a half; at the maximum the party lost between four and five points because of the energization of the issue. At the end, though, the combination of persuasion and priming left the party only slightly worse off than it had been just before the debates.

For the Liberals, according to Figure 8-4, three factors stood out: the FTA, John Turner, and expectations. For the FTA (solid), Figure 8-4 gives the "unprimed' (no marker) as well as the "primed" (marker) line. The unprimed line, which stays closest to zero, reflects how small the pre-debates effect was: had the FTA not been primed, opinion shifts would have made almost no difference to the Liberal share. But the issue *was* primed and at the maximum, FTA shifts induced about two points of the total Liberal gain. By the end of the campaign, though, the FTA induction was gone. John Turner's evaluation surge, as primed, was also worth nearly two points at the maximum, but this asset was also wasted.

One asset which did not waste, at least not entirely, was the self-fulfilling one of expectations, as represented by poll standings. At its peak the Liberals' poll surge, represented by the dashed line, was worth nearly six points, about 60 percent of the total gain. By the time the polls peaked, the FTA and Turner readings were on the way down. By election day, the poll induction was also telling against the Liberals but was still worth some three points relative to the 23 October baseline.

The phenomenon at work here was strategic voting. Shifts in polls and expectations helped consolidate the anti-FTA vote. Recall from Figure 1-1 that the Conservatives could expect to benefit from the fragmentation of the rest of the vote. Blocking a Conservative majority required both that the Conservatives' own vote share be cut and that the rest of the vote be consolidated.

There may still have been an irony in this consolidation of the national Liberal total, which we can only sketch here in outline. It may be true that national information defined who could form a majority government. It may also be true that national poll information registered in voters' consciousness more clearly than did local information. Even so, stopping the Conservatives had to be done one constituency at a time. To this objective, local information was critical to defining the locally feasible alternatives. To the extent that national information overrode local information, voters may have been induced to support a party, whatever its national standing, whose local chances were still negligible. In particular, the Liberal wave in the west, documented in chapter 1, may have saved some Conservative candidates from defeat by the NDP.

The general point is not that national expectations by themselves overrode local ones. The Liberal surge also reflected John Turner's rehabilitation. But perceptions of leaders and expectations for the national outcome had this in common: the *dynamic* component in each was geographically uniform. Given the geographically non-uniform starting points for the surge, the operation of the two spatially homogeneous factors, where the Liberals were initially weak, tugged *against* the logic of the electoral system.

Was the Liberal party simply "famous for being famous," the beneficiary of accidental good fortune? In one sense this had to be true. In fact the NDP had undoubted advantages: it ought to have been more credible than the Liberals on the FTA; Ed Broadbent's standing was much higher than John Turner's and chapter 6 indicated that this was not obviously the result of his party's irrelevance. Table 8-1 indicates that Mr Broadbent ceased to be a factor in the campaign only as his party was dealt out of the race. On the other hand the NDP had two major strategic disadvantages that its exalted standing on the eve of the debates papered over: its historic weakness in French Canada, and its identification with the union movement. Its own base of identifiers was still small – only half the size of the Liberals'. But the Liberals could mobilize their base only if they could solve their leadership problem. Many of those who entered the Liberal fold after the debates were just coming home, a pattern to which we return at the end of this chapter. It was not so much that Liberal expectations were artificially high at the end as that they had been at an historic low earlier on.

ONE ELECTORATE OR TWO?

In most essentials, French and English Canada were similar or complementary. In two ways, however, the electorates differed. Issue positions and leader ratings actually shifted more – and thus imparted more dynamics – in French than in English Canada. And one factor, the polls, behaved quite differently between electorates. These patterns emerge from Tables 8-2 and 8-3, which repeat the basic time-series–cross-section analysis separately for Quebec francophones and for English Canada, and Figures 8-5 and 8-6, which flesh out the story with pictures.

The impact of a unit shift on the FTA was more important in English Canada than in francophone Quebec. In cross-sectional

Table 8-2
"English Canada." Time Series-Cross Section Estimation: Vote Intentions

	(Generalized least squares estimation; BON = 1,690)					
	Conservative		Liberal		NDP	
FTA Position						
Pre	0.121	(0.017)	−0.047	(0.014)	−0.007	(0.011)
Pre x Debate	0.071	(0.017)	−0.052	(0.016)	−0.005	(0.013)
Post	0.025	(0.011)	−0.025	(0.012)	−0.041	(0.010)
Meech Lake Position						
Pre	0.041	(0.011)	−0.006	(0.010)	−0.022	(0.010)
Pre x Debate	−0.039	(0.012)	0.007	(0.012)	0.026	(0.011)
Post	0.008	(0.006)	0.003	(0.007)	−0.002	(0.006)
Mulroney Rating						
Pre	0.195	(0.038)	−0.082	(0.046)	−0.079	(0.038)
Pre x Debate	−0.110	(0.039)	0.013	(0.045)	0.044	(0.038)
Post	0.066	(0.022)	−0.034	(0.026)	−0.037	(0.025)
Turner Rating						
Pre	−0.084	(0.040)	0.195	(0.047)	−0.089	(0.042)
Pre x Debate	−0.011	(0.045)	0.053	(0.054)	0.015	(0.047)
Post	0.003	(0.019)	0.020	(0.023)	0.044	(0.020)
Broadbent Rating						
Pre	−0.080	(0.037)	−0.145	(0.042)	0.207	(0.036)
Pre x Debate	0.097	(0.039)	−0.025	(0.044)	−0.056	(0.038)
Post	−0.061	(0.021)	0.007	(0.025)	0.101	(0.022)
Liberal % Last Poll	0.024	(0.116)	0.378	(0.137)	−0.231	(0.124)
Party Identification						
Conservative	0.343	(0.022)	−0.150	(0.018)	−0.092	(0.015)
Liberal	−0.097	(0.015)	0.409	(0.024)	−0.130	(0.016)
NDP	−0.095	(0.016)	−0.218	(0.021)	0.577	(0.024)
Constant	0.329	(0.045)	0.203	(0.053)	0.230	(0.047)
R^2	0.860		0.748		0.713	

Standard errors in parentheses.

terms, the reverse appears to have been true; at any cross-section the FTA was a better predictor of party choice among Quebec francophones than among English Canadians. The debates primed the issue to almost exactly the same degree in each electorate. In both French and English Canada, the FTA was pivotal.

But recall that for the FTA the debates were more persuasive in

Table 8-3
Quebec Francophones. Time Series-Cross Section Estimation: Vote Intentions

	N = 400) (Generalized least squares estimation; BON = 400)					
	Conservative		Liberal		NDP	
FTA Position						
Pre	0.068	(0.036)	0.039	(0.019)	−0.104	(0.024)
Pre x Debate	0.079	(0.042)	−0.088	(0.028)	0.005	(0.033)
Post	0.093	(0.028)	−0.090	(0.021)	−0.011	(0.021)
Meech Lake Position						
Pre	0.042	(0.029)	−0.066	(0.021)	0.059	(0.020)
Pre x Debate	−0.045	(0.037)	0.105	(0.029)	−0.057	(0.032)
Post	0.002	(0.018)	−0.001	(0.010)	−0.029	(0.018)
Mulroney Rating						
Pre	0.424	(0.106)	−0.072	(0.074)	−0.185	(0.082)
Pre x Debate	−0.154	(0.016)	−0.146	(0.087)	0.167	(0.100)
Post	0.042	(0.038)	−0.012	(0.031)	−0.014	(0.011)
Turner Rating						
Pre	−0.026	(0.095)	0.302	(0.072)	−0.298	(0.097)
Pre x Debate	−0.027	(0.110)	0.013	(0.086)	0.061	(0.112)
Post	−0.061	(0.075)	(0.141)	(0.053)	0.032	(0.075)
Broadbent Rating						
Pre	−0.194	(0.093)	−0.238	(0.074)	0.413	(0.087)
Pre x Debate	0.202	(0.103)	−0.050	(0.069)	−0.123	(0.087)
Post	0.027	(0.068)	0.008	(0.057)	−0.046	(0.066)
Liberal % Last Poll	−0.574	(0.351)	0.783	(0.272)	−0.118	(0.353)
Party Identification						
Conservative	0.211	(0.041)	−0.009	(0.022)	−0.063	(0.031)
Liberal	−0.158	(0.043)	0.366	(0.037)	−0.089	(0.033)
NDP	−0.216	(0.048)	−0.084	(0.031)	0.501	(0.053)
Constant	0.502	(0.129)	−0.034	(0.098)	0.286	(0.120)
R²	0.819		0.734		0.754	

Standard errors in parentheses

French than in English Canada; the post-debates drop was bigger and more abrupt in francophone Quebec (Figure 5-6). Figures 8-5 and 8-6 show how this fed through to the vote. At the maximum, the FTA cut three points off the Conservative share in English Canada, while in francophone Quebec the maximum impact was about five points. Outside Quebec the FTA recovery began immediately

Figure 8-5
English Canada Key Factors – Conservative Share

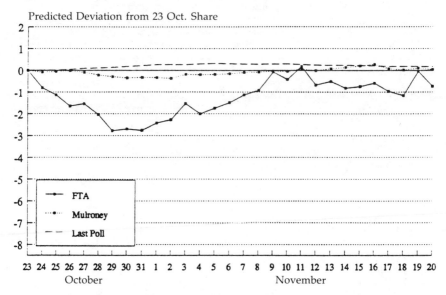

Predicted Deviation from 23 Oct. Share

7-day moving average

and this, too, is reflected in Figure 8-5. In francophone Quebec, conversely, the FTA reversal did not start until the campaign's second-last weekend.

In neither group was Meech Lake significant. Almost every aspect of the issue was identical between the two groups: the same trivially small post-election (cross-section) coefficient; the same pre-debates coefficient; and the same flattening of the effect after the debates. The fact that the issue was dormant even in francophone Quebec was a tribute to the effectiveness of the elite consensus.

For leaders the pattern was complementary. The marginal impact of each leader was greater in the electorate in which he was less at home, where his evaluations were the most problematic. A unit shift in Brian Mulroney's evaluation was twice as important dynamically outside Quebec as inside the province, and exactly the opposite was true for Ed Broadbent; for each leader the ratio was the same before and after the debates. Shifts in John Turner's ratings were one and a half times as important in Quebec as in English Canada, a ratio which diminished slightly after the debates.

But Figures 8-5 and 8-6 remind us yet again that marginal impact is not the only way to look upon a factor. The figures compare

Figure 8-6
Quebec Francophones Key Factors – Conservative Share

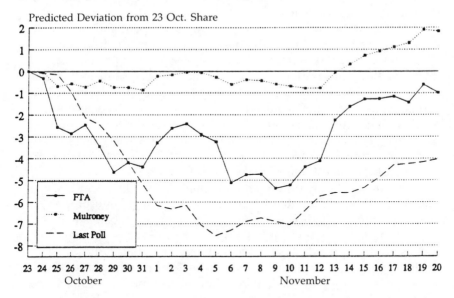

Predicted Deviation from 23 Oct. Share

7-day moving average

Mr Mulroney's impact between electorates. Evaluations of him had virtually no impact in English Canada, and very little in Quebec until the end, when the Quebec electorate evidently rallied to him – a rally worth two points over the 23 October baseline.

The two electorates differed profoundly in one crucial way: in the structure of poll effects. Outside Quebec, polls motivated strategic voting; the tradeoff was between the two anti-FTA parties, the Liberals and the NDP. In French Canada, Liberal poll standing had no real effect on the NDP share. Its effect on the Liberals' own share was huge. But the Liberals' poll standing also affected the Conservative share. Figures 8-5 and 8-6 drive the point home. In English Canada the small positive coefficient is reflected in a poll effect which barely rises above the zero line. If the Liberals' poll standing did anything in this electorate, it forced a consolidation of the pro-FTA vote. In fact, the only really sustainable interpretation is that polls had no independent impact on the subsequent Conservative vote. Among Quebec francophones polls accelerated the Conservative post-debates decline. At the maximum, poll indications of Liberal strength stripped about seven points off the Conservative share. The modest strengthening of the Conservative poll share (the result of shifts in English Canada) helped bring the Conservatives back up, eventually, in French Canada. By election day the net poll-induced loss was about four points.

This is evidence for a bandwagon. Earlier chapters indicated that bandwagons have not been the historical norm in Quebec. Concertation of behaviour has always made sense for Quebec francophones. But concertation has not traditionally been to follow the English-Canadian lead. Only with Brian Mulroney's accession to the Conservative leadership did both major parties become acceptable in French Canada. Once both were acceptable, the logic of francophone Québécois concertation could shift and a bandwagon psychology become possible. A bandwagon may have occurred in 1984 and no other interpretation makes sense for 1988.

If one focused only on the Liberal equation for Quebec, the coefficient on the poll variable would admit a strategic interpretation. The fact that the poll coefficient is bigger in the Liberal than the Conservative estimation suggests that two processes – strategic voting as well as a bandwagon – were at work for that party.

But no strategic story can be told for the Conservative share. There was no last-choice threat that required abandonment of the Conservatives in favour of the better-placed Liberals. The effect cannot be explained away by sampling variance in the small Quebec francophone subsample. The poll measure is, as we have said, truly exogenous, all the more so for being dominated by the behaviour of English-Canadian commercial-poll respondents. Every alternative hypothesis is already represented directly in the estimation.

A bandwagon is not necessarily a stampede. Had the 1988 version carried through, it would not have produced the Liberal hegemony in Quebec typical of earlier elections; the Liberal starting point was just too far back. At its maximum the poll induction would have brought the Conservatives from somewhere in the 50 percent range down to somewhere in the high 40s. The 1988 bandwagon just made Quebec more competitive; ironically, it became more like the rest of the electorate. In any case, the bandwagon stalled. It began with the first post-debates polls and peaked with the 7 November Gallup rogue poll.

EXTERNAL SOURCES OF CAMPAIGN DYNAMICS

Debates

We know already that direct exposure to a debate was critical to judgments on the leaders, at least for the first few days after the

Figure 8-7
Debate Viewership and the Liberal Vote

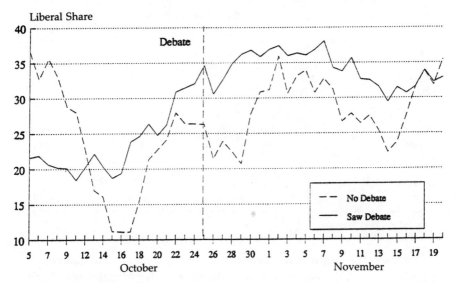

Liberal Share

7-day moving average
Debate viewership from post-election

event. Direct exposure was not critical, however, to opinion on the
FTA. Judgments on leaders and opinions on the FTA, in turn, had
a direct impact on the vote. After the debates the FTA became more
important and judgments on two of three leaders less important.
Exactly what role did the debates play in this priming and distracting
of voters? To answer this question we focus on the debates' prime
beneficiary, the Liberal party.

Seeing a debate made a sizable short-run difference to the vote,
according Figure 8-7. Debate viewership is assessed, again, from
the post-campaign question to help separate the impact of the debate
proper from abiding characteristics of people who are motivated to
watch debates. Recall, for instance, that Liberal and Conservative
identifiers were disproportionately represented in the debate audience. The daily pattern is a familiar one: in the days right after the
debates the Liberal share began to grow immediately in the debate-
viewer group, whereas no growth was evident in the non-viewer
group. By about 29 October the vote gap between those who had
seen a debate and those who had not was over ten points. Then it
began to close and by 3 November it had effectively disappeared.

The debates had a direct impact on their audience and an indirect
effect on those not in the audience. Were those who saw a debate

Table 8-4
Persuasion, Priming, and Debate Exposure Liberal Vote Intentions

| | (Selected coefficients from full estimation) | | | |
	No Debate		Saw Debate	
FTA				
Main	0.002	(0.021)	−0.044	(0.015)
Interaction	−0.070	(0.024)	−0.064	(0.017
Total	−0.068		−0.108	
TURNER				
Main	0.343	(0.069)	0.133	(0.048)
Interaction	−0.163	(0.070)	0.154	(0.060)
Total	0.180		0.287	
POLLS				
Main	0.600	(0.248)	0.364	(0.140)

Standard errors in parentheses.

and those who did not affected in the same way by persuasion and priming? Or did debates prime only those who actually watched them? To answer this question we must "go inside the heads" of each group. Table 8-4 and the charts based on it, Figures 8-8 and 8-9, do this. Although the focus in Table 8-4 is on three variables only – the FTA, ratings of John Turner, and the last poll reading – the table is based on an estimation in each group identical to that in tables 8-1 to 8-3. The main effect coefficient can be read as indicating the general responsiveness of the group to persuasion on a factor. The interaction indicates how responsive each group is to the fact that the debate happened. As the interaction is, in effect, averaged across the whole post-debates period, it is less than ideal as an indicator of the short-run impact of debate exposure. But it is the best we can do under the circumstances.

The FTA was clearly much more important dynamically for viewers of the debates than for non-viewers. Indeed, before the debates, non-viewers simply did not connect shifts of FTA position to Liberal vote intentions. Each group was primed after the debates by roughly the same amount. This still left the pre-election FTA coefficient about two-thirds again as large among viewers as among non-viewers. Before the debates, John Turner appears to have been more important for non-viewers than for viewers. After the debates he became less important for those who did not actually see one. For debate viewers, Turner ratings were primed. Of course, this priming accompanied that group's re-evaluation of Mr Turner. Finally, non-

Figure 8-8
Simulated Impact of Key Factors: Debate Viewers

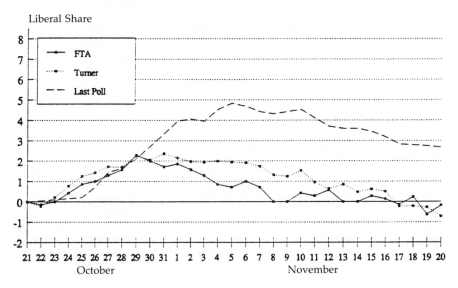

Liberal Share

7-day moving average
Debate viewership from post-election

viewers were more responsive to polls than were viewers. And poll information, as a potential factor in Liberal choice, did not begin to change until four days after the English debate.

Figures 8-8 and 8-9 take the critical factors into the daily tracking. The FTA and Turner lines in each figure represent the effect of movement in opinion or evaluation as primed – to the extent that the factor was indeed primed – by the debates. Accordingly, these lines have daily markers. As the impact of poll standing is unprimed, no markers appear.

For debate viewers, movement in Liberal intentions was a compound of factors. Critically, the two factors which moved immediately for debate viewers – FTA opinion and evaluations of John Turner – were important in lifting the Liberal line right after the debates. Polls also helped and in the long run supplied the only enduring dynamic boost. But, as estimated here, they could not begin to work until 30 October.

For non-viewers, polls were the key factor. Although FTA opinion did move among non-viewers, its impact on vote intentions was not as dramatic, even when primed, as for viewers. Evaluations of John Turner had no more than a marginal impact and were slow to

Figure 8-9
Simulated Impact of Key Factors: Debate Non-Viewers

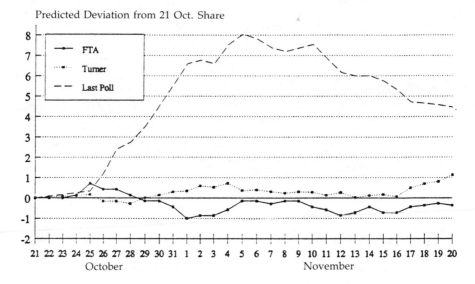

Predicted Deviation from 21 Oct. Share

7-day moving average
Debate viewership from post-election

change in this group. Once polls kicked in, however, they took the Liberal share in this group even further up than they had for debate watchers. Where debate viewers sharpened their opinions of John Turner and the FTA and tightened the links between these opinions and their vote preference, the non-viewer group, (who not only missed the debates but who were generally less interested in the campaign and knew less about it), relied on the hoopla, including polls, generated by John Turner's debate performance – rather than the performance itself – to increase their support for the Liberals. This resembles the way in which victories in American presidential primaries and caucuses increase support for candidates even among voters who know little about them (Bartels, 1988; Brady and Johnston, 1987).

If non-watchers were reacting to others' post-debate reactions, were debate watchers reacting to the event they actually witnessed? The answer must be a qualified positive. On the FTA, watchers were not primed any more than non-watchers. Conceivably, a temporally more fine-grained setup might indicate that debate watchers were primed more quickly than non-watchers, even if the total post-debates effect was the same for each group. On the estimation here, however, we must conclude that much of the exposure group difference inheres in the groups themselves. In other words, the kind of person who seeks a debate out is the kind of person to whom the campaign's key issue matters a lot.

On John Turner, however, the picture is different and, taken together with information from chapter 6, makes a case for true priming from direct debate exposure. Only for debate viewers did John Turner become more important after the debates (why John Turner actually became less important for non-watchers is a mystery). As well, chapters 4 and 6 revealed that debate viewers were much quicker than non-viewers to re-evaluate John Turner. Moreover, the aspect of Mr Turner most vitally affected by the debates was his competence. The debates evidently exerted their greatest direct impact on the biggest question about the Liberal party: was its leader up to the job? The compounding of a re-evaluation of Mr Turner and priming of that re-evaluation as a factor in the Liberal vote was exclusive to voters exposed to the debates and appears to be the effect, not the cause, of that exposure.

The Media

Here we concentrate on the Conservative vote. For the critical post-debates period, the Liberal vote, roughly, complemented the Conservative one. The NDP was dealt out of the game and was neither a target nor a major contributor in the central battle over John Turner and the FTA. We open with a comprehensive setup, quickly pare it down, and then look at the tracking generated by the pared-down estimation.

The comprehensive estimation appears in Table 8-5. As in estimations for opinion on the FTA, the two FTA media variables just do not have much cumulative, interpretable effect. Third-party advertising on the FTA has the right sign cumulatively but exhibits huge standard errors and, concomitantly, highly unstable individual coefficients. News treatment of the FTA seems more stable but has a perverse effect: positive coverage of the FTA reduces the Conservative vote share. Estimates here may have succumbed to the multicollinearity remarked on when these variables were introduced in chapter 5. The two Turner variables have plausible effects, just as they did in earlier chapters. Both groups have the right sign and the cumulative advertising effect seems especially stable. Once again, the indication is obvious: further estimations should employ Turner media variables only.

Table 8-5
The Media and the Conservative Vote, Whole Sample

| | (Generalized least squares estimation; $N=2{,}760$) | | | |
	Turner		FTA	
News				
1	−0.000	(0.007)	0.054	(0.034)
2	−0.001	(0.007)	−0.027	(0.029)
3	0.001	(0.007)	0.039	(0.036)
4	−0.011	(0.007)	−0.102	(0.031)
5	−0.001	(0.007)	0.133	(0.036)
6	−0.010	(0.007)	−0.038	(0.028)
Total	−0.022	(0.017)	0.059	(0.079)
Advertisements				
1	0.001	(0.003)	0.002	(0.003)
2	−0.010	(0.004)	0.007	(0.004)
3	0.004	(0.004)	−0.001	(0.005)
4	−0.006	(0.005)	−0.011	(0.004)
5	0.009	(0.005)	−0.010	(0.005)
6	−0.019	(0.005)	−0.007	(0.006)
Total	−0.021	(0.011)	−0.020	(0.011)
Covariates				
PC Ident	0.461	(0.019)		
Lib Ident	−0.286	(0.019)		
NDP Ident	−0.305	(0.020)		
Quebec	0.108	(0.014)		
Education	0.009	(0.003)		
Intercept	0.307	(0.028)		
R^2	0.657			

Standard errors in parentheses.

These are embodied in Table 8-6. Now *news* treatment of John Turner dominates. The effect remains as plausible as before and now seems much more stable than the advertising pattern. Advertising has virtually disappeared from view. Conceivably, the power of Turner advertising in Table 8-5 is the adventitious product of the presence of the perverse effects from FTA news and advertising. That news and advertising should be functionally linked to each other and across domains is entirely reasonable; this was a theme in chapter 4, after all. But that Turner advertising should somehow be designed to offset perversities in other advertising or news channels makes no sense. Why, for instance, would Liberals boost positive mentions of John Turner to offset good news about the FTA if that good news *harms* the Conservatives? The path of least re-

Table 8-6
Turner Media Variables and the Conservative Vote, Whole Sample
and by Media Exposure

	Total		Low		High	
		(Generalized least squares estimation)				
News						
1	0.001	(0.005)	0.019	(0.007)	−0.026	(0.007)
2	−0.002	(0.005)	−0.022	(0.008)	0.004	(0.006)
3	−0.008	(0.006)	0.002	(0.009)	0.007	(0.008)
4	−0.014	(0.006)	−0.016	(0.009)	−0.000	(0.007)
5	−0.010	(0.006)	−0.014	(0.009)	−0.008	(0.007)
6	−0.005	(0.005)	0.001	(0.008)	−0.023	(0.007)
Total	−0.038	(0.013)	−0.030	(0.020)	−0.060	(0.017)
Advertisements						
1	0.003	(0.003)	0.002	(0.004)	0.006	(0.003)
2	−0.001	(0.002)	0.008	(0.004)	−0.004	(0.003)
3	0.002	(0.003)	−0.002	(0.004)	0.005	(0.003)
4	−0.001	(0.002)	−0.012	(0.004)	0.008	(0.003)
5	−0.002	(0.002)	−0.001	(0.004)	−0.002	(0.003)
6	−0.002	(0.002)	0.003	(0.003)	−0.005	(0.003)
Total	−0.001	(0.006)	−0.002	(0.009)	0.008	(0.007)
Covariates						
PC Ident	0.457	(0.019)	0.457	(0.027)	0.473	(0.026)
Lib Ident	−0.288	(0.020)	−0.323	(0.027)	−0.245	(0.026)
NDP Ident	−0.318	(0.020)	−0.335	(0.027)	−0.292	(0.027)
Quebec	0.104	(0.015)	0.089	(0.021)	0.120	(0.019)
Education	0.007	(0.003)	0.001	(0.004)	0.012	(0.003)
Intercept	0.325	(0.024)	0.375	(0.033)	0.268	(0.032)
R^2	0.639		0.662		0.688	
N	2,760		1,190		1,566	

sistance seems to be to accept that Turner advertising, however important it was to opinion on the FTA and to opinion on John Turner himself, did not produce straightforward effects on the vote bottom line. The most reasonable view is that the greatest direct effect on the vote came from how John Turner was treated in the news. We will outline the shape of the news effect in a moment.

Claims about media effects are more plausible the more obviously they are conditioned on respondents' actual exposure to the very media in question. Arguments here need to be made with some care. There is a powerful case to be made that, confounded with the effect of exposure, is an effect that might be called "yielding"; factors which increase one's probability of exposure to a stimulus also decrease one's likelihood of yielding to its persuasive content.

The earliest formulation of something like this argument was in the Yale studies of attitude change and social influence (see especially Hovland and Janis, 1959, and the brilliant synthesis in McGuire, 1969). The earliest political application was Converse (1962), although at the time Converse himself apparently did not see the parallel between his own work and the Yale studies. It has since been drawn explicitly by Zaller (1990; 1991).

As it happens, exposure effects, also part of Table 8-6, stand by themselves. Exposure is measured by the simple addition of scores on the following items: number of days in the past week the respondent watched television news; the score on an item asking how much attention the respondent paid to campaign news on television; whether or not the respondent saw television commercials for any party; the number of days in the past week the respondent read a daily newspaper; and the score on an item asking how much attention the respondent paid to newspaper articles on the campaign. For simplicity of presentation the index is split as closely to the median as possible.

News of John Turner had a dramatically bigger effect in the high-exposure than in the low-exposure group. The cumulative news effect was twice as large and the pattern of individual coefficients was clearer. In the low-exposure group, party identification played a slightly larger role.

What this produces dynamically appears in Figure 8-10. The Conservative share is predicted to hit bottom earlier in the high-exposure group and to drop further. The predicted net drop is 60 percent larger in the high-exposure group and the predicted net recovery is also slightly larger. Although the pattern of overshooting that began to appear in chapter 1 is visible for both exposure groups, the peak was reached earlier in the high-exposure group.

The news pattern mirrors the vote only imperfectly, however. It works best where competing explanations for shifts are also most plausible: right after the debates. The news treatment predicts a Conservative recovery, indeed almost all of the net recovery that actually occurred. But the predicted time path for recovery departs significantly from the actual one. There is some evidence in both exposure groups for a surge predicted near the beginning of the last week. But its size is small, much less than actually occurred.

So far as our estimations go, the late Conservative surge and Liberal collapse do not seem to be simple media phenomena. The impact of the media appears to be have been indirect, to have worked through perceptions of John Turner and, most critically, FTA opinion. These factors were each affected by both advertising and news.

Figure 8-10
The News and the Conservative Share: Simulated Impact by Exposure Level

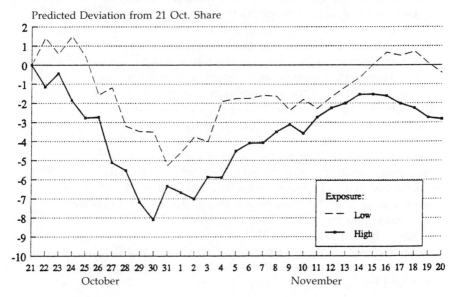

Predicted Deviation from 21 Oct. Share

Exposure:
- - Low
—•— High

21 22 23 24 25 26 27 28 29 30 31 1 2 3 4 5 6 7 8 9 10 11 12 13 14 15 16 17 18 19 20
October   November

7-day moving average

For John Turner, advertising was critical to the late drop in his ratings and this drop was estimated to induce about one point of the total Liberal drop (Figure 8-4). Both advertising and news figured in the recovery of FTA support at the campaign's end (Figure 5-12). The FTA surge was clearly important to the Conservatives' own surge; Figure 8-3 indicates that about two points of the total surge were attributable to the sudden movement in FTA opinion.

As we estimate them, media effects seem more critical for anterior issue and leader factors than directly for the vote itself. This pattern can be read in either methodological or substantive ways, which shade into each other. We may have reached the limits of our statistical microscope when we try to discern the impact of media variables – especially of advertising, which was restrained from having any impact until the last half of the campaign – on a dependent variable as grossly measured and as distant from the media stimulus as the voting decision. Both FTA opinion and leader ratings are more finely measured than the vote and, for that reason alone, more sensitive to media effects. These two factors were also more proximate, in voters' own minds, to the media variables and closer in content to the specific types of media stimuli. Indeed, it would be

disturbing if news and advertising about John Turner had their greatest impact on anything other than evaluation of the man himself. It
is also substantively appropriate that next in line should be the FTA.
All negative advertising about John Turner was also about the FTA:
he was said to be misleading the Canadian people about the agreement and doing so to save his own job, not anybody else's. Much
of Mr Turner's positive news coverage followed the English debate,
where his rhetorical competence was demonstrated in the FTA context. Finally, there is a question of chronology. The issue and leader
factors that carried media effects into the vote did not themselves
always move on the same time path as the vote. Advertising and
the rhetoric carried by the news do not just tell people how to vote,
they give specific reasons, about leaders and issues. The critical thing
for parties is to get the reasons in place and to get them in place
early enough. If the reasons are there, the vote will follow, but a
few days may be required for the issue-leader-vote nexus to crys-
tallize. The implication for this chapter's estimations is that coefficients may be small and unstable. This should not distract us from
the power of the media effects further back up the chain, on the
FTA and on evaluations of John Turner.

THE CAMPAIGN AND THE ALIGNMENT OF PARTIES

Was the result simply preordained and all the talk of debates and
media little more than a diversion? There is no denying the striking
similarity between the distribution of identifications in Table 3-1 and
Figure 3-1 and the final weekend's distribution of vote intentions
in Figure 1-4. Perhaps party identification really is, as we characterized it earlier, *deus ex machina*.

The study of elections continues to feel a powerful influence from
the first studies of campaigns, the "Columbia School" volumes
(Lazarsfeld et al., 1968; Berelson et al,. 1954). These studies argued
that the active features of the campaign had no more than minimal
effects, that the dynamics vote intentions did exhibit were the product of voters awakening to their prior partisan commitments. Although, as we acknowledged in the introduction, the view
articulated in those volumes no longer holds sway among communications researchers (Chaffee, 1975), students of elections – of
American elections, at least – still emphasize the power of long-term
factors, of elements in place before a campaign commences. The
1988 campaign itself supplies ample evidence for the directive force
of background party commitments. Chapter 5 showed how FTA

Figure 8-11
Defection Rates for Liberal and Conservative Identifiers

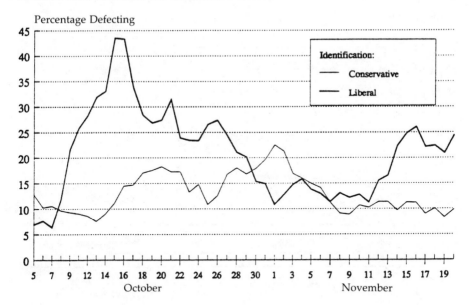

Percentage Defecting

Identification:
—— Conservative
—— Liberal

October   November

7-day moving average

opinion became more consistently partisan over the campaign. Chapter 6 indicated that the re-evaluation of John Turner was greatest in the group with the most at stake in re-evaluating him – 1984 apostates.

Perhaps, then, only issues and perceptions that reinforce prior party commitments will ever be activated. Their activation may not even require the application of external stimuli to the electorate beyond the scheduling of a date by which voters must focus their minds. Alternatively, the absence of force and, thus, of activation may not matter because issues and perceptions are only epiphenomena, where the essential thing is party identification.

Figure 8-11 tracks defection rates for the two main parties and invites us to ask if what we see is merely the inevitable restoration of a partisan equilibrium. An argument along these lines might be teased out of the Conservative tracking. The middle of the campaign certainly produced a surge in defection, but the endgame restored the already very low defection rate that prevailed at the opening. No such argument can be constructed for the Liberals. The defection rate at the end was slightly smaller than it was on the eve of the debates, but was strikingly larger than it had been for the first two

Figure 8-12
Vote Intentions of Non-partisans

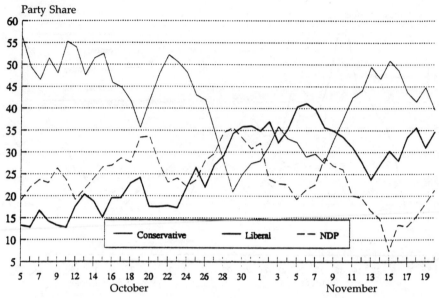

7-day moving average

weeks in November. Nor can it be said that the Liberal defection surge in the last week itself restored defection rates to some sort of notional equilibrium value. Given the party identification breakdown in Table 3-1, the rate of Liberal defection in the last week was much higher than such a simple restoration would imply. Although we should expect smaller parties to have higher rates of defection than larger parties, the difference in Figure 8-11 is grossly out of scale with the ratios implicit in Table 3-1.[7] On party identification grounds alone the Liberals should have done better, or the Conservatives, worse than they actually did.

Besides, roughly one-third of our sample resisted the lure of party identification. Not surprisingly, according to Figure 8-12 the amplitude was greater for non-partisans' swings than for identifiers' defection rates. But the discrepancy between identifiers and non-partisans was pronounced in only one place: after the debates. In Conservative intentions, non-partisans fell two and a half to three times as far as Conservative identifiers. Liberal identifiers, conversely, surged back to their party at a faster clip than non-partisans. Thus far, non-partisans supplied yeast to the mix even as party identification groups behaved according to type.

At the end, though, identifiers were no less responsive to the short-term forces of the campaign than non-partisans. The late Conservative surge and Liberal decline spanned ten to fifteen points in each group. Non-partisans supplied the overreaction at the beginning of the last weekend, but they also, so to speak, corrected themselves. By the last weekend the net gain and loss was hardly distinguishable between identifiers and non-partisans. Whatever the campaign did at the end, it did to partisans and non-partisans alike. Within party identification groups the pattern is not one of preordained equilibration. Party identifiers, although far more likely than non-partisans to support their long-standing preference, were nonetheless dynamically available, at the margin. In 1988, at least, the votes that made the difference between winning and losing had to be fought for.

DISCUSSION

The 1988 campaign, then, substantiates claims for the importance of strategy and counter-strategy. Post-debate movement in evaluation of the leaders was consistent with the near-consensus on what happened in the debates. Opinion shifts on the FTA responded to parties' rhetorical initiatives. The very emphasis on the FTA was far from inevitable; the subject dominated because party organizations laboured to make it do so. And they worked hard at the task because their strategic interests forced them to. While parties commonly work to activate interests in their own camp and thus to reinforce long-standing patterns, they also work to split other party camps and they choose which interests within their own camp to activate. Party identification sets bounds on the possible but ample scope remains for strategic manipulation.

Voters are sensitive to that manipulation. Sensitivities are organized by prior party commitment but the organization is not airtight. The campaign can penetrate partisan boundaries. Coalitions can be split. Voters are strikingly sensitive to news about the campaign, and voters who report an interest in the news are responsive to information they gather and not just so as to reinforce their predispositions. But news is episodic, and cannot be controlled indefinitely by any party. Advertising can be controlled, at least for a week or so. Although voters almost certainly do not seek advertising out, it does ultimately catch up with many of them and it does permit repetition of a message which has been found to be persuasive. The impact of advertising on the bottom line – the vote – may be indirect but it is not obviously trivial.

Many voters, in any case, are perfectly capable of taking in politically relevant information directly. They watch debates in great
numbers and, in 1988 at least, converged quickly on an interpretation
of the event. Convergence was quickest for those who had actually
seen a debate. The effacement of the debate's impact was not automatic. In the early going all effacement was, so to speak, cross-
sectional: the convergence of non-viewers on viewers.[8] The impact
of actual exposure to a debate was most distinctive for evaluation
of the men who participated in it.

Had the debates not happened, there is every indication that the
Conservatives would have coasted home. It is even possible that the
NDP would have formed the official opposition. Had the NDP done
so, its frontrunner strategy would have been vindicated. Chapters 3 and 6 indicated that a leadership emphasis and an under-
playing of the FTA made sense for the NDP. To the extent that they
could control events, they seem to have made the correct choice.
They could not control events, of course, but John Turner's debate
victory was no more preordained than the subsequent dissipation
of the advantage that the victory gave him. The Liberals, after all,
did not need an outright seat majority to win. But they did need to
energize the FTA and, in the same event, to establish their credibility
on the issue. The debate gave John Turner the chance to do both
things and he seized it.

Shifts after the debates – the reversal of FTA opinion, Turner perceptions, and vote shares – were not automatic, nor did they appear
to be the inevitable decay of an ephemeral impulse. The time path
of the shift suggests that the Conservatives had to work to win the
election back. The media analyses indicate some of the routes by
which the task was accomplished. Merely to establish that media
factors played a role is an important first step toward a theory of
campaign dynamics. The analyses also reveal how much distance
still needs to be travelled. The chronology of the campaign alerts us
to the possibility that movement in key factors – including in media
variables – does not necessarily track linearly and additively into
movement in votes. Vote shifts may be anticipated by shifts in other
factors, but when they finally arrive, they can do so with astonishing
speed.

Party Strategy and the Dynamics of Campaigns

The 1988 Canadian campaign poses fundamental challenges to electoral studies. The discipline's most highly formalized and elegant theoretical paradigm predicts that on key issues parties will converge on the median voter. In 1988 the parties converged on one key issue but divided sharply over the other. At the same time, it seems to be widely held in the discipline that campaigns do not matter. The 1988 campaign did. The way in which 1988 mattered suggests that, at some level, *all* campaigns matter, even when they do not exhibit the spectacular ups and downs of 1988.

The 1988 election also poses a challenge to the Canadian people. The issue the parties suppressed, the national question in its 1988 guise as the Meech Lake Accord, has always lurked in the background of Canadian politics, and has often surged to the foreground. Tension over the national question, especially if accompanied by economic distress, seems to be the midwife of party realignment. Since 1988 it may have played this role again.

The 1988 campaign revolved around fundamental differences over the Canada-US Free Trade Agreement. Why? Spatial models of party competition tell us that parties usually steam to the safe harbour of the median position, where differences are obscured and votes maximized. This is exactly what the parties did with the Meech Lake agreement in 1988. Why haven't they always done so? Why didn't they do the same with free trade?

The way we tell the story, the parties emphasized their differences on free trade rather than obscuring them. The Conservative choice to support free trade forced the Liberals and the NDP to fight over the opposite position. The NDP had to oppose the agreement, even though it was not the best issue the party could could muster. The NDP preferred to focus on leadership, and tried to do this, with modest success, throughout the campaign. Although the Liberals had more freedom of action, John Turner needed to demonstrate his leadership ability and decided to elbow the NDP aside by strongly opposing the FTA. The Liberals and Conservatives went out of their way to dramatize their differences; many voters changed their minds on the free trade issue as a result of these efforts. Even for voters who did not change their position on free trade, the issue became more important to their decision-making. We have called this increase in the importance of an issue *priming*. The econometric evidence for priming is impressive. Now we must ask what lies behind the econometric results, why parties sometimes stray from the protective calm of the median.

Two theoretical explanations, at least, can be found for the robust priming effects in chapter 8. One comes from social choice theory, and it suggests that politicians will sometimes emphasize a particular issue to gain strategic advantage over their opponents. Riker (1983) calls this heresthetic: "The point of an heresthetical act is to structure the situation so that the actor wins, regardless of whether or not the other participants are persuaded" (p. 60). Another explanation comes from combining recent work on decision-making and choice with the older Columbia University research on campaign effects. Out of this combination comes an emphasis on accessibility, priming, and selective attention. The recent work emphasizes the limitations of human information processing and the likelihood that people will focus on "accessible" considerations. The term priming also comes out of this work. The Columbia research and its progeny (most notably Festinger, 1957) focused on selective exposure, selective perception, and selective retention. It suggested that the major targets of priming ought to be voters who are tentatively committed but who have cognitive dissonance to reduce. In an electorate the targets should be party identifiers. Both heresthetics and priming took place in 1988. This is as it should be, for the two types of explanation are closely related to one another – so closely that it is hard to disentangle them empirically. Indeed, we believe that the different languages of spatial modelling and social choice theory, on one hand, and of the campaign effects and political communications literatures, on the other, should be melded together.

HERESTHETICS

In 1988 the Conservatives sought to shift the ground for the electoral battle. They apparently succeeded in erasing any trace of their traditional antipathy to French Canada. Indeed, with the Meech Lake Accord they dragged the whole party system towards the position of Quebec provincial elites. By inducing this convergence, the Conservative party effectively suppressed the national question which, in various guises, had dominated party choice to the Conservatives' disadvantage. At the same time, the party moved itself even further towards the pro-American pole on commercial policy. In effect they stretched the commercial policy dimension. In doing so, they forced an issue which appealed to the newer parts of their coalition (farmers and French Quebec), finessed the issue which threatened to blow their newly built coalition apart, and made Liberals and New Democrats fight over the opposite pole on commercial policy. In short, by what looks like a classic heresthetic move the Conservatives upset the existing equilibrium.

There is one problem with this explanation, however. The most highly developed examples for Riker and his colleagues are from legislatures and similar elite gatherings: the US Senate, the Roman Senate, and the US Constitutional Convention; the nearest we get to mass politics is Athenian democracy and the Lincoln-Douglas debates. Before an attentive and sophisticated audience, politicians can raise a new concern and attempt to change the issue space simply by standing up and making a case for it. The audience may resist the attempt, but it is certainly likely to be aware of it. And where the body has a formal decision-making function, the rules may allow politicians to force the issue by making a motion or by amending a motion on the floor.[1] It is not clear that what works in a small forum will work with mass publics. Riker (1983), in fact, notes that "while heresthetic and rhetoric were initially entwined in classical thought, as the democratic assembly – the one place where political strategy could be easily observed – disappeared from classical institutions, only rhetoric in the sense of persuasion was left to be observed and classified". He returns to this point again and again in his 1983 article, and he implies, but does not say directly, that there is something different about mass publics.

It is much harder to get a message out to the mass public than it is to colleagues in a deliberative body; mass publics cannot be made to pay attention in quite the same way. This leads us back to rhetoric and to the forum for rhetoric, campaigns. From the 1920s to the

1950s, political scientists believed that propaganda, the modern cousin of rhetoric, had an enormous, even mesmerizing, impact on mass publics. The authors of the Columbia studies were surprised to find very little persuasion during political campaigns. Minimal communications effects and small campaign impacts then became the common wisdom.

In the last twenty years, however McCoombs and Shaw, Iyengar and Kinder, and other students of communications have shown that the mass media work less by persuading than by focusing attention on certain issues. They use the same term that Riker uses, "agenda setting," for the way the media can direct people to certain issues. But they are less concerned with issue choice and strategic advantage than with how news and media messages can be used to affect what people perceive to be the agenda. They do not presume that politicians play before an attentive audience. They believe that it takes considerable effort to set or change the agenda, and they show how this can be done through the mass media.

The two different notions of agenda setting converge in the electoral setting. Sophisticated politicians will work hard to find heresthetical advantages, but they cannot just state their position. They must then work even harder to use the mass media to make their agenda stick. Heresthetics explains *why* they set the agenda; modern communications research wants to show *how* they can set it, but research in the area is in its infancy.

ACCESSIBILITY, PRIMING, AND SELECTIVE ATTENTION

There is still another problem with the agenda-setting argument, however. Spatial models, at least in the two-party case, suggest that it makes sense to focus on a new dimension only if doing so catches the opposing party far from the median. Why would the opposing party not be at the median? One possible explanation is that the party might be shackled to the position by history. If parties abandon long-held positions to woo new voters, prospective supporters will doubt whether the party's movement towards their position is real. Meanwhile old supporters may now be forced to entertain doubts.

The NDP was fixed to its FTA position because of its links to organized labour and to voters in non-market occupations. The Liberals, however, were not so fixed and John Turner had wide latitude over which to range. Spatial theory suggests that he should have chosen a position somewhere between the Conservatives and the NDP. This would have placed him near the median voter, not far from the centre of his own party, and, one would think, in an excellent position to gain support. Yet he chose to be almost exactly where the NDP was – a location far from the median voter, indeed far from his own partisan base. Why did he do this?

It is hard to reconcile Mr Turner's positioning with heresthetics and spatial theory. Something more was at work. We think Mr Turner had to pick a fight to win the election. Going towardss the median would have provided him with little to fight about. Nobody would have paid any attention to him if he had chosen the middle way. Indeed, doing this would have played into the hands of those who claimed he was a weak leader. Free trade allowed him to prime, to arouse, basic sentiments among Liberal party members and to give those members reasons for voting for him. In this formulation, priming is less important as a way to upset a pre-existing equilibrium than as a way to provide people with a foundation for supporting the party. Priming is about picking fights – carefully. Parties must make noise to get noticed. The spatial model assumes too readily that voters will immediately perceive where the parties stand. This is the nub of the issue, where the spatial modelling approach and recent work in cognitive psychology part company. By taking positions away from the median, parties get attention, simplify the cognitive task confronting voters, and give voters reasons for supporting them.

We suspect that partisans are especially vulnerable to priming. One of the fundamental findings of the Columbia studies, remember, was that people tend to listen to and be affected by communications which support their point of view. From this, Lazarsfeld and his colleagues inferred that campaign effects must be limited. But parties and politicians can choose which issues to prime and which voters to target. Moreover, to the extent that selective processes produce asymmetry in who hears a message, a party can gain by taking a position away from the median; the gains should outweigh the losses.

Rhetoric, then, does play an important role in campaigns, but not just by persuading people. Rhetoric also plays a role – possibly its biggest role – by directing voters towards a specific agenda and considerations surrounding that agenda. In 1988 that meant directing people away from Meech Lake and towards free trade, especially its impact on social programs and Canadian prosperity, and towards leadership considerations. Some of this was heresthetical – there were strategic advantages to be gained from bringing up these issues – but it was also rhetorical because it gave people reasons for voting one way or another.

ALTERNATIVE EXPLANATIONS

This combination of heresthetics and priming is not the only possible explanation of party differences, but we believe that it makes more sense than the others which come to mind. We are aware of four alternatives:

- The most straightforward explanation comes right out of spatial theory. In spatial models with plurality voting, three mobile alternatives, and one issue, "at least one [party] will be outside or on the boundary of the interquartile range of the electorate's distribution of ideal points" (Cox, 1987, p. 102). This hardly fits 1988. First, both the Conservatives and the NDP had relatively extreme, fixed positions before the campaign. Moreover, with the other two parties fixed, the Liberals were free to choose just about any position. They chose to take a position on free trade far from the median.

- Another explanation, a wrinkle on spatial theory, is that catering to party activists (Aldrich, 1983) leads to differences among parties: the more a party converges on the median the fewer reasons it gives its workers and financial angels, who are typically far away from the median, for helping it. At first glance this looks like our own account of "giving reasons." But our account is one of giving reasons to ordinary voters, not to activists. And in 1988 such an explanation just does not wash: John Turner was *more* opposed to the FTA than the elite of the Liberal party, not to mention the party's own identifiers.

- An ingenious explanation for party differences which also seems to fit the stylized facts of the 1988 campaign has been offered by Chappell and Keech (1986). To the extent that an event such as a debate is about leadership, it may yield gains to a party independently of policy distances. In this case, "failure to select a median policy no longer unduly risks defeat in the case of very large numbers of voters, since a candidate may win anyway if he or she is fortunate enough to win the debate" (p. 895). But this suggests that parties risk taking extreme positions only because other factors than issues decide the election. Leaders say what they think because, after all, it doesn't really matter. Some of this might go on, but it does not fit our picture of risk-averse politicians. It might fit with a picture of politicians who have their own policy goals as well as a desire to get elected. John Turner may have had a strong dislike of the FTA in 1988, but it is hard to believe that he would have risked the future of his party and his whole career on this dislike. In any case, Mr Turner staked out his position well in advance of the debates. And in the debates, as on 20 July, John Turner demonstrated his leadership capacity by the very act of occupying one pole of the debate.

– Finally, there is an alternative entirely separate from spatial theory: directional theory (Rabinowitz and Macdonald, 1989; Macdonald, Listhaug, and Rabinowitz, 1991). Here it is argued that the spatial model is flawed at its very foundation. People do not support the party closest to them; rather they support the party that is on the same side of the status quo as they are. Macdonald, Listhaug, and Rabinowitz recognize that this could lead to absurdities: for example, someone slightly to the left of centre supporting a very left-wing party because it is on the correct side while rejecting a slightly right of centre party. To solve this problem they add a penalty for "extreme parties." Although other problems arise with the directional model, it does have very strong empirical support. And we find persuasive the claim that "a key feature of party strategy is the attempt by politicians to shape the issues used to evaluate themselves and their opponents" (Macdonald, et al., 1991, p. 1108). But if spatial theory failed to account for the specific way in which centrifugal pressures worked in Canada in 1988, directional theory stumbles over the centripetal force. The penalty the directional model imposes on extreme parties seems contrived, a political science version of Ptolemy's epicycles. And divergence is not the only pattern parties exhibit. Figure 3-2, after all, was a picture of perfect convergence on one dimension, even if it also exhibited marked divergence on the other.

The three modifications of spatial theory and a fourth, directional theory, fall short. Spatial theory still seems to be the place to begin. It incorporates a natural centripetal force on the parties: they simply cannot get too far from the median voter. At every place on the policy continuum parties must feel the pull of the median, not just when they get to some arbitrarily defined "too extreme" point. What must be added to spatial models is a force that drives parties away from the centre. That force is the need for priming. Parties prime, we believe, because they must provide voters with reasons for voting for them. Not just any reasons will do, however. They must be reasons with enough force that they will cause people to vote for the party. Reasons connected to the mainsprings, to the basic cleavages, of the political system are excellent candidates. Among these, the best reasons are ones that resonate with the pre-existing partisan ties of the electorate. Free trade passed this test; Meech Lake did not.

Riker (1984) contrasts rhetoric and heresthetic by saying that "rhetoric involves converting others by persuasive argument, whereas heresthetic involves structuring the situation so that others accept it willingly" (p. 8). Both persuasion and heresthetic took place in the 1988 campaign, although we have said little about persuasion in this chapter. Yet neither persuasive arguments nor clever heresthetic positioning suffice in modern campaigns. In his definition of rhetoric as persuasion, Riker leaves out another aspect of rhetoric – its ability to arouse people by setting agendas and priming considerations. Priming and agenda setting operate by mobilizing a party's partisans. They do this both by emphasizing issues that activate partisan sensibilities and by demonstrating the leadership ability and decisiveness of the party and its leader. In John Turner's case, priming brought apostate Liberals who had voted for Brian Mulroney in 1984 back to the party. The net result was a rejuvenation of the Liberals and a solid second-place finish.

THE STUDY OF ELECTIONS

We believe that this study questions, possibly even overturns, some political science shibboleths. But we only have one case, the campaign and election of 1988, and we must be clear about its limitations. How typical is the case?

As an historical event, it is probably atypical, even for Canada. But then each election is atypical in some way. And if 1988 was atypical, it was so in a very special way: virtually every imaginable element in the calculus of voting exhibited dynamics and virtually every element mattered to the final choice. Even if 1988 demonstrated more than is likely in a garden-variety campaign, it nonetheless demonstrated what is possible, what we should get in the habit of looking for even if we do not always expect to find it. As we accumulate cases, the boring and trivial along with the dynamic and pivotal, we can map out a full theory of campaign effects. What we know at this point is that an instrument designed specifically to be sensitive to campaign effects found them. This naturally raises the question: to what extent is the discipline's slighting of campaign effects mainly the result of failure to look for them? We believe that we have uncovered some general principles about campaigns. These principles should make re-examination of older studies fruitful.[2] As for future work, the technology now exists to bring politics and citizens back into electoral studies, to catch heresthetic manipulation, agenda setting, and priming. Sometimes the instruments will encounter campaigns that are dull and tepid, where little happens. But other times they will meet campaigns filled with strategic and rhetorical moves that reverse the balance of forces and determine the election. One or two studies may even run into a campaign that alters permanently the basic alignment of political forces.

Whatever the shape of any particular campaign, all campaigns matter merely by existing. They represent the moment at which the mass electorate comes closest to being a legislative body. Citizens are most likely to pay attention to politics when they are called upon to take responsibility for their opinions and make a politically consequential choice. Politicians may hope that they have structured the choice to their own maximum strategic advantage before the campaign unfolds. The 1988 Canadian campaign indicated that they do not always succeed. Even when political strategists do succeed in anticipating campaign contingencies, their strategizing cannot be accounted for other than by reference to the campaign to come. Only when we take campaigns seriously, and begin to accumulate evidence about voters' cognitive psychology in them, will we be able to make the spatial model adequate to electoral reality.

THE 1988 CAMPAIGN AND THE CANADIAN PARTY SYSTEM

Even when parties successfully cover the contingencies for a given campaign, they may only create hostages to fortune for the next one. Although the Canadian parties did not anticipate all that would follow from their emphasis on free trade, they all succeeded handsomely in avoiding the dangers posed by the national question. No party had its coalition split by the opening up of that issue. But 1988 may have only been a stay of execution.

Of all parties, the biggest beneficiary of the suppression of the national question was the Conservative party. Figure 3-2 showed that this question divided the Conservatives' electoral coalition more than it did any other party's. The Liberals and the NDP may have been doing themselves a favour by converging on the Conservative position. Only by doing so could each keep open the possibility of building its own pan-regional coalition. But by converging on the Conservative position they also deprived potentially dissident Conservative identifiers of an avenue of escape.

In chapter 3 we wondered how long the Conservative balancing act could continue, how long francophones could be harnessed to francophobes. Events since 1988 suggest: not long. As we write, the Conservative electoral coalition has cracked. On its English Canadian flank has appeared the Reform Party, so far a mainly extraparliamentary force but one that must be taken seriously. The Reform party's success in the first Alberta by-election after the 1988 general campaign bore witness to the complementarity of emphasis on free trade and suppression of the national question: so long as supporting Reform threatened to undermine a pro-free trade parliamentary majority, the new party remained weak; the moment the FTA ceased to be at risk, Reform began to mushroom. As the agenda came once again to be dominated by the national question, Reform grew still more. The years after 1988 are eerily reminiscent of the years after 1911. The 1911 election also bottled up western and anglophone discontent (discontent which 1896 anticipated) by a polarization over commercial policy. When the discontent could no longer be contained, it shattered the foundations of party choice. Meanwhile, tension over the national question has produced a threat on the Conservatives' other flank, the Bloc Québécois. In contrast to Reform, the Bloc is parliamentary in origin, made up principally of former Conservative MPs. Where the Bloc fits in the concertation logic which, in one variant or the other, has been so important in Quebec remains to be seen. Clearly, the threat the Bloc poses is primarily to the Conservatives.

In the inter-election period, the new entrants have fragmented voter intentions. Neither of the two new parties wants to play the pan-regional coalition game. Some observers sense that the very presence of these parties has ended that game, at least in its electoral form; it may recur as a parliamentary game, akin to those played in European parliaments. If the electoral game has really changed, old parties may adapt their own strategies. Most intriguing in this respect is the NDP. Figure 3-2 disguised the fact that, despite its pretentions in 1988, the NDP was still a party of English Canada, at that point the only party which could make such a claim. In 1988 it scrupulously avoided doing so. Now that the Reform party has shown the mileage to be gained, the NDP might be tempted to assert that it, too, is an authentic voice for English Canada.

Will the fragmentation of the years after 1988 persist into the next election? The logic of the single-member plurality electoral system is hostile to such fragmentation. The 1988 campaign revealed that Canadian voters could derive sensible expectations and act on them. The primary story about expectations was strategic, but the bandwagon evidence for Quebec is also relevant. Both stories reflected the powerful logic of the electoral system. And both stories indicated that strategic contingencies can shift and that the shifts feed on themselves.

The Canadian parties are now engaged in strategic manoeuvres rather as they were in the run up to 1988. This time the stakes are even higher. One or more of the currently visible alternatives may be erased as a result of a misstep. Indeed, each actor may play its role in the strategically optimum way and yet one or more may disappear. The victim could readily be an old party. The victim may also be the country. Whatever happens, the site for the critical events is likely to be next campaign.

APPENDICES

The 1988 Canadian Election Study Sample

The 1988 Canadian Election Study (CES) had three parts: a campaign-period telephone study; a post-election telephone study; and a self-administered mailback questionnaire.

The campaign wave of the CES was administered as a rolling cross-section. The total campaign-wave sample was broken into forty-seven replicates. A fresh replicate, large enough to yield about seventy-seven ultimate completions, was released each day. The bulk of the completions were recorded within three days of release, but telephone numbers were kept open for two weeks and for as many as fifteen callbacks (a few completions took even more callbacks than this). The first few fieldwork days saw fewer than seventy-seven completions, as the system warmed up. By fieldwork day 4 (7 October) the daily pattern was set: forty to fifty completions from that day's release, ten to twenty from the previous day's release, five to ten from two days before, and scattered completions from a range of earlier releases. As the end of campaign approached, the clearance period for new daily samples shortened and thus the response rate tailed off. The impact of this was trivial until the last two days, however. On those days response rate was sacrificed for number of completions and for stability in their daily composition. The day on which a respondent was interviewed was thus, to all intents and purposes, a random event. Altogether, 3,609 interviews were completed during the campaign. The response rate is conservatively estimated to be 57 percent.

The sample was stratified by province of residence, to overrepresent smaller provinces. As interviews were initiated in French for the Quebec sample and in English for all other provinces, we were concerned that official language minority populations would be undersampled. Official language minorities were also of substantive interest to the investigators. Accordingly, extra numbers were released for exchanges in which linguistic minorities were known to be numerous in the three provinces with the biggest minority populations – Ontario, Quebec, and New Brunswick.

All analyses in this book used a weighted version of the sample. Weights corrected for household size, the sampling fraction in the province, and for minority-language oversampling. The household weight was an inverse function of the number of adult citizens identified for the household as part of the interview's front end. Province and minority-language weights used census data to offset the two forms of stratification. Weights were designed to produce table counts close to the original values. Any table reporting data by province uses cases weighted only for household size and, if necessary, minority-language status. For this reason, apparent discrepancies between province-by-province and total-sample numbers can creep into tables; this a problem mainly for chapter 3. The discrepancy reflects further weighting of provincial strata in the calculation of the national number.

The post-election sample of 2,922 respondents (a reinterview rate of 81 percent) was a proper subset of the campaign wave. It thus is biased by panel mortality: it tends to be a politically more engaged group than the campaign wave. Urban respondents were moderately less likely to be reinterviewed than rural ones, but no weighting for panel mortality was attempted.

Variables from the self-administered mailback questionnaire were not used at any point in this book.

Further details on the sample and on other technical features of the 1988 CES can be found in Northrup and Dram (1989).

APPENDIX B

Two Notes on Estimation

WHY THE LINEAR PROBABILITY MODEL?

Throughout this book we use the linear probability model to estimate the impact of various factors on nominal dependent variables (Aldrich and Nelson, 1984; Maddala, 1983). For example, in chapter 8 we predict the probability of preferring a particular party by regressing a dichotomous variable, one if the party is supported by the respondent and zero otherwise, on a set of independent variables, including level of support for the free trade agreement, evaluations of the leaders, and expectations about which party will form the government. Our major reason for using the linear probability model is its ease of interpretation. For a unit change in the independent variables, the regression coefficient is the change in probability of voting for the party. Another virtue is that it uses a familiar statistical method, ordinary least squares, to obtain the coefficients.

We could have chosen other methods for estimating these equations. Probit, logit, and even other models have been proposed for dealing with nominal dependent variables. Each method has its strengths and weaknesses. Proponents of probit and logit often note that with these methods it is impossible to get predicted probability values outside the natural zero-one range of probability measures. This is a virtue, but with our regressions, we typically had only about ten predicted values outside this range – less than 0.3 percent of the entire sample.

Another argument for probit and logit is that they are more sensitive to high and low probabilities than the linear probability model. This is really an argument about the appropriate functional form between the underlying tendency to vote for a party, say, and the probability of voting for the party. We do not believe that anyone knows the proper relationship between the underlying tendency and the probability. Our best guess, in fact, is that the truth lies somewhere between the linear probability model and probit, or its close cousin, logit. Using the linear probability model amounts to assuming that the error term in the regression is uniformly distributed, whereas using the probit model amounts to assuming a normally distributed error. Normal distributions have very "thin" tails and are unbounded. Uniform distributions have very "thick" tails – in fact, the tails and the middle of the distribution have the same thickness – and are bounded. It seems likely to us that errors are always bounded and the tails of the error distribution are thicker than the normal distribution allows, but not so thick as in the uniform distribution. Whatever the true functional form, in the situations where we have estimated equations using both the linear probability model and probit, we have found no essential difference in our results. This is a common occurrence. There is, then, no clear-cut reason for preferring one functional specification over the other.

A final criticism of the linear probability model is that if just ordinary least squares are used, the errors will be heteroscedastic. Throughout we use a Goldberger correction (Goldberger, 1964) which corrects for this problem by first obtaining consistent estimates of the probabilities with ordinary least squares, using these estimates to determine the variance of the errors, and using these estimates of variance in errors to adjust for the heteroscedasticity in a second stage. This method is described in Aldrich and Nelson (1984) and Achen (1986, chapter 3).

We not only use the linear probability model for dichtomous variables, we also use it for polytomous variables such as party choice. Just as with two choices in the dichotomous case we need only estimate one equation, with three choices in the trichotomous case we need only estimate two equations (Aldrich and Nelson, 1984, p. 23). Nevertheless, we usually present three equations, one for each party. We only do this to simplify comparsions across the parties although it is always true that any two of the three equations contain all the information in the data.

SEPARATING TEMPORAL AND INDIVIDUAL VARIATION

Why Have We Tried to Separate These Effects?

We have tried throughout to disentangle temporal and individual variation. We have decomposed free trade opinion, for example, into its cross-sectional and time-series components, and we have shown that they affect voting preference in different ways. Why have we gone to this trouble?

Our major purpose has been to find true campaign dynamics and to avoid treating cross-sectional covariation as time-series covariation. We find, for example, that gender and voting intention are (somewhat) correlated in our sample. This does not mean, however, that gender and voting intention play any dynamic role in the election. Because the gender composition of the electorate does not vary over the campaign, there is no way there could be a time-series effect. (Gender could interact with some dynamic elements of the campaign, but this is another matter.) Gender only varies in the cross-section but not in the time-series. The same might be true for free trade opinion or leadership evaluations except that sampling or measurement error might create the appearance of variation in these measures over time. As with gender and voting intention, if we just correlated free trade opinion with voting intention we would find a relationship, but it might have nothing to do with campaign dynamics. Separating the two components and entering them in a regression separately might then reveal that only cross-sectional variation significantly affects voting preference.

It seems unlikely that there is no real time-series variation in free trade opinion or leadership evaluations, and a more likely problem is that a cross-sectional variation in free trade opinion might be a proxy for a great many other things that also vary in the cross-section and covary cross-sectionally with the vote; party identification is an obvious example. If we fail to control for all these things in the cross-section – and it is virtually impossible to control for everything – then we will get a spurious correlation between free trade opinion and the vote. There is good reason to believe, however, that party identification and many other things that are correlated with free trade opinion do not vary rapidly over time, so that any correlation between time-series variation in free trade opinion and voting preference is a truer reflection of the actual relationship between opinion and vote.

In fact, a negative or a positive judgment about free trade might get absorbed into party identification after a while so that if we did control for party identification and other factors, free trade opinion might appear in the cross-section to have little real impact when, in fact, there is a great deal; the impact just would be entirely mediated by variation in party identification.

It is still possible, of course, that even time-series variation in our respondents' reports on their opinions is nothing more than projection from other variables such as vote intention, so that we obtain a spurious correlation with the time-series component as well. One way to deal with this problem would be to model the projection process explicitly, as in Brady and Sniderman (1985). Another way is to show that our independent variables – free trade opinion and leadership evaluations – have a life apart from vote intentions. This we have shown throughout the book. A related approach is to choose independent variables – advertising time, media coverage, and poll results – that are not based upon reports from our respondents, and we have also done this.

How Should We Disentangle Time Series and Cross-Sectional Variation?

Time-series cross-sectional method.   We have taken two approaches to dealing with time-series cross-sectional data, depending upon whether or not we have post-election as well as pre-election measures. If we do not have adequate post-election measures, we have formed the average for the seventy to eighty people interviewed on a given day and called this average the time-series component. This measure suffers from two kinds of error. There is substantial sampling error because of the small number of responses upon which the average is based, and there is measurement error because of the vagaries of survey response. If we think of each individual response as composed of a true opinion and an uncorrelated measurement error, then the variance due to sampling error will be the variance of true opinion divided by the daily sample size of seventy to eighty. The variance due to measurement error will be the variance of this error divided by the daily sample size. If an item has a reliability of about one-half, then these two sources of error will be equal. One of the problems in this set-up is that the sampling variation in the time-series component will reflect the particular cross-section of people interviewed on that day. This could create a false correlation between the time-series component and the dependent variable such as voting intention if both depend in the cross-section on the same factors such as party identification. This will tend to increase the coefficient for the time-series effect beyond what it should be.

The cross-sectional or "individual" component in this set-up is the difference between individual responses and the time-series component. Although the cross-sectional component defined in this way will carry along the sampling and measurement error from the time-series component, these will be small (on the order of one over the sample size) compared to the measurement error. If the measure is somewhat unreliable, this will typically depress the coefficient for the cross-sectional effect.

Pre-post control method.   If we have a post-election measure for an item, we can take a different approach. We can define the time-series effect as the difference between the pre-election and the post-election measure. Because the post-election measures were all collected during the relative calm of the post-election period, this difference controls for the individual differences of respondents. It provides the (almost) perfect way to control for the sampling differences that occur from one day to the next because the post-election measure, by definition, embodies all those factors which might affect the respondent's position on the item. This approach does have one defect, however. Because both the pre-election and post-election items are undoubtedly measured with error, their difference incorporates this double dose of error. This is a nuisance, but random error in this time-series measure cannot create a spurious correlation in the same way as the sampling error in the time-series cross-sectional method can.

In practice, we do not actually take the difference between the pre-election and the post-election measure. Instead, we just include both the pre-election and the post-election measures in our estimations. It is not hard to show that the coefficients of the pre-election measure represent the time-series impact, and the coefficients of the post-election measure plus those of the pre-election measure represent the cross-sectional impact. Because we invariably focus on the time-series impact, this is a convenient way to perform the estimations.

For those cases where we have post-election measures, we have tried the time-series cross-sectional method as well as the the pre-post method. We have invariably found similar results, although the time-series coefficients tend, as we would expect from the discussion above, to be smaller for the pre-post method.

APPENDIX C

Coding of Media Quantities

A videotape record was kept of prime time (6 p.m. to midnight) broadcasting on CBC and CTV Toronto and Radio-Canada (SRC) Montreal from 2 October to 20 November. Taping was performed by an informal network of VCRs which could not be mobilized before the second day of the campaign. Power failures in Quebec in November also eliminated some readings; there, however, the lack of readings arguably mirrored the broadcast media reality for most Quebec voters on those days. From these tapes were derived content analyses of national news programs. All advertisements placed by parties on these channels could also be identified, located, and analysed according to a coding scheme like that developed for the news.

An archive of fourteen metropolitan daily newspapers was turned over to us by the library at l'Université Laval. This was the basis for the account of headlines in chapter 4 and for the creation of the daily series for third-party advertising on the FTA.

The third-party advertising series was a straightforward count of the area devoted to advertisements on one side or the other by day. The television news and advertising series were more complex and merit separate description.

Television News Coverage

A news broadcast is broken up into items; the boundaries between items are obvious to most viewers. According to Table C-1, each wing of the CBC broadcast two to three hundred campaign items over the 2 October–20 November span. Each item has been cut into smaller pieces, which we

Table C-1
"Items" and "Units," English (CBC) and French (SRC)

	English	French
Number of items	223	295
Number of units	2,714	2,685
Total time (seconds)	41,470	39,273
Average seconds per unit	15.27	14.62

call units. A unit deals with one subject, mentions no more than one actor, and rests on one source of information. Units vary in length and thus the length of a unit is a variable in its own right. Each unit was coded for content on several dimensions. Some of the codes reflect mundane factual questions. Some reflected rhetorical themes that figure elsewhere in this book. Altogether, 518 items were recorded on the two networks and these items were broken down into 5,399 units. An average unit is about fifteen seconds long.

For this book's purposes, units are weighted by their length in seconds. One purpose of this weighting is to calculate the proportion of time devoted to different topics. The other purpose is in daily tracking. For instance, in Figure 4-2, the weighted direction of FTA reportage was computed as follows: for a given day, each unit with FTA content was identified; the unit was coded as pro-FTA ($+1$) or anti-FTA (-1) and then weighted by its length in seconds; all units so identified and weighted were then added together; the repetition of this exercise by day produced the series in Figure 4-2. Further detail on specific directional coding appears in the notes.

Televison Advertising

We began by identifying each advertisement on CBC and CTV Toronto and SRC Montreal. Each advertisment was then analysed following the coding scheme devised for the news. Once the vector of numbers for each advertisment had been created, it could be read into a daily file as many times as the advertisement appeared on the day and channel in question. From this, daily aggregates could be created for rhetorical dimensions, such as the treatment of John Turner.

APPENDIX D

Comparing Questions about the FTA

What was the "true" balance of opinion on the FTA? The closest we can get to answering this question is by comparing our FTA questions with those used by others. The "Mulroney" version of our question was constructed in the specific expectation that it would depress support for the FTA. The "Canada" version was originally conceived as a baseline but may have placed a mild burden of proof on rejecting the FTA and thus may have induced supportive response.

Table D-1 compares our versions with the two most readily comparable alternatives, the Gallup and Environics items asked during the campaign. Environics mentioned Canada in its item, Gallup did not. FTA support was smaller in response to the Gallup item than to our "Canada" item. The difference was greatest in the early campaign, before opinions were firmly established. This time path is consistent with our findings for the experiment and for the challenges and with the logic of campaign rhetoric. The Environics/Gallup comparison is more equivocal. Environics, like the CES "Canada" version, did seem to induce more support for the FTA. The Environics item also induced more opposition; it simply attracted more response. Still, the Environics version did yield a balance of opinion more favourable to the FTA than did Gallup, another indication that including the word "Canada" induced FTA support.

Of course, the "Mulroney" version of our item did its work and depressed response. The distribution it produced was not markedly more negative than Gallup's, however. The two CES biases tended to cancel each other and yielded a summary distribution that fell between the Environics and Gallup readings. By the end, the differences were minuscule.

Table D-1
Response to Free Trade Items: Percentage Supporting FTA

	1	2	3	4	5	1	2	3	4	5	1	2	3	4	5
October															
2–10	47	37	41	44		36	36	36	42		17	27	23	14	
22–25	43	38	40		34	35	43	39		42	22	19	21		24
28–30	35	26	31	31		52	54	53	51		13	20	16	18	
November															
2–5	35	34	34		26	40	46	43		50	25	20	22		24
3–8	37	32	35	39		42	47	45	51		21	20	21	11	
9–12	38	36	37		32	48	45	47		45	13	19	16		23
14–17	26	34	31		34	50	47	49		41	24	18	21		24

1: CES: "Canada"
2: CES: "the Mulroney government"
3: CES: both versions combined
4: Environics
5: Gallup

APPENDIX E

Measurement of Expectations

Expectations were tapped by items $f1a$ to $f1c$ (local) and $f2a$ to $f2c$ (national) in Appendix F. The measures were adapted from recent US National Election Studies. For more detail on the American items, see Bartels (1988) or Brady and Johnston (1988).

Scores were not constrained to add up to 100 within the local and national batteries and, in fact, rarely did. For national expectations, for instance, only 16 percent came up with a total of 100; the mean total was 138. The upward bias probably stemmed from the item wording itself, which encouraged respondents to score an even chance at 50. Strikingly, the modal three-party totals were 100 (526 cases) and 150 (375 cases). A similar pattern has been observed in the United States: according to Bartels (1988, p. 322), the average 1984 US respondent assigned a total probability of more than 200 to candidates' chances in presidential primaries. In light of this scaling variance it seemed prudent to normalize response by dividing scores for specific parties by the three-party total and then multiplying the result by 100 to restore the 0–100 range.

Selected CES 1988 Survey Items

(a6) Did you see the last TV debate among the party leaders?

(a6a) In your opinion, which leader performed the BEST in that debate?

(a6b) And which leader performed the WORST?

(b2) Which party do you think you will vote for: the Conservative party, the Liberal party, the New Democratic Party, or another party?

(b3) Perhaps you have not made up your mind. But which party are you leaning toward now?

(b10) What is your opinion on Quebec independence? Do you SUPPORT IT COMPLETELY, SUPPORT IT SOMEWHAT, OPPOSE IT SOMEWHAT, OPPOSE IT COMPLETELY, or don't you really have an opinion on it?

(d2) Now let's talk about your feelings towards the political parties, their leaders and their candidates.

I'll read a name and ask you to rate a person or a party on a thermometer that runs from 0 to 100 degrees. Ratings between 50 and 100 degrees mean that you feel favourable toward that person. Ratings between 0 and 50 degrees mean that you feel unfavourable toward that person. You may use any number from 0 to 100 to tell me how you feel.

(d2a – d2c) How would you rate [Leader Name]?

(d3 – d5) Now, we'd like to know about your impressions of the party leaders. I am going to read a list of words and phrases people use to describe political figures. After each one, I would like you to tell me how much the word or phrase fits your impressions ... How much would you say [insert word] fits your impression of [insert leader name]: A GREAT DEAL, SOMEWHAT, A LITTLE, or NOT AT ALL?

(f1a – f2c) Now let's talk about how the election is going for each party. We will be using a scale which runs from 0 to 100, where 0 represents NO chance for the party, 50 represents AN EVEN CHANCE, and 100 represents CERTAIN VICTORY.

(Using the 0 to 100 scale), what do you think the [party name] party's chances are of winning the election IN THE WHOLE COUNTRY (IN YOUR RIDING)?

(h1a) Some people feel that too much is being done to promote the French language in Canada. Others feel that not enough is being done to promote French. How much do you think should be done to promote French: MUCH MORE, SOMEWHAT MORE, ABOUT THE SAME AS NOW, SOMEWHAT LESS, MUCH LESS, or haven't you thought much about it?

(h1b – h1d) Where does the FEDERAL [LIBERAL, CONSERVATIVE, NDP] party stand on this question? Does the FEDERAL [LIBERAL, CONSERVATIVE, NDP] party think that MUCH MORE, SOMEWHAT MORE, ABOUT THE SAME AS NOW, SOMEWHAT LESS, or MUCH LESS should be done to promote French?

(h2a) Some people believe that Canada should have closer ties with the United States. Others feel that Canada should distance itself from the United States. How about you? Do you think Canada should be: MUCH CLOSER to the United States, SOMEWHAT CLOSER, ABOUT THE SAME AS NOW, SOME-WHAT MORE DISTANT, MUCH MORE DISTANT, or haven't you thought much about this?

(h2b – h2d) Where does the FEDERAL [LIBERAL, CONSERVATIVE, NDP] party stand on this question? Does the FEDERAL [LIBERAL, CONSERVATIVE, NDP] party think that Canada should be MUCH CLOSER to the United States, SOMEWHAT CLOSER, ABOUT THE SAME AS NOW, SOMEWHAT MORE DIS-TANT, or MUCH MORE DISTANT?

(h3) Some people believe that Canada must have stronger trade unions to protect workers. Others feel that Canada's trade unions are too strong already, and that the power of trade unions should be curbed. How much power do you think trade unions should have: MUCH MORE, SOMEWHAT MORE, ABOUT THE SAME AS NOW, SOMEWHAT LESS, MUCH LESS, or haven't you thought much about this?

(h4a) Most experts argue that if we want more government services we must increase taxes and if we want to lower taxes we must reduce services. If you had to choose, should the level of taxes and services be MUCH HIGHER, SOMEWHAT HIGHER, about the SAME, SOMEWHAT LOWER, or MUCH LOWER than now?

(i1) Thinking of federal politics, do you usually think of yourself as a Liberal, Consevative, NDP, or none of these?

(l2) As you know, [Canada/the Mulroney government] has reached a free trade agreement with the United States. All things considered, do you SUPPORT the agreement or do you OPPOSE it?

(l2a1) Some people say that under this agreement Canada will lose its ability to control key sectors of the economy, such as energy. Does this make you

LESS SUPPORTIVE of the agreement, or does it make NO DIFFERENCE to how you feel?

(l2a2) Some people say that this agreement will make it very hard for us to maintain our social programmes, such as medicare. Does this make you LESS SUPPORTIVE of the agreement, or does it make NO DIFFERENCE to how you feel?

(l2a3) Some people say that under this agreement many Canadians will lose their jobs, in industries such as textiles, automobiles and services. Does this make you LESS SUPPORTIVE of the agreement, or does it make NO DIFFER-ENCE to how you feel?

(l2b1) Some people say that this agreement will defend us against American protectionism, such as happened in the softwood lumber dispute. Does this make you LESS OPPOSED to the agreement, or does it make NO DIFFERENCE to how you feel?

(l2b2) Some people say that this agreement will lower the cost of many of the goods that Canadian families need. Does this make you LESS OPPOSED to the agreement, or does it make NO DIFFERENCE to how you feel?

(l3) As you may know, Canada belongs to NATO, a military alliance which includes the United States and many western European countries. Do you think that Canada should stay in NATO or get out of NATO?

(l4a – l4d) Now I would like to ask you about the Meech Lake Accord, reached last year by the federal and provincial governments.

(l4a) [No consideration supplied]

(l4b) Under this accord, Quebec is recognized as a distinct society.

(l4c) Under this accord, the government of Quebec has agreed to accept the new Constitution of Canada, as the other nine provinces did in 1981.

(l4d) Under this accord, the powers of provincial governments are strength-ened in various ways.

Do you support the accord or oppose it?

(l5) Some people think that the government of Canada should tighten up its immigration policy. Others think that Canada should welcome even more immigrants. How about you? Should Canada admit MORE immigrants or FEWER immigrants than at present?

(l6) [Prefatory sentence at random to half sample only:

According to the Supreme Court, the Charter of Rights says that govern-ments cannot make abortions absolutely illegal.]

Of the following three positions, which is closest to your own opinion: one, abortion should NEVER be permitted, two, should be permitted ONLY AFTER NEED has been established by a doctor, or three, should be a matter of the WOMAN'S PERSONAL CHOICE? [NB: order of positions randomized]

(l7) The government intends to sell shares in Air Canada to private bidders. On balance, do you FAVOUR or OPPOSE the privatization of Air Canada?

(l8) The [no mention of party/Conservative] government has made a number of amendments to the Official Languages Act. These amendments extend services for the French outside Quebec and for the English inside Quebec. Do you FAVOUR or OPPOSE the extension of such services?

(l9) As you may know, the government intends to buy eight or more nuclear submarines for the Navy [no consideration/to assert our sovereignty in the Canadian North/at a cost of $ 8 billion or more]. All things considered, do you SUPPORT or OPPOSE buying nuclear submarines?

(l14) And now a question about child care. Which of the following three statements comes closest to your own opinion?

1. If parents want child care, they should pay for it THEMSELVES.
2. The government should help PARENTS pay for child care.
3. The government should provide financial help to DAY CARE centres.

(n11) What is your religious affiliation? Is it Protestant, Catholic, Jewish, something else or no religion?

(n11a) [If Protestant] What church or denomination is that?

(n12) How often do you attend your place of worship?

(n15) To what ethnic or cultural group do you belong/did your ancestors belong on first coming to this continent?

Post-Election Questionnaire

(l2e) The agreement is necessary to make sure we have large market for our products.

Notes

PROLOGUE

1 Emphasis added. Christopher Waddell, "Block free trade bill, Turner tells Senate: Liberal leader seeking to force election," *Globe and Mail*, 21 July 1988, p. A1.
2 The primacy of the voter seems especially dominant in US studies. Consider *The People's Choice* (Lazarsfeld et al., 1968 [originally 1944]); *Voting* (Berelson et al., 1954); *The American Voter* (Campbell et al., 1960); *The Changing American Voter* (Nie et al., 1976); and *Retrospective Voting in American National Elections* (Fiorina, 1981). There is also *The People Elect a President* (Campbell and Kahn, 1952); *The Voter Decides* (Campbell, et al., 1954); *Voter's Choice* (Pomper, 1975); or *The Reasoning Voter* (Popkin, 1991). Among major US works the outstanding exception is Burnham's *Critical Elections and the Mainsprings of American Politics* (1970), where the title emphasizes the aggregate outcome.

The aggregate situation – or anticipations of it – appears to be a dominant motif in British studies, from the earliest Milne and Mackenzie volumes, *Straight Fight* (1954) and *Marginal Seat* (1958), to Butler and Stokes, *Political Change in Britain* (1969) and Sarlvik and Crewe, *Decade of Dealignment* (1983). British studies in the later 1980s seem to have converged on the American type: *How Voters Decide* (Himmelweit et al., 1984); *How Britain Votes* (Heath et al., 1985); and *How Voters Change* (Miller et al., 1990).

The title of the most comprehensive Canadian volume has an American ring: *Political Choice in Canada* (Clarke et al., 1979). The two other survey-based general books strike a different, rather cynical note: Laponce (1969), *People vs Politics*, and Clarke et al., (1984), *Absent Mandate*.

The definitive article on national styles in titles for election studies remains to be written.

3 Attribution theory, for example, shows that people invariably find explanations for the behaviour of others even when there is every indication that the behaviour was simply random. See Nisbett and Wilson (1977).

4 Perhaps the case most similar to John Turner in 1984 is an American one, Edward Kennedy in 1979. In his famous interview with Roger Mudd, Kennedy provided no new information about Chappaquiddick (a scandal from his past) and could seem to provide no reason why he wanted to be president. Before the interview, Kennedy, partly because of his distinguished political lineage, was leading the incumbent president, Jimmy Carter, in the polls. After the interview, Kennedy's support declined precipitously. Popkin (1991) notes that "what better common event with which to express doubts felt by millions than an interview in which the senator himself seemed to reveal real doubts?" (p. 112). Popkin argues that the incident itself was probably less decisive than many pundits believe and that incidents such as these "become important only when they draw upon many other related incidents and concerns."

5 Note the "people" in question are members of the electorate at large. Unlike Aldrich (1983), our argument does not rely on activists to motivate non-centrist position-taking.

6 Aldrich (1980) and Bartels (1988) consider strategic candidates and rational voters in presidential primaries, but they consider neither priming nor how history sets campaigns up.

7 For comprehensive, politically acute accounts, see Monahan (1991) and Cohen (1990).

8 Ross Howard, "Turner tactic to force vote spectacular brinkmanship," *Globe and Mail*, 22 July 1988, p. A1.

9 The study could never have been completed without the herculean efforts of the Institute of Survey Research, York University, Toronto. The ISR and its staff performed brilliantly under tight deadlines. Northrup and Oram (1989) discuss the technical aspects of the study. A description of the fieldwork can be found in Appendix A of this book.

Two rolling cross-sections have been executed as part of US National Election Studies. The 1988 study was only for the primaries. The 1984 study extended through the general election period, but only about sixty-five interviews were completed per week and there was no post-election reinterview.

10 The CES also has a third wave, based on a self-administered mailback questionnaire, mainly devoted to basic values and attitudes. No mail-back items are used in this book.

11 Lazarsfeld et al., (1946), Preface to the second Edition.

12 The quotation is from Chaffee (1975), p. 19. The full quotation is "the limited effects model is simply not believed by the authors of the chapters that follow." Sears and Kosterman (1987) are more restrained although they come to a similar conclusion: "[T]his general idea of minimal media effects still has much truth today, although recent re-search has identified some long-term effects, and highlighted the com-monalities among the rare instances of short-term effects … Exceptions to the minimal effects model usually depend upon massive exposure (as in long-term, repetitive coverage or a short-term barrage) combined with weak prior predispositions as with a complex issue or a crowded field of candidates" (pp. 44–5).

13 Canadian debates tend to be sequences of one-on-one confrontations. A question will be posed to one leader, with a second leader having a right to comment. The third leader is off-screen. Then roles reverse between the first two. Once this pairing is finished, the third leader steps in and one of the original two steps out. The round robin con-tinues for two to three hours.

14 Research on the 1960 Kennedy-Nixon debates came to this conclusion and all subsequent work has upheld it. For the 1960 debates, see Katz and Feldman (1962). For a more recent confirmation, see Sigelman and Sigelman (1984).

15 Ranney (1983), pp. 25–6.

16 Abramowitz (1978) and Chaffee and Dennis (1979). But see Patterson (1987), who argues that the news media often obscure the issues by their emphasis on winners and losers.

17 Fraser (1989) entitled his chapter on the impact of the debate "The Ground Moves." Lee (1989) chose "Dambusters."

18 "To force an election," *Globe and Mail*, 21 July 1988.

19 Christopher Waddell, "Block free trade bill, Turner tells Senate," *Globe and Mail*, 21 July 1988, p. A1.

20 The phrase "hijacker of democracy" was used by Ross Howard, "Turner tactic to force vote spectacular brinkmanship," *Globe and Mail*, 22 July 1988, p. A1.

1. THE CAMPAIGN ROLLER-COASTER

1 The estimates are based on the following regressions:

$$S_{pc,t} = 48.7 + 0.018(V_{pc,t})^2 - 0.020(V_{lib,t})^2 + \varepsilon;$$
$$S_{lib,t} = 12.2 - 0.009(V_{pc,t})^2 + 0.028(V_{lib,t})^2 + \varepsilon;$$

where:

S is a party's percentage of House of Commons seats;

V is a party's share of the national popular vote; and

ε is a disturbance term which subsumes all unmeasured variation. Estimates were based on elections from 1935 to 1984 inclusive. Coefficients of determination for the Conservative and Liberal estimations were, respectively, 0.96 and 0.95. The NDP share is assumed to be the residual. The quadratic setup was suggested by Duff Spafford.

2 See chapter 2.

3 If these claims seem hard to swallow, consider some recent examples. The NDP majority government formed in Ontario in 1990 received only 38 percent of the popular vote. Had the Liberal vote share in that election been a bit lower and the Conservative vote share a bit higher, the NDP majority would have been even greater. In the 1979 Canadian general election, the Conservatives received 36 percent of the popular vote, four points less than the Liberals, and yet returned 48 percent of the seats, only five seats short of a majority. This was, it must be admitted, something of an outlier in Canadian elections: from Figure 1-1, the seat share predicted from a Conservative vote of 36 and a Liberal vote of 40 is in the low 40s.

4 Figure 1-2 implies that the Liberals have a markedly greater seat growth potential than the NDP: as the Liberals sink and, presumably, the NDP rises, NDP domination over the Liberals would become clearer, but the Conservatives would also be major beneficiaries; an NDP opposition would be numerically weak. Estimates in Figure 1-2 for Liberal shares close to 20 and below should probably be taken cautiously. A Liberal share that low would probably signal a realignment more profound than any yet seen in the Canadian system (again see chapter 2), one which would probably render the equations in note 1 above no longer applicable.

5 Campbell and Pal (1991), p. 189.

6 Indeed, this seems to have been the conclusion of the NDP's own research. See Fraser (1989), p. 319.

7 Entries are for the week of fieldwork, so far as it can be identified, not of publication. The first entry is the Liberal share in the last poll whose fieldwork took place before the campaign. Usually this was right on the eve of the campaign, but sometimes (especially for the early campaigns) the fieldwork occurred some months before. For none of the campaigns was there a Gallup poll each week. Sometimes the imputation of fieldwork week was a guess. Readers should thus resist the temptation to overinterpret the exact time path of a campaign. The last entry reflects the Liberal share from official returns. All entries but one are cast as deviations from the average Liberal

share for 1962–80, 41 percent. The one exception is for the 1957 line, which is cast as the deviation from the 1935–53 average of 47 percent. The reasoning behind the 1962–80 and 1935–53 periodizations stems from the account in chapter 2.

8 In the sense that the leading party's vote-intention share at the beginning of the campaign was large enough, by the estimates underlying Figures 1-1 and 1-2, to return that party a majority of seats.

9 The issue is confused in a few cases. Three times the Liberal share appeared to surge early in a campaign. Only in 1979, where the last pre-campaign poll was conducted less than a month before the campaign, is this at all plausible. In the 1968 and 1980 elections, the appearance of a surge was an artifact of the lapse of time between the last pre-campaign published poll and the actual start of the campaign. In 1968 the poll predated the Liberal leadership convention that chose Pierre Trudeau and thus did not reflect the early phase of the surge that Mr Trudeau's accession induced. The first campaign-period poll did pick the surge up. In 1980 the last published poll was conducted in early November of 1979. The Liberals were acting on more recent information in their decision to bring the Clark government down (Simpson, 1980).

10 The same might be said of vote intentions early in the campaign. This is an issue for later in this chapter and for subsequent chapters.

11 This has to be argued with care. The difference between official returns and the earlier polls may be a compound of statistical artifacts. First, we have set the baseline in precisely the way that minimizes the variance around the rightmost point in Figure 1-3: the mean for a distribution is *defined* as a moment which minimizes the next larger moment, the variance. Secondly, election outcomes, unlike the poll readings, are not subject to sampling error.

12 In every campaign from 1945 to 1953 inclusive, the Liberal share did not shift at all over the campaign.

13 On 1962 and 1965, see Smith (1973), chapters 5 and 11 respectively.

14 Whether anything lay behind the story is still a matter of controversy. For different angles on the matter, see Fraser (1989) and Lee (1989).

15 The daily reading was based on response to an initial vote-intention item, b2, and a follow-up, b3, each of which can be found in Appendix F. Note that for the first two and the last two observations in a series, the number of observations averaged drops to three and four. More detail on the sample can be found in Appendix A.

16 For an extended treatment of the graphical use of moving averages, see Cleveland (1985).

17 Our tracking of the movement in shares, if not of their precise level, is consistent with the record of published polls.

18 In the days just before the debates the NDP share seems to have dropped to the benefit of both other parties. This is not consistent with published polls (on which see chapter 4) from the same days. Figure 3-1, a daily tracking of party identification, suggests that some of the apparent NDP drop is due to sampling error.

19 Murray Campbell, "Party ads woo voters tomorrow," *Globe and Mail*, 22 October 1988, pp. A1,5.

20 For instance, Caplan et al. (1989) pp. 158ff, devote one paragraph to the French debate and eight to the English. Some of their commentary on the media and popular reaction to the debates refers to both debates, but more often than not "debate" appears in the singular. Lee (1989) discusses only the English debate in his chapter 11, "Shaking the Booga-Wooga Stick."

21 Our reading on the NDP is consistent with three of the four polls published in the wake of the debates. Only the Insight-CTV poll gave the NDP less than 26 percent. The first clear published indication that the NDP was dropping came with the second Insight-CTV poll, broadcast on 4 November. See Table 4-1.

22 The poll gave the Liberals 43 percent and the Conservatives 31 percent. By the equation in note 1, the Liberals would have received 55 percent of House seats.

23 Even to the point that the Conservative leadership leaked its own polls to hasten the process of rebuilding morale. See Fraser (1989), pp. 411–15.

24 Brander (1989) indicates that some of the TSE drop reflected movements on the New York Stock Exchange, movements which could not plausibly be connected to Canadian politics. The TSE movement that Brander specifically attributed to published polls was not obviously in response to trade-related matters.

25 The quotation from Mr Mulroney is taken from Matthew Fisher, "Ex-jurist's attack aimed at Turner, Mulroney says," *Globe and Mail*, 5 November 1989, p. A1. For more detail on the rhetoric of the period, as reported, see chapter 4.

26 See Hugh Winsor, "Last ad blitz costing PCs $2 million," *Globe and Mail*, 16 November 1989, p. A1.

27 Fraser (1989) reports that the Canadian Alliance for Jobs and Opportunities budgeted $1.3 million for the late campaign and that the *Toronto Star* alone accepted $550,000 in pro-FTA advertising.

28 Benoît Aubin, "Bourassa makes another strong pitch for free-trade deal," *Globe and Mail*, 17 November 1988, p. A3.

29 The 57 percent share is slightly less than the equation in note 1 would have predicted.

30 In fact, the trend is slightly negative, implying a net loss of 2 percentage points.

2. THE ELECTORAL BACKGROUND

1 This generalization, of course, has its exceptions. Two language-community issues which figured prominently in national politics in the early period were the controversy in 1885–6 over the execution of the leader of the Northwest Rebellion, Louis Riel, and the debate over whether French should be an official language in the North-West Territories, which came to a head in 1890.

2 It remained so through the 1941 census.

3 The winner is here defined as the party that won a plurality of seats. Once, in 1925, the plurality winner, the Conservatives, did not form the government. Also plotted for this series is the winner's-share average for each of four periods, 1878–1917, 1921–30, 1935–58, and 1962–80. Note that the 1962–80 average is projected through 1984.

4 On the South African War, see Stacey (1977) and Penlington (1965). Both Laurier's position on Canada's entry into The First World War and King's handling of the advent of The Second World War showed a preoccupation with the lessons of 1899. On these see, respectively, Stacey (1977) and Stacey (1981).

5 This is the gist of two classic theorems in trade theory, the Heckscher-Ohlin and Stolper-Samuelson (see Stolper and Samuelson, 1941). For an application of this logic to electoral politics, see Rogowski (1987).

6 A good capsule account of the 1891 election is Waite (1971), pp. 221–7.

7 The tariff reductions were not, strictly speaking, exclusive to the Empire. The legislation offered reciprocal reductions to any country willing to match them. The United States was not among these, as it had just enacted the Dingley tariff. Britain was granted the preference by virtue of its standing policy of free trade. For some Liberals the legislation was appealing as an inducement to American reciprocation. For others the unlikelihood of the latter was a considerable relief. For all, the imperial gloss was no less happy for being something of an accident. See Colvin (1955).

8 On the American side, the incentive for the agreement seems to have been to give a sop to Progressives, who were still smarting from the enactment of the Payne-Aldrich tariff. The classic source on the agreement is Ellis (1939).

9 As it happens, the Conservative party did not campaign in its own right in the francophone parts of Quebec, but was happy to count Nationalists returned on the naval issue in its parliamentary ranks, at least for a while.

10 Johnston and Percy (1980).

11 The period-average entry in Figure 2-2 is calculated for the 1896–1911 period. It did not make sense to include 1917 itself in the calculation.

It made visual sense, though, to carry the 1896–1911 average through to 1917 to put the 1917 and 1921 results in proper perspective.

12 Stacey (1981), p. 235.

13 Lipset (1968) is a useful review of anti-party tendencies in agrarian politics.

14 See Allen (1971), Bliss (1968), and Morton (1950).

15 Fowke (1957), p. 169ff.

16 Perhaps it would be more correct to say, after Young (1969), that the CCF and NDP, although styling themselves as much a movement as a party, also accepted, or had influential cadres who accepted, the necessity of being a party.

17 Quoted in Stacey (1981), at p. 119.

18 On the prewar and wartime period, see Granatstein (1967).

19 Bothwell et al. (1981), p. 145.

20 On early economic policy, see Drummond (1974). On the Bennett New Deal, see Wilbur (1964).

21 The fall in grain prices was accompanied by drought in much of the region. And recovery was slower in agriculture than elsewhere. See Marr and Paterson (1980), pp. 393–4.

22 See Ward and Smith (1990) for a poignant account of the waning influence of the minister of agriculture, Jimmy Gardiner, in the King and St Laurent cabinets.

23 The 1957–8 swing of + 14.7 points was second only to the + 16.3 gain from 1921 to 1925. Confining our attention to 1958 understates the shift: from 1953 to 1958 the total Conservative surge was 23 points.

24 The largest, at 57 percent, was in 1917. This comparison is unfair to 1958, as Mr Diefenbaker's landslide had no taint of coalition about it.

25 The 1963–4 export volume was 550 million bushels. Never before had Canadian exports exceeded 400 million bushels.

26 Berthelet (1985), p.11. See also Skogstad (1987) and Bothwell et al. (1981).

27 The largest drop, of 26.7 points, came in 1921. The 1917 Conservative share included returns for Liberal Unionists. The second-largest drop, of 19.1 points, was from 1930 to 1935.

28 The full-period average disguises a Conservative slippage in those provinces, however, following Mr Diefenbaker's displacement as leader.

29 These were the elections of 1917, 1921, 1925, and 1945.

30 They dropped in Alberta and British Columbia as well, but not by a greater margin than in the rest of English Canada. These had been provinces of chronic Liberal weakness for many decades.

31 The case here needs to made very carefully. The NDP was – and is – not the majority or even the plurality choice among union house-

holds. But union households made up a clear majority of NDP supporters and affiliation by a local is an major factor in the NDP share in the corresponding ridings (Archer, 1985).

32 The logic of this has been formalized in Bates (1981) and Bates and Rogerson (1981).

33 See, for instance, the acerbic commentary on Suez in Robinson (1957) and in Grant (1965). Bothwell et al. (1981), report a Gallup poll which indicated that a majority of Canadians *supported* the Anglo-French invasion of Egypt (p. 144).

34 This account of the Liberal transformation is a synthesis of Wearing (1981), Smith (1973), Smith (1981), and Kent (1988).

35 In the 1970s Canada maintained domestic oil prices below world levels. Eastern Canadian consumption of offshore oil was subsidized by a tax equivalent to the difference between the domestic and world prices levied on exports to the United States from the west, mainly Alberta. This scheme was roughly self-financing as long as Canadian exports and imports were in balance. As the 1970s progressed, the trade in oil went out of balance and the fiscal foundations of the policy were undermined.

36 FIRA was renamed Investment Canada. At the renaming the government announced that "Canada [was] open for business."

37 The lowest was the Conservative share in 1945, 27.4 percent.

38 Although the Conservatives' parliamentary share in 1979 was close to a majority, the party's popular vote share was rather smaller than the Liberals'. Indeed, the 1979 Conservative vote, 36 percent, was the smallest for any seat plurality winner in Canadian history.

39 This is not to deny that the NDP has also sought consciously to moderate its appeal. Still, there is no mistaking the direction from which the moderation proceeds.

40 The government's popularity in late 1984 and early 1985 was fairly typical of the honeymoon in the first three quarters after a majority result, as was the subsequent modest decay in its standing. See Nadeau (1990), especially Table 1.

41 See, for instance, the review of 1974–80 poll standings in Irvine (1981) or the quarterly tracking in Monroe and Erickson (1986), Appendix A. Nadeau's (1987) exhaustive analysis makes two key points: first, this pattern makes no sense under Canada's frequent minority governments (p. 295ff); and, secondly, that even where analysis is confined to majority-government periods the mere passage of time simply has no effect on government popularity (p. 702).

42 For a review of European experience, see Lewis-Beck (1988). The American literature is voluminous; the most comprehensive review is Hibbs (1987).

43 In the paragraphs which follow, we have drawn heavily upon the narrative in Campbell and Pal (1991), chapter 3.
44 Recall that the same logic may have applied in 1911.

3. THE BACKGROUND OF THE PARTY SYSTEM

1 Johnston (1992). The same problem may afflict British election studies.
2 The item, i1, can be found in Appendix F.
3 The problem was compounded by the fact that the surveys commonly overestimated the winning party's vote share, the more so the larger and the less regionally differentiated the winning party's seat share.
4 For Liberal and NDP identification, the daily variance in identification was almost exactly that expected from sampling error alone. Conservative identification was slightly more volatile.
5 A compelling critique of the European discussion of the party identification literature, along lines similar to ours, is Richardson (1991).
6 In the 1988 non-Quebec sample Anglican, United, or Presbyterian respondents made up 82 percent of Protestants and 40 percent of the total. Another 32 percent were Catholics. Thus, only four denominations took up 72 percent of the non-Quebec total. Most of the remaining 28 percent were in non-Christian denominations or identified with no denomination at all. Small Protestant groups made up only about 8 percent of the sample.
7 Earlier studies, such as Irvine (1974) and Irvine and Gold (1980) found that frequency of church attendance had little impact on the width of the Catholic-Protestant cleavage. In the 1988 survey frequency of attendance did have a modest effect. It worked mainly at the very high (weekly) end and only to mobilize identification with the denominationally indicated party, not to reduce identification with the other party.
8 The percentage in the 1988 sample who claimed no religious affiliation was higher than in earlier Canadian studies. We believe that this reflects the fact that we made a measurement decision parallel to that for party identification: to give and thus validate, a "none of the above" option. Items in earlier studies tended to enumerate religious options only.
9 This reflects primarily a Jewish base for the party. Most Jews, however, identify with the Liberals.
10 The classification was based on item n15 (see Appendix F). Only 7 percent outside Quebec could not give a single ethnic answer. The numbers in the specific non-British/non-French groups were too small for detailed analysis. Northern European represents mainly those of

Dutch, German, and Scandinavian origins. Eastern European includes all the Eastern bloc countries and nationalities. "French" here means the ethnically French, regardless of language use. Southern Europe includes all countries other than France which border on the Mediterranean, as well as Portugal. In the sample, this group is overwhelmingly Italian. The "Other" group is mainly non-European and mostly Asian. It also includes those who gave Jewish as an ethnic category.

11 This is the long-term effect of the *Ne Temere* decree of 1908 which required that children of interfaith marriages be brought up Catholic. The steady growth in the Catholic share in English Canada thus reflects more than immigration and birth-rate differentials.

12 Religion also cuts through region. In Ontario, Protestants are nineteen points more likely to be Tories and Catholics are nineteen points more likely to be Liberals. The most seemingly archaic cleavage continued to be most powerful in the province that is most urbanized, most complex, and (in its own collective mind) socially most advanced. The cleavage is also marked in the prairies and in British Columbia.

13 The number of farm respondents in the other regions was too small for analysis.

14 The relationship between church attendance and non-partisanship did not appear to be monotonic, however.

15 The two factors are closely related: younger respondents were much less likely to report weekly attendance than older ones. Even so, each has a significant *ceteris paribus* impact.

16 The other factor which most caught the eye in Blais and Nadeau's analyses was union membership. This did not have any impact worth mentioning on federal identifications in 1988.

17 The group and policy items were in sections **h** and **l**. Not every item in these sections could be used. Left-right self-placement could not be used as too few respondents actually placed themselves. Any item that referred to a party or a leader by name risked picking up party identification directly. Similarly an item that referred to the government and seemed either to invite an evaluation of its performance or to invite merely partisan response was left aside. All other policy items in the campaign-wave pool appear in our analysis. The absence of partisan references should enhance the credibility of claims we make below for the dimensional bases of party identification.

18 Discriminant analysis was performed by the program in SPSS:X. Variable selection was based on Wilk's *lambda*; equal initial probabilities were assumed for each party.

19 We would never expect to attain a 100 percent prediction rate. Idiosyncratic reasons for partisan identification undoubtedly account for a substantial number of responses, and even if true positions on the is-

sues we include explain completely true partisan identification, the measurement error in the items for these issues would substantially decrease our predictive ability. When these factors are taken into account, correct predictions in 62 percent of the cases seems very good, especially when only a few items are used.

20 These figures are obtained by taking the percentage correctly predicted for a model with the items for a dimension and comparing it with a model without the items for this dimension. A number of comparisons are possible because we can look at pairs of models with or without other dimensions. The figures given in the text are the average across all the possible comparisons for each dimension.

21 The options were: Support it completely, support it somewhat, oppose it somewhat, and oppose it completely. Respondents with no opinion (25 percent of the total) were in the middle, at zero, and the distribution was scaled from -2 to $+2$.

22 These loadings are from a solution constrained to two dimensions. Loadings are higher where three and four factors are allowed to emerge.

23 We are not claiming that class does not count in Quebec; it just did not emerge as an organizing dimension in our factor analysis. In plots of occupations on the union power item (not reported here), differences were sharp and altogether like those outside Quebec. The weak statistical associations among issues may reflect the political weakness of an obvious potential organizing focus, the NDP.

24 These figures can be obtained either by taking the percentage predicted correctly by a pair of the items alone over chance, or by taking the percentage predicted correctly by all four items minus that predicted correctly by the other two items alone. The figures in the text are the average of these alternative calculations.

25 About 55 percent of the sample could place the parties on the French Canada item and about 75 percent could do so on the United States item.

26 The lack of group differences is especially encouraging, as respondents' estimates of group or party positions on issues can involve complex psychological processes which turn on respondents' own group or party locations (Brady and Sniderman, 1985). No doubt, bias runs through response here but it appears to be dominated by pressure towards convergent perception.

27 Political circumstances since 1988 may have made single-party government less attainable. If this is so, then the NDP's incentive to aim solely for non-Quebec votes may have sharpened. Our sense is that the party's leadership has responded accordingly.

4. THE CAMPAIGN IN THE MEDIA: ILLUSION OR
REALITY?

1 See also Frizzell and Westell (1989).
2 This is the argument in Robinson and Sheehan (1983), chapter 3, and in Brady and Johnston (1988). Soderlund et al. (1984) found bias in the Canadian coverage for 1979 and 1980, however.
3 For a summary of the findings in the domain, see Robinson and Levy (1986).
4 Even the wire service can be edited to suit local tastes.
5 Robinson and Sheehan (1983, chapter 2) came to similar conclusions for the United States.
6 For more detail on news coding, see Appendix C. Despite differences of method, the pattern here corresponds substantially to the findings in Frizzell and Westell (1989).
7 In contrast with the patterns reported for earlier campaigns by, for instance, Wilson (1980–81), Soderlund et al. (1984), and Wagenburg et al. (1988).
8 The pattern on *Le téléjournal* was similar but with generally more positive readings.
9 The categorization of content anticipates the discussion in the next chapter. The original coding admitted more detail than appears in Figure 4-3. "Sovereignty," for instance, was divided in two: references to the substance of loss of control over sectors of the economy were separated from more general references to sovereignty. American protectionism and references to prices were treated as separate categories but the volume of references to these categories was too small to warrant separate treatment here.
10 As much of the coverage was of issues and leaders simultaneously, we could not present a figure which partitions coverage between them. We can partition *among* actors, however, as our analytic units are defined in terms of singular actor referents. See Appendix C.
11 Here a unit was coded from -2 to $+2$, depending on both direction and intensity. The coded value was then weighted by duration in seconds. We should be clear about what we mean by the favourable or unfavourable character of an analytic unit. Direct comment on a leader's competence or character was rarely at issue. More common were factual accounts of the circumstances of a leader's tour: if, for example, a report indicated that Mr Turner was booed at a meeting, the unit would receive a leader code and a negative value.
12 See Fraser (1989) and above, chapter 1.
13 Newspaper polls (Gallup, Reid, Environics) are recorded for the day

of appearance. Polls reported by the CBC and CTV are registered the day after they were released, as results were not presented until the late evening news. Where more than one poll was reported on the same day, the simple average of poll readings is presented; there seemed to be no reason to assume that voters weighted polls for sample size. Multiple-poll days were: 17 October (Gallup and CBC from the night before); 19 November (Reid and Gallup). Note that some other days might appear from Table 4-1 to be multiple-poll days but these are days on which a television and newspaper poll coincided. The CTV poll published on 19 November is recorded as taking effect on the 20th.

14 The only exception was the very first (Gallup) poll, in which the Liberals clearly led the NDP.

15 The fit was not exact, though. Altogether, the publication of the twenty-two polls required eighteen separate days. Not all eighteen generated secondary television commentary, and a few television horse-race items were on other aspects of the campaign.

16 This is also true of American coverage of primary campaigns and is likely to be the case generally for campaign coverage. See Brady and Johnston (1988).

17 Moving averages in these figures are the conventional centred ones, to give a sense of the weight of advertising at the moment. Putting in daily quantities would make Figure 4-9 unreadable. For most purposes, "buy" is the correct way to describe the advertising commitment. Note, though, that some of the advertising was free.

18 Lee (1989) and Fraser (1989). This paragraph is also based on informal conversations with party informants.

19 The 1945 election, which saw a CCF breakthrough (see Figure 2-3), witnessed a pointed third-party anti-socialist campaign. See Young (1969), p.117, and Caplan (1973), chapter 8.

20 *National Citizens Coalition Inc.* v. *AG Canada*.

21 Only for a few days in October (before Figure 4-11 picks the campaign up), when anti-FTA forces placed a few perfunctory advertisements, did the line drop below zero.

22 See especially, Kraus (1962) and (1979), and Ranney (1979).

23 See Schrott (1990).

24 We are grateful to Ian McKinnon for suggesting this. See also Graham Fraser, "Mulroney camp expects history to repeat itself," *Globe and Mail* (Toronto), 22 October 1988, p. D2–3: "A couple of days after the event ... a delighted Tory organizer reflected on the [1984] debate. "I could tell that Brian had won when he uttered the two most beautiful words in the French language," he said, "Chez nous.""

25 If anything Lanoue (1991) may have underestimated their impact; he was forced to rely on data collected some months after the event. As we show below, the passage of time tends to efface distinctions between those who saw debates and those who did not. Lanoue helped himself out by using performance variables, which we also make much of below. LeDuc and Price (1990) are more sceptical, but employ a setup that minimizes the possibility of finding debate effects.

26 Hugh Winsor, "The battle of the potential network stars," *Globe and Mail*, 22 October 1988, pp. D1–2.

27 As examples of diffident interpretations of the 25 October debate, see Jeffrey Simpson, "His Best Hour," and Hugh Winsor, "Opposition leaders' aggressive strategy may have backfired," *Globe and Mail*, 26 October 1988, p. A6 and p. A11, respectively. The account of journalists' reactions to the post-debate manipulatory assault is in Lee (1989), chapter 11.

28 Denis Bastien and Yves Bernier, "Relevé des manchettes des 16 quotidiens," Université Laval, memo (December 1988).

29 See the summary in Frizzell and Westell (1989), pp. 78–9.

30 We cannot be sure, obviously, that all 55 percent were making a correct claim; some respondents may have had news coverage of the debates in mind. It is striking, however, that the proportion who claimed to have seen a debate did not increase as the campaign wore on. If there was bias in recall of debate exposure, it did not increase as time passed.

31 The high initial level of the "saw debate" line is not just an artifact of pooling observations. This said, there is a hint that some in the audience needed prodding: the raw reading for 26 October, although nearly twenty points above the "did not see debate" reading for that day, is lower than the next two readings. Over the few days after the debates an additional 10 percent or so of those who had seen a debate may have been moved by the post-debates commentary to see Mr Turner as the winner. Then again, the reading for the 26th may be low simply from sampling error.

32 Even in this group, Mr Turner was the most frequent choice from the beginning; growth in his share came at the expense not so much of the other leaders as of uncertainty.

33 Where the dependent variable is dichotomous, we employ a form of generalized least squares (GLS) regression, in which observations are weighted. In the jargon of the trade, estimates are "Goldbergerized" (Goldberger, 1964; a brief and clear exposition of the technique can be found in Achen, 1986, p. 40ff). This lets us take advantage of the easy interpretability of least-squares coefficients, at the same time as it off-

sets the impact of heteroscedastic disturbances. We are not convinced that the alternative estimation strategies, logit or probit, are superior econometrically to GLS. We are convinced, however, that those strategies present unnecessary difficulties of interpretation for a lay audience. For more detail, see Appendix B. Where the dependent variable is not dichotomous (the usual situation for media analyses in chapters 5 and 6), estimation is by ordinary least squares (OLS).

34 The strategy runs the risk of collinearity, given the number of values for adjacent days. Collinearity is a problem for news reporting of the FTA and for third-party advertising. It is not a problem for either of the Turner quantities, the ones analysed in this chapter.

5. FREE TRADE AND THE CONTROL OF THE AGENDA

1 Campbell (1989), p. 4.
2 The Environics item was: "Please tell me whether you strongly agree, somewhat agree, somewhat disagree or strongly disagree that there should be free trade between Canada and the US?"
3 The Gallup item was: "Do you think Canada would be better off or worse off if US goods were allowed in here without tariff or customs charges and Canadian goods were allowed in the US free?"
4 The Decima wording was: "I am going to read you two statements. Please listen carefully and then tell me which one you agree with more. Canada should enter into a free trade agreement with the United States that would eliminate any trade barriers and tariffs on goods flowing between the two countries ... or, Canada should protect Canadian industry from American competition through tariffs and limiting the amount of goods entering Canada through the United States." The figures were 57 to 39 in 1982, and 55 to 42 in 1983 (Johnston, 1986).
5 The Gallup series does not permit a pre/post-agreement comparison as their item was modified at this point by a preamble; "Subject to the restrictions agreed upon ..."
6 The Environics FTA item was: "Do you strongly favour, somewhat favour, somewhat oppose, or strongly oppose the Free Trade agreement that has been negotiated between Canada and the United States?"
7 The FTA item had two versions, to which respondents were assigned at random. See Appendix F for the wording of the item and below for further discussion. See Appendix D for a comparison of our item with items from published polls. The balance of opinion was more opposed to the FTA in the whole sample than in the subsample with active preferences.

8 The tearsheet in the ad was titled: "I support the fight against the Mulroney trade deal." Other organizations upped the ante by referring to the "Mulroney/Reagan" deal. See, for instance, handouts by the Council of Canadians and by the (British Columbia) Coalition against "Free" Trade. Note that the latter coalition was careful to imply that trade under the agreement would be only notionally free; trade that was truly free seemed rhetorically difficult to attack.

9 On the impact of this presumption, see Appendix D.

10 Schuman and Presser (1981) and Zaller (1984). As Zaller puts it: "Question wording changes which introduce new ideas, stimulate memory, or otherwise alter the context in which an issue is viewed often influence survey responses. Question wording changes which cannot plausibly be argued to have done any of these things less often affect survey responses" (p. 23).

11 A theme emerged later in the campaign, which we had not anticipated correctly: a concern over access to a large market. We framed a market-size item for the post-election wave and refer to it below.

12 The challenges to supporters were items l2a1, l2a2, and l2a3. The challenges to opponents were l2b1 and l2b2. See Appendix F.

13 Reassuringly, respondents who claimed that the challenge's consideration might make them reconsider were more likely than respondents who said that the challenge would make no difference to take a different position on the FTA after the election.

14 A weekly breakdown indicates that the "key sectors" and "jobs" challenges eroded by the end; in the last week their ability to provoke reconsideration was no higher than that for the "US protectionism" challenge.

15 Down to 25 October the mean Conservative position was 0.51 and the mean Liberal one −0.20. For non-partisans the mean was 0.14.

16 The items (l2a to l2e) retained the campaign wave wording except for the "some people say that ..." introduction. agreement/disagreement was on a five-point scale. See Appendix F.

17 The Conservatives seemed to sense that mention of active protectionism might only arouse anti-American sentiment. The protectionism challenge was the only one that provoked more than a trivial number of (unprompted) "more opposed" responses. For the specific wording of the post-election market-size item, l2e, see Appendix F.

18 For example, the detailed account of the 1984 primary season in the media by Brady and Johnston (1988) is entirely devoted to news coverage. The same is true of the media analyses in the major book-length study of primaries by Bartels (1988).

19 See Fraser (1989), for instance.

20 They were of little further substantive interest, given their statistical
fragility. Equally important, however, is a concern about fitting predicted to observed values where observations are not numerous. The
equation in Table 5-5 has twenty-nine free parameters – twenty-four
media terms and five covariates. This is not of grave concern with
2,760 respondents, but when we make predictions to the daily average rating we are down to forty-six observations, the number of days
on which large numbers of interviews were completed. Even if the
overall equation is nonsense, twenty-nine parameters can still make a
good fit to forty-six observations. By dropping the twelve FTA terms
we cut the total number of parameters to seventeen, and for six of the
terms still in the equation, the Turner advertising variables, there was
no variance before 23 October at the earliest.

6. TRAITS, DEBATES, AND LEADERS' FATES

1 See for instance, Clarke et al. (1979), chapters 7 and 11; Clarke et al.
(1984), chapters 5 and 6; and Kay et al. (1991).
2 Quoted in Martin et al. (1983), p. 84.
3 For the items, **d2a to d2c**, see Appendix F.
4 Only those people who could place themselves and each leader are
included.
5 The items are batteries **d3, d4**, and **d5**. See Appendix F.
6 If one or more of the component traits was missing, we took the average of the remaining traits. Alternative treatments of missing values
made little difference to the overall picture.
7 These observations also hold for the raw daily tracking. Even there
the debate simply burns through the noise of sampling error.
8 The non-partisan group is intrinsically more diverse than either the
Conservative or Liberal ones. When non-partisans are broken down
by FTA support/opposition, a contrast emerges in Turner competence
dynamics.

7. EXPECTATIONS: SELF-FULFILLING PROPHECIES?

1 For electoral studies, the canonical formulation is the "calculus of voting," which originated with Downs (1957), was formalized by Riker
and Ordeshook (1968) and McKelvey and Ordeshook (1972), and was
extended to multi-party systems by Cain (1978) and Black (1978).
2 See also Ferejohn and Fiorina (1974).
3 We owe this perspective to Duff Spafford (1974; and personal communication).

4 The idea of a bandwagon has not received the scholarly attention that strategic voting has, but it does have a scholarly pedigree. See especially Straffin (1977). See also Brams and Riker (1972), Collat, Kelley, and Rogowski (1981), and Nadeau, Cloutier, and Guay (1989).

5 Compare the Conservative tracking in Figure 1-4 with the publication dates in Table 4-1 or the synthesized poll information in Figure 4-7.

6 This may occur in part because many voters outside Quebec feel compelled to act strategically and go along with Quebec's bloc preference. This would help obscure underlying first preferences in English Canada. See Johnston (1991).

7 But then so was 1984. The generation of the Quebec Conservative majority in that campaign deserves extended analysis.

8 For constituency-level strategic voting in Canada, see especially Black (1978). For Britain, see Cain (1978) and Spafford (1973). For national and provincial effects, see Johnston (1991).

9 The items referred to in this chapter are **f1a** to **f2c**; they can be found in Appendix F. Appendix E gives more detail on the items and their coding.

10 By Gallup on the 27th and Environics on the 28th.

11 This is not to dismiss the heights that the NDP share had attained in the early going. Indeed, the next chapter argues that the NDP had a very good chance to form the opposition, a result that the party's leadership would have greeted with glee. But the expectations item was not about forming the opposition; it was about winning. By this standard the NDP's early chances, like the Liberals', were poor.

12 As Table 7-1 reports two sets of dummy variables (party variables as well as the regional ones), the reference category for the equation is non-partisan Ontario residents.

13 Coding rules for the last poll were described in chapter 4. Also in the estimation is a three-day "debate" dummy variable: respondents interviewed from 26 to 28 October inclusive scored one; all others scored zero. The variable is of no particular interest in its own right. It appears to offset a possible bias in the last-poll variable: we know already that expectations began to rise *before* the first post-debates polls. Had we failed to allow for this, we would have overestimated the impact of the last poll.

14 See above, chapter 4. The general pattern of poll attention is similar to that found for Britain by Miller et al. (1990), p. 256.

15 This is true: among poll-aware respondents, 70 percent also saw a debate. Among the unaware, the corresponding percentage was 30.

16 Not that the unaware missed the aftermath entirely. The Liberal rating did drop back sharply, although it then began another slow climb.

The Conservative rating made only a slight recovery.

17 In voters' defence, Figure 1-1 indicates that the Liberals are still at a
   disadvantage when the two old parties level peg in the high thirties.

18 Edwards (1982), p. 358.

8. ASKING THE RIGHT QUESTION

1 In mid-December 1988 the Supreme Court of Canada struck down restrictions on commercial signs in Quebec's Charter of the French Language, popularly known in English as Bill 101. Thereupon the
  government of Quebec invoked the "notwithstanding clause" (s. 33) of
  the Constitution Act, 1982 to reimpose a variant of the restrictions.
  The episode triggered a tit-for-tat period which revealed the contingent nature of Canadians' attitudes on linguistic accommodation
  (Sniderman et al., 1989; 1990) and which caused the accord to unravel
  (Cohen, 1991; Monahan, 1991). Fear of such an eventuality reinforced
  electoral calculations to produce the elite consensus embodied in Figure 3-2.

2 The difference in Figure 8–1 was slightly compounded by a difference
  in initial placements: 2 to 3 percent more respondents could not place
  themselves on the French Canada scale than on the pro-United States
  one.

3 We suspect that much of this shift reflected the same concession of
  the government's right to proceed as the opposition parties made.

4 One indicator of the problem with taking daily means is the difference
  in time-series coefficients between the pre-post setup that we actually
  report below and daily-means setups that were estimated but not reported: on most variables, estimates for time-series coefficients are
  roughly twice as large in the daily-means setup as in the pre-post one.
  See also Appendix B.

5 For readability's sake the coefficients and standard errors for poll
  standing and for feeling thermometers have been multiplied by 100.
  This is tantamount to taking the 100-point range on the variables and
  compressing it into the same 0–1 range as the dependent variable
  spans. It has no effect on estimates of significance for coefficients or of
  the robustness of the overall equation. Coefficients on variables which
  were measured with arithmetically small ranges (for instance, the
  party identification dummy variables or the FTA variable, which
  ranges from -1 to $+1$) were left in their original form.

6 Roughly, a initial unit shift in party standing, if nothing comes along
  to disturb the system, should ultimately induce a further two-thirds of
  a point shift, as the sum of an infinite series. For more detail, see
  Johnston et al. (1991).

7 The best introduction to the arithmetic of defection and recruitment remains Butler and Stokes (1969).
8 This explains the lack of differences between viewers and non-viewers that LeDuc and Price (1990) report from their essentially cross-sectional post-election setup.

EPILOGUE

1 Rules designed to suppress certain motions bear witness to the vulnerability of voting bodies to heresthetical moves.
2 The best candidates for this kind of analysis are the 1940 and 1948 Columbia studies, the 1980, 1984, and 1988 (the Super Tuesday component) US National Election Studies, Patterson's study of the 1976 campaign, and the 1987 British Election Study. All of these involved either campaign-wave panels or continuous monitoring.

Bibliography

Abramowitz, Alan I. 1978. "The Impact of a Presidential Debate on Voter Rationality." *American Journal of Political Science* 22: 680–90.

Achen, Christopher H. 1986. *The Statistical Analysis of Quasi-Experiments.* Berkeley, Los Angeles, and London: University of California Press.

Akenson, Donald Harman. 1984. *The Irish in Ontario: A Study in Rural History.* Montreal: McGill-Queen's University Press.

Aldrich, John H. 1980. *Before the Convention: Strategies and Choices in Presidential Nomination Campaigns.* Chicago: University of Chicago Press.

– 1983. "A Downsian Spatial Model with Party Activism." *American Political Science Review* 77: 974–90.

Aldrich, John H. and Forrest Nelson. 1984. *Linear Probability, Probit, and Logit Models.* Beverly Hills, CA: Sage.

Aldrich, John H., John L. Sullivan, and Eugene Borgida. 1989. "Foreign Affairs and Issue Voting: Do Candidates 'Waltz Before a Blind Audience'?" *American Political Science Review* 83: 123–41.

Allen, Richard. 1971. *The Social Passion: Religion and Social Reform in Canada 1914–28.* Toronto: University of Toronto Press.

Archer, Keith. 1985. "The Failure of the New Democratic Party: Unions, Unionists, and Politics in Canada." *Canadian Journal of Political Science* 18: 353–66.

Arrow, Kenneth J. 1951. *Social Choice and Individual Values.* New York: Wiley [republished by Yale University Press, 1963].

Bartels. Larry M. 1988. *Presidential Primaries and the Dynamics of Public Choice.* Princeton, NJ: Princeton University Press.

Bates, Robert H. 1981. *Markets and States in Tropical Africa: The Political Basis of Agricultural Policies*. Berkeley, Los Angeles, and London: University of California Press.

Bates, Robert H. and William P. Rogerson. 1981. "Agriculture in Development: A Coalitional Analysis." *Public Choice* 35: 513–27.

Bean, Clive and Anthony Mughan. 1989. "Leadership Effects in Parliamentary Elections in Australia and Britain." *American Political Science Review* 83: 1165–79.

Beck, Paul Allen. 1974. "A Socialization Theory of Party Realignment," in Richard G. Niemi, ed. *The Politics of Future Citizens*. San Francisco: Jossey-Bass.

Berelson, Bernard R., Paul F. Lazarsfeld, and William N. McPhee. 1954. *Voting*. Chicago: University of Chicago Press.

Berthelet, D. 1985. "Agriculture Canada Policy and Expenditure Patterns 1868–1983." *Canadian Farm Economics* 19: 5–15.

Black, Duncan. 1958. *The Theory of Committees and Elections*. Cambridge: Cambridge University Press.

Black, Jerome H. 1978. "The Multicandidate Calculus of Voting: Application to Canadian Federal Elections." *American Journal of Political Science* 22: 609–38.

Blais, André and Richard Nadeau. 1984. "L'appui au Parti québécois; évolution de la clientèle de 1970 à 1981," in Jean Crête, ed., *Comportement électorale au Québec*. Chicoutimi: Gaetan Morin.

Bliss, J.M. 1968. "The Methodist Church and World War I." *Canadian Historical Review* 49, reprinted in Carl Berger, ed., *Conscription 1917*. Toronto: University of Toronto Press, [1969].

Bothwell, Robert, Ian Drummond, and John English. 1981. *Canada since 1945: Power, Politics, and Provincialism*. Toronto: University of Toronto Press.

Brady, Henry E. and Richard Johnston. 1987. "What's the Primary Message: Horse Race or Issue Journalism?" in Gary R. Orren and Nelson W. Polsby, eds., *Media and Momentum: The New Hampshire Primary and Nomination Politics*. Chatham, NJ: Chatham House.

Brady, Henry E. and Paul M. Sniderman. 1985. "Attitude Attribution: A Group Basis for Political Reasoning." *American Political Science Review* 79: 1061–78.

Brams, Steven J. and William H. Riker. 1972. "Models of Coalition Formation in Voting Bodies," in J.F. Herndon and J.L. Bernd, eds., *Mathematical Applications in Political Science IV*. Charlottesville: University of Virginia Press.

Brander, James A. 1989. "Election Polls, Free Trade, and the Stock Market: Evidence from the 1988 Canadian General Election." University of British Columbia: ms.

Brodie, M. Janine and Jane Jenson. 1980. *Crisis, Challenge, and Change: Party and Class in Canada*. Toronto: Methuen.

Brody, Richard A. 1991. *Assessing the President: The Media, Elite Opinion, and Public Support*. Stanford: Stanford University Press.

Burnham, Walter Dean. 1970. *Critical Elections and the Mainsprings of American Politics*. New York: Norton.

Butler, David and Dennis Kavanagh. 1988. *The British General Election of 1987*. Basingstoke: Macmillan.

Butler, David E. and Donald E. Stokes. 1969. *Political Change in Britain*. New York: St. Martin's.

Cain, Bruce E. 1978. "Strategic Voting in Britain." *American Journal of Political Science* 22: 639–55.

Camp, Dalton. 1970. *Gentlemen, Players and Politicians*. Toronto: McClelland and Stewart.

Campbell, Angus and Robert L. Kahn (with the editorial assistance of Sylvia Eberhart). 1952. *The People Elect a President*. Ann Arbor: Survey Research Center, Institute for Social Research, University of Michigan.

Campbell, Angus, Gerald Gurin, and Warren E. Miller. 1954. *The Voter Decides*. Evanston, IL: Row, Peterson.

Campbell, Angus, Philip E. Converse, Warren E. Miller, and Donald E. Stokes. 1960. *The American Voter*. New York: Wiley.

Campbell, Robert Malcolm. 1989. "Post-Mortem on the Free Trade Election." *Journal of Canadian Studies* 24: 3–4, 163–6.

Campbell, Robert M. and Leslie A. Pal. 1991. *The Real Worlds of Canadian Politics: Cases in Process and Policy*. Peterborough: Broadview.

Caplan, Gerald L. 1973. *The Dilemma of Canadian Socialism: The CCF in Ontario*. Toronto: McClelland and Stewart.

Caplan, Gerald, Michael Kirby, and Hugh Segal. 1989. *Election: The Issues, the Strategies, the Aftermath*. Scarborough: Prentice-Hall.

Carty, R. Kenneth. 1988. "Three Canadian Party Systems: An Interpretation of the Development of National Politics," in George C. Perlin, ed., *Party Democracy in Canada; The Politics of National Party Conventions*. Scarborough: Prentice-Hall.

Chaffee, Steven H. 1975. "Asking New Questions about Communication and Politics," in Stephen H. Chaffee, ed., *Political Communication*. Beverly Hills: Sage (Sage Annual Reviews of Communication Research, Volume 4).

Chaffee, Steven H. and Jack Dennis. 1979. "Presidential Debates: an Empirical Assessment," in Ranney, ed., *The Past and Future of Presidential Debates*, 75–101.

Chappell, Henry W. and William R. Keech. 1986. "Policy Motivation and Party Differences in a Dynamic Spatial Model of Party Competition." *American Political Science Review* 80: 881–99.

Clarke, Harold D., Jane Jenson, Lawrence LeDuc, and Jon H. Pammett. 1979. *Political Choice in Canada*. Toronto: McGraw-Hill Ryerson.

– 1984. *Absent Mandate: The Politics of Discontent in Canada*. Toronto: Gage.

Cleveland, William S. 1985. *The Elements of Graphing Data*. Monterey, CA: Wadsworth.

Cohen, Andrew. 1990. *A Deal Undone: The Making and Breaking of the Meech Lake Accord*. Vancouver: Douglas and McIntyre.

Collat, Donald S., Stanley Kelley, and Ronald Rogowski. 1981. "The End Game in Presidential Nominations." *American Political Science Review* 75: 426–35.

Colvin, J.A. 1955. "Sir Wilfrid Laurier and the British Preferential Tariff System." Canadian Historical Association, *Report*, reprinted in Carl Berger, ed. *Imperial Relations in the Age of Laurier*. Toronto: University of Toronto Press, 1969: 34–44.

Converse, Philip E. 1962. "Information Flow and the Stability of Partisan Attitudes." *Public Opinion Quarterly* 26: 578–99.

Cox, Gary W. 1987. "Electoral Equilibrium under Alternative Voting Institutions." *American Journal of Political Science* 31: 82–108.

Downs, A. 1957. *An Economic Theory of Democracy*. New York: Harper and Row.

Drummond, Ian M. 1974. *Imperial Economic Policy 1917–1939: Studies in Expansion and Protection*. Toronto: University of Toronto Press.

Edwards, Ward. 1982. "Conservatism in Human Information Processing," in Kahneman, Slovic, and Tversky, eds., *Judgment under Certainty*.

Ellis, L.E. 1939. *Reciprocity 1911*. New Haven: Yale University Press.

Enelow, James M. and Melvin J. Hinich. 1984. *Spatial Analysis of Elections*. New York: Cambridge University Press.

Ferejohn, John A. and Morris P. Fiorina. 1974. "The Paradox of Not Voting: A Decision Theoretic Analysis." *American Political Science Review* 68: 525–36.

Fiorina, Morris P. 1977. "An Outline for a Model of Party Choice." *American Journal of Political Science* 21: 601–25.

– 1981. *Retrospective Voting in American National Elections*. New Haven: Yale University Press.

Fletcher, Frederick J. 1981. "The Contest for Media Attention: The 1979 and 1980 Federal Election Campaigns," in *Politics and the Media: An Examination of the Issues Raised by the Quebec Referendum and the 1979 and 1980 Federal Elections*. Toronto: The Reader's Digest Foundation of Canada.

Fowke, V.C. 1957. *The National Policy and the Wheat Economy*. Toronto: University of Toronto Press.

Franklin, Charles H. 1984. "Issue Preferences, Socialization, and the Evolution of Party Identification." *American Journal of Political Science* 28: 459–78.

Fraser, Graham. 1989. *Playing for Keeps: The Making of the Prime Minister, 1988*. Toronto: McClelland and Stewart.

Frizzell, Alan, Jon H. Pammett, and Anthony Westell. 1989. *The Canadian General Election of 1988*. Ottawa: Carleton University Press.

Frizzell, Alan and Anthony Westell. 1989. "The Media and the Campaign," in Frizzell, et al. *The Canadian General Election of 1988*, 75–90.

Goldberger, Arthur S. 1964. *Econometric Theory*. New York: Wiley.

Graham, Ron. 1986. *One-Eyed Kings: Promise and Illusion in Canadian Politics*. Toronto: Collins.

Grant, George. 1965. *Lament for a Nation: The Defeat of Canadian Nationalism*. Toronto: McClelland and Stewart.

Gunderson, Morley and W. Craig Riddell. 1988. *Labour Market Economics: Theory, Evidence and Policy in Canada*. Toronto: McGraw-Hill Ryerson.

Heath, Anthony, Roger Jowell, and John Curtice. 1985. *How Britain Votes*. Oxford: Pergamon.

Hibbs, Douglas A. 1987. *The American Political Economy: Macroeconomics and Electoral Politics in the United States*. Cambridge, MA and London: Harvard University Press.

Himmelweit, Hilde T., Patrick Humphreys, and Marianne Jaeger. 1984. *How Voters Decide*. Milton Keynes: Open University Press.

Horowitz, Gad. 1968. *Canadian Labour in Politics*. Toronto: University of Toronto Press.

Hovland, Carl I. and Irving L. Janis. 1959. *Personality and Persuasibility*. New Haven: Yale University Press.

Irvine, William P. 1974. "Explaining the Religious Basis of the Canadian Partisan Identity: Success on the Third Try." *Canadian Journal of Political Science* 7: 560–3.

– 1981. "The Canadian Voter," in Howard R. Penniman, ed., *Canada at the Polls, 1979 and 1980: A Study of the General Elections*. Washington, DC: American Enterprise Institute for Public Policy Research.

Irvine, W.P. and H. Gold. 1980. "Do Frozen Cleavages Ever Go Stale? The Bases of the Canadian and Australian Party Systems." *British Journal of Political Science* 10: 187–218.

Iyengar, Shanto and Donald R. Kinder. 1987. *News That Matters: Television and American Opinion*. Chicago: University of Chicago Press.

Jenson, Jane. 1975. "Party Loyalty in Canada: The Question of Party Identification." *Canadian Journal of Political Science* 8: 543–53.

Johnston, Richard. 1986. *Public Opinion and Public Policy in Canada: Questions of Confidence*. Toronto: University of Toronto Press.

– 1991. "The Geography of Class and Religion in Canadian Elections," in Wearing, ed., *The Ballot and Its Message*, 108–35.

– 1992. "Party Identification Measures in the Anglo-American Democracies: A National Survey Experiment." *American Journal of Political Science* 36: 542–59.

Johnston, Richard and Michael B. Percy. 1980. "Reciprocity, Imperial Sentiment, and Party Politics in the 1911 Election." *Canadian Journal of Political Science* 13: 711–729.

Johnston, Richard, André Blais, Henry E. Brady, and Jean Crête. 1991. "Free Trade and the Dynamics of the 1988 Canadian Election," in Joseph Wearing, ed., *The Ballot and Its Message*. Toronto: Copp Clark Pitman.

Kahneman, Daniel, Paul Slovic, and Amos Tversky, eds. 1982. *Judgment under Uncertainty: Heuristics and Biases*. Cambridge: Cambridge University Press.

Katz, Elihu and Paul F. Lazarsfeld. 1955. *Personal Influence*. New York: Free Press.

Katz, Elihu and Jacob J. Feldman. 1962. "The Debates in the Light of Research: A Survey of Surveys," in Kraus, *The Great Debates*.

Kay, Barry J., Steven D. Brown, James E. Curtis, Ronald E. Lambert, and John M. Wilson. 1991. "The Character of Electoral Change: A Preliminary Report from the 1984 National Election Study," in Wearing, *The Ballot and Its Message*, 283–314.

Kent, Tom. 1988. *A Public Purpose: An Experience of Liberal Opposition and Canadian Government*. Montreal: McGill-Queen's University Press.

Kinder, Donald R. 1983. "Presidential Traits." Pilot Study for the 1984 Planning Committee and the NES Board of Overseers.

Kinder, Donald R., Mark D. Peters, Robert P. Abelson, and Susan T. Fiske. 1980. "Presidential Prototypes." *Political Behavior* 2: 315–37.

Klapper, Joseph T. 1960. *The Effects of Mass Communication*. New York: Free Press.

Kraus, Sidney, ed. 1962. *The Great Debates: Background, Perspective, Effects*. Bloomington, IN: Indiana University Press.

– ed. 1979. *The Great Debates: Carter vs. Ford*. Bloomington, IN: Indiana University Press.

Krosnick, Jon A. and Donald R. Kinder. 1990. "Altering the Foundations of Support for the President through Priming." *American Political Science Review* 84: 497–512.

Lanoue, David J. 1991. "Debates that Mattered: Voters' Reaction to the 1984 Canadian Leadership Debates." *Canadian Journal of Political Science* 24: 51–65.

Laponce, Jean A. 1969. *People vs Politics*. Toronto: University of Toronto Press.

Lazarsfeld, Paul F., Bernard R. Berelson, and Hazel G. Erskine. 1944. *The People's Choice*. New York: Duell Sloan, and Pearce; reprinted 1968, New York: Columbia University Press.

LeDuc, Lawrence. 1981. "The Dynamic Properties of Party Identification: a Four-Nation Comparison." *European Journal of Political Research* 9: 257–68.

– 1984. "Canada: The Politics of Stable Dealignment," in Russell J. Dalton,

Scott C. Flanagan, and Paul Allen Beck, eds., *Electoral Change in Advanced Industrial Democracies: Realignment or Dealignment?* Princeton, NJ: Princeton University Press.

LeDuc, Lawrence and Richard Price. 1985. "Great Debates: The Televised Leadership Debates in Canada." *Canadian Journal of Political Science* 18: 135–53.

– 1990. "Campaign Debates and Party Leader Images: The 'Encounter '88 Case." Presented to the Annual Meeting of the Canadian Political Science Association, Victoria.

Lee, Robert Mason. 1989. *One Hundred Monkeys: The Triumph of Popular Wisdom in Canadian Politics.* Toronto: Macfarlane, Walter and Ross.

Lewis-Beck, Michael S. 1988. *Economics and Elections: The Major Western Democracies.* Ann Arbor: University of Michigan Press.

Lipset, Seymour Martin. 1968. *Agrarian Socialism.* New York: Doubleday.

Lipset, Seymour Martin and Stein Rokkan. 1967. *Party Systems and Voter Alignments.* New York: Free Press.

Lodge, Milton, Kathleen M. McGraw, and Patrick Stroh. 1989. "An Impression-driven Model of Candidate Evaluation." *American Political Science Review* 83: 399–419.

McCoombs, Maxwell E. and Donald L. Shaw. 1972. "The Agenda-Setting Function of the Mass Media," *Public Opinion Quarterly* 36: 176–87.

McDonald, Roderick P. 1985. *Factor Analysis and Related Methods.* Hillsdale, NJ: Erlbaum.

Macdonald, Stuart Elaine, Ola Listhaug, and George Rabinowitz. 1991. "Issues and Party Support in Multiparty Systems." *American Political Science Review* 85: 1107–31.

McGuire, William. 1969. "The Nature of Attitudes and Attitude Change," in Gardner Lindzey and Elliot Aronson, eds. *The Handbook of Social Psychology*, volume 3. Reading, MA: Addison-Wesley [second edition], 136–314.

McKelvey, Richard D. and Peter C. Ordeshook. 1972. "A General Theory of the Calculus of Voting," in J.F. Herndon and J.L. Bernd, eds., *Mathematical Applications in political Science IV.* Charlottesville: University of Virginia Press.

Mackintosh, W.A. 1964. *The Economic Background of Dominion-Provincial Relations.* Toronto: McClelland and Stewart [Carleton Library Edition].

Maddala, G.S. 1983. *Limited Dependent and Qualitative Variables in Econometrics.* Cambridge: Cambridge University Press.

Marr, William L. and Donald G. Paterson. 1980. *Canada: An Economic History.* Toronto: Macmillan.

Martin, Patrick, Allan Gregg, and George Perlin. 1983. *Contenders: The Tory Quest for Power.* Scarborough: Prentice-Hall.

Meehl, Paul E. 1977. "The Selfish Voter Paradox and the Thrown-Away Vote Argument." *American Political Science Review* 71: 11–30.

Miller, Arthur H., Martin P. Wattenberg, and Oksana Malanchuk. 1986. "Schematic Assessments of Presidential Candidates." *American Political Science Review* 80: 521–40.

Miller, William, Harold D. Clarke, Martin Harrop, Lawrence LeDuc, and Paul F. Whiteley. 1990. *How Voters Change: The 1987 British Election Campaign in Perspective*. Oxford: Clarendon Press.

Milne, R.S. and H.C. Mackenzie. 1954. *Straight Fight*. London: The Hansard Society.

– 1958. *Marginal Seat*. London: The Hansard Society.

Monahan, Patrick J. 1991. *Meech Lake: The Inside Story*. Toronto: University of Toronto Press.

Monroe, Kristen and Lynda Erickson. 1986. "The Economy and Political Support: The Canadian Case." *Journal of Politics* 48: 616–47.

Morton, W.L. 1950. *The Progressive Party in Canada*. Toronto: University of Toronto Press.

Nadeau, Richard. 1987. "Modélisation et analyse empirique des fluctuations de courte terme du comportement électorale: le cas canadien." Montréal: Université de Montréal, PH.D. dissertation.

– 1990. "L'effet lune de miel dans une contexte parlementaire: le cas canadien." *Canadian Journal of Political Science* 23: 483–97.

Nadeau, Richard, Edouard Cloutier, and Jean Guay. 1989. "Bandwagoning and Underdogging on North American Free Trade: A Quasi-Experimental Study of Opinion Movement." *International Journal of Public Opinion Research* 1: 206–20.

Nie, Norman H., Sidney Verba, and John R. Petrocik. 1976. *The Changing American Voter*. Cambridge, MA: Harvard University Press.

Nisbett, Robert E. and T.D. Wilson. 1977. "Telling More than We Can Know: Verbal Reports on Mental Processes." *Psychological Review* 84: 231–59.

Northrup, David and Anne Oram. 1989. *The 1988 National Election Study: Technical Documentation*. North York, Ontario: York University, Institute for Social Research.

Ordeshook, Peter C. 1986. *Game Theory and Political Theory: An Introduction*. Cambridge: Cambridge University Press.

Patterson, Thomas E. 1980. *The Mass Media Election*. New York: Praeger.

– 1987. "Television and Presidential Politics: Proposal to Restructure Television Communication in Election Campaigns," in Alexander Heard and Michael Nelson, eds., *Presidential Selection*. Durham, NC: Duke University Press, 302–29.

Penlington, Norman. 1965. *Canada and Imperialism 1896–1899*. Toronto: University of Toronto Press.

Pinard, Maurice. 1971. *The Rise of a Third Party: A Study in Crisis Politics*. Englewood Cliffs, NJ: Prentice-Hall.

Polsby, Nelson W. and Aaron Wildavsky. 1991. *Presidential Elections: Contemporary Strategies of American Electoral Politics*. New York: Free Press.

Pomper, Gerald M. 1975. *Voters' Choice: Varieties of American Electoral Behavior*. New York: Dodd, Mead.

Popkin, Samuel L. 1991. *The Reasoning Voter: Communication and Persuasion in Presidential Campaigns*. Chicago: University of Chicago Press.

Przeworski, Adam and John Sprague. 1986. *Paper Stones: A History of Electoral Socialism*. Chicago: University of Chicago Press.

Rabinowitz, George and Stuart Elaine Macdonald. 1989. "A Directional Theory of Issue Voting." *American Political Science Review* 83: 93–121.

Ranney, Austin, ed. 1979. *The Past and Future of Presidential Debates*. Washington, DC: American Enterprise Institute for Public Policy Research.

– 1983. *Channels of Power*. New York: Basic Books.

Richardson, Bradley M. 1991. "European Party Loyalties Revisited." *American Political Science Review* 85: 751–75.

Riker, William H. 1982. *Liberalism Against Populism: A Confrontation between the Theory of Democracy and the Theory of Social Choice*. San Francisco: Freeman.

– 1983. "Political Theory and the Art of Heresthetics," in Ada Finifter, ed., *Political Science: The State of the Discipline*. Washington, DC: American Political Science Association.

– 1984. "The Heresthetics of Constitution-Making: The Presidency in 1787, with Comments on Determinism and Social Choice." *American Political Science Review* 78: 1–16.

Riker, William H. and Peter C. Ordeshook. 1968. "A Theory of the Calculus of Voting." *American Political Science Review* 63: 25–43.

Robinson, Judith. 1957. *This Is on the House*. Toronto: McClelland and Stewart.

Robinson, John P. and Mark R. Levy. 1986. *The Main Source: Learning from Television News*. Beverly Hills: Sage.

Robinson, Michael J. and Margaret A. Sheehan. 1983. *Over the Wire and on TV: CBS and UPI in Campaign '80*. New York: Russell Sage.

Rogowski, Ronald. 1987. "Political Cleavages and Changing Exposure to Trade." *American Political Science Review* 81: 1121–37.

Sarlvik, Bo and Ivor Crewe. 1983. *Decade of Dealignment: The Conservative Victory of 1979 and Electoral Trends in the 1970s*. Cambridge: Cambridge University Press.

Schrott, Peter R. 1990. "Electoral Consequences of 'Winning' Televised Campaign Debates." *Public Opinion Quarterly* 54: 567–85.

Schuman, Howard and Stanley Presser. 1981. *Questions and Answers in Attitude Surveys: Experiments in Question Form, Wording and Content*. New York: Academic Press.

Sears, David O. and Rick Kosterman. 1987. "Mass Media and Political Persuasion." Los Angeles, CA: University of California – Los Angeles, ms.

Shepsle, Kenneth A. 1991. *Models of Multiparty Electoral Competition*. Chur: Harwood Academic Publishers.

Siegfried, André. 1907. *The Race Question in Canada.* Toronto: McClelland and Stewart [Carleton Library Edition, 1966].

Sigelman, Lee and Carol K. Sigelman. 1984. "Judgments of the Carter-Reagan Debate: The Eyes of the Beholders." *Public Opinion Quarterly* 48: 624–8.

Simpson, Jeffrey. 1980. *Discipline of Power: The Conservative Interlude and the Liberal Restoration.* Toronto: Personal Library.

Skogstad, Grace. 1987. *The Politics of Agricultural Policy-Making in Canada.* Toronto: University of Toronto Press.

Smith, Denis. 1973. *Gentle Patriot: A Political Biography of Walter Gordon.* Edmonton: Hurtig.

Smith, David E. 1981. *The Regional Decline of a National Party: Liberals on the Prairies.* Toronto: University of Toronto Press.

– 1985. "Party Government, Representation, and National Integration in Canada," in Peter Aucoin, ed., *Party Government and Regional Representation in Canada.* Toronto: University of Toronto Press.

Sniderman, Paul M., Joseph F. Fletcher, Peter H. Russell, and Philip E. Tetlock. 1989. "Political Culture and the Problem of Double Standards: Mass and Elite Attitudes toward Language Rights in the Canadian Charter of Rights and Freedoms." *Canadian Journal of Political Science* 22: 259–84.

– 1990. "Reply: Strategic Calculation and Political Values – The Dynamics of Language Rights." *Canadian Journal of Political Science* 23: 537–44.

Soderlund, Walter C., Walter I. Romanow, E. Donald Briggs, and Ronald H. Wagenberg. 1984. *Media and Elections in Canada.* Toronto: Holt, Rinehart and Winston.

Spafford, D.S. 1973. "Electoral Systems and Voters' Behavior." *Comparative Politics* 5: 129–134.

– 1974. "'Wasted' Votes in Three-Party Contests." Presented to the Canadian Political Science Association, 1974 annual meeting, Toronto.

Stacey, C.P. 1977. *Canada and the Age of Conflict, Vol. 1: 1867–1921.* Toronto: Macmillan.

– 1981. *Canada and the Age of Conflict, Vol. 2: 1921–1948.* Toronto: University of Toronto Press.

Stolper, Wolfgang Friedrich and Paul A. Samuelson. 1941. "Protection and Real Wages." *Review of Economic Studies* 9: 58–73.

Straffin, Philip D. 1977. "The Bandwagon Curve." *American Journal of Political Science* 21: 695–709.

Sundquist, James L. 1973. *Dynamics of the Party System: Alignment and Realignment of Political Parties in the United States.* Washington, DC: The Brookings Institution.

Wagenberg, R.H., W.C. Soderlund, W.I. Romanow, and E.D. Briggs. 1988. "Campaigns, Images and Polls: Mass Media Coverage of the 1984 Canadian Election." *Canadian Journal of Political Science* 21: 117–29.

Waite, Peter B. 1971. *Canada 1874–1896: Arduous Destiny*. Toronto: McClelland and Stewart.

Wallsten, Thomas S. 1980. *Cognitive Processes in Choice and Decision Behavior*. Hillsdale, NJ: Erlbaum.

Ward, Norman and David Smith. 1990. *Jimmy Gardiner: Relentless Liberal*. Toronto: University of Toronto Press.

Wearing, Joseph. 1981. *The L-Shaped Party: The Liberal Party of Canada 1958–1980*. Toronto: McGraw-Hill Ryerson.

– ed. 1991. *The Ballot and Its Message*. Toronto: Copp Clark Pitman.

Wilbur, J.R.H. 1964. "H.H. Stevens and the Reconstruction Party." *Canadian Historical Review* 45, reprinted in Ramsay Cook, ed., *Politics of Discontent*. Toronto: University of Toronto Press, 1967.

Wilson, R. Jeremy. 1980–81. "Media Coverage of Canadian Election Campaigns: Horse-race Journalism and the Meta-Campaign." *Journal of Canadian Studies* 15:56–68.

Young, Walter D. 1969. *The Anatomy of a Party: The National CCF*. Toronto: University of Toronto Press.

Zaller, John. 1984. "Toward a Theory of the Survey Response." Paper presented to the American Political Science Association 1984, annual meeting, Washington, DC.

– 1990. "Bringing Converse Back In: Modeling Information Flow in Political Campaigns," in James A. Stimson, ed., *Political Analysis*. 1: 181–234.

– 1991. "Information, Values, and Opinion." *American Political Science Review* 85: 1215–37.

Index

Abortion: as a campaign issue, 25, 96

Advertising, 113; as a reactive phenomenon, 139; strategy for estimating impact of, 136. *See also* Media, mass

Advertising by political parties: allocation to parties, 27; and balance of opinion on FTA, 163–4; coding of, 267; daily totals, 125–6; first appearance (23 October), 27; on the FTA, 127–8; and leader ratings, 187–90; and perceptions of debates, 138; and vote intentions, 236

Advertising, "third-party," on the FTA, 9, 128–9; and balance of opinion on the FTA, 163–4; expenditures on, 280n27; and vote intentions, 235

Age and party identification in Quebec, 91

Agenda-setting and the mass media, 248

Agricultural policy: in the first transition, 51; in the second

party system, 56; in the second transition, 58–9. *See also* Commercial policy; National Policy

Alberta: and the first transition, 50; in the Liberal coalition, 43

Aldrich, John H., 250, 276n6

Bandwagon, 14; defined, 198–9; evidence for, in Quebec, 230; and expectations, 198–9; folk wisdom about, in Quebec, 199. *See also* Expectations; Polls

Bartels, Larry M., 276n6

Blais, André, 285n16

Bloc québécois, 110

Brady, Henry E., 286n26, 288n16

Brander, James A., 280n24

British connection: as a factor in elections, 37–8; party positions on, 38, 66

Broadbent, Ed: background, 170–1; CBC campaign coverage of, 119–21; "feeling thermometer," ratings of, 174, 221–5; in party advertising, 129; perceived performance in debates, 133; popu-